ZEW Economic Studies

Publication Series of the Centre for
European Economic Research (ZEW),
Mannheim, Germany

ZEW Economic Studies

Vol. 1: O. Hohmeyer, K. Rennings (Eds.)
Man-Made Climate Change
Economic Aspects and Policy Options
1999. VIII, 401 pp. ISBN 3-7908-1146-7

Vol. 2: Th. Büttner
Agglomeration, Growth, and Adjustment
A Theoretical and Empirical Study
of Regional Labor Markets in Germany
1999. XI, 206 pp. ISBN 3-7908-1160-2

Vol. 3: P. Capros et al.
Climate Technology Strategies 1
Controlling Greenhouse Gases.
Policy and Technology Options
1999. XVIII, 365 pp. ISBN 3-7908-1229-3

Vol. 4: P. Capros et al.
Climate Technology Strategies 2
The Macro-Economic Cost and Benefit
of Reducing Greenhouse Gas Emissions
in the European Union
1999. XIII, 224 pp. ISBN 3-7908-1230-7

Vol. 5: P. A. Puhani
Evaluating Active Labour Market Policies
Empirical Evidence for Poland During Transition
1999. XVI, 239 pp. ISBN 3-7908-1234-X

Vol. 6: B. Fitzenberger
Wages and Employment Across Skill Groups
An Analysis for West Germany
1999, XII, 251 pp. ISBN 3-7908-1235-8

Vol. 7: K. Rennings et al.
Social Costs and Sustainable Mobility
Strategies and Experiences in Europe
and the United States
1999, VI, 212 pp. ISBN 3-7908-1260-9

Vol. 8: Legler et al.
Germany's Technological Performance
2000, X, 191 pp. ISBN 3-7908-1281-1

Oliver Bürgel

The Internationalisation of British Start-up Companies in High-Technology Industries

With 11 Figures
and 58 Tables

Physica-Verlag
A Springer-Verlag Company

Zentrum für Europäische
Wirtschaftsforschung GmbH
Centre for European
Economic Research

Series Editor
Prof. Dr. Wolfgang Franz

Author
Dr. Oliver Bürgel
London Business School
Sussex Place
London NW1 4SA
United Kingdom

ISBN 3-7908-1292-7 Physica-Verlag Heidelberg New York

Cataloging-in-Publication Data applied for
Die Deutsche Bibliothek – CIP-Einheitsaufnahme
Bürgel, Oliver: The internationalisation of British start-up companies in high-technology industries / Oliver Bürgel. ZEW, Zentrum für Europäische Wirtschaftsforschung GmbH. – Heidelberg; New York: Physica-Verl., 2000
  (ZEW economic studies; Vol. 9)
  ISBN 3-7908-1292-7

This work is subject to copyright. All rights are reserved, whether the whole or part of the material is concerned, specifically the rights of translation, reprinting, reuse of illustrations, recitation, broadcasting, reproduction on microfilm or in any other way, and storage in data banks. Duplication of this publication or parts thereof is permitted only under the provisions of the German Copyright Law of September 9, 1965, in its current version, and permission for use must always be obtained from Physica-Verlag. Violations are liable for prosecution under the German Copyright Law.

Physica-Verlag is a company in the BertelsmannSpringer publishing group.
© Physica-Verlag Heidelberg 2000
Printed in Germany

The use of general descriptive names, registered names, trademarks, etc. in this publication does not imply, even in the absence of a specific statement, that such names are exempt from the relevant protective laws and regulations and therefore free for general use.

Cover design: Erich Dichiser, ZEW, Mannheim
SPIN 10763545   88/2202-5 4 3 2 1 0 – Printed on acid-free paper

To Emma and Magda

Acknowledgements

Doing a PhD on internationally operating, entrepreneurial companies ended up becoming a veritable act of cross-border entrepreneurship in itself.

It all began about three and a half years ago, when, apparently against all reason, I decided to turn down the security of a three year fully-funded PhD grant from another university to come to Warwick Business School. At the time, I was tempted by Warwick's research reputation, its structured PhD programme and my assigned supervisor, Gordon Murray, who appeared to be somewhat more entertaining and communicative than the other academics I interviewed. (Time proved that I wasn't wrong on any of these questions.)

I was intrigued by the idea that tiny start-up firms could build up international activities. Like an entrepreneur who had all but his idea for a promising product, I started communicating with future and existing backers. Numerous applications for funding were written during my first year and my parents had to be convinced that this was not just the latest well-crafted plot of their oldest son to avoid the hardships of working life.

There were many initial drawbacks, starting from the comment of a leading British professor in international business who told me "Young man, the firms you're trying to research don't really exist" up to being a bit too honest during a grant interview and – not surprisingly – being turned down by the trustees of the foundation. I also soon realised that additional expertise in empirical research on start-ups and their analysis was required. Help appeared in the form of Georg Licht from the Centre for European Economic Research in Mannheim, Germany, who immediately expressed interest in the topic. After initial discussions, we decided to start a comparative Anglo-German research project on the internationalisation of new, technology-based firms. Despite my frequent laments and complaints, the funding saga ended like Gordon ("Cheer up, Oliver!") predicted. Like venture capitalists who seem to ignore applications below a certain threshold, the potential funding organisations reacted more positively to a professional project that stretched over two countries and proposed both a large scale survey and a considerable number of case studies (The fact that it was proposed by two renowned research institutions rather than a lonely PhD student surely helped).

The remaining parts of the story are quickly told. After receiving financial support - the vital ingredient for a PhD - we started developing a questionnaire and identified a suitable primary database of start-ups. The various mailshots covered a period of five months. I will never forget how the entire Frost family (Sheila, Ian, Jo and Mark) came to my help during a long week-end when I underestimated the time it took to prepare 2000 envelopes. All these hardships were forgotten as soon as the dataset was cleaned-up and ready for analysis. During the summer 1998, the project team, with the help of Ferdinand Porak and Hans Nyctelius (both MBA students at Warwick), carried out 40 interviews with managers of high-tech start-ups. The results of the case studies are not part of the thesis, but the process of analysing them has influenced me immensely in my thinking. Finally, I can now present the end product to a larger audience. The long awaited moment to thank everybody who helped me during that process has thus come.

Above all, this project would not have been possible without the financial support from various organisations. The German Academic Exchange Service funded the first two years of my PhD studies. Financial support in order to carry out the Anglo-German research project has been provided by the Anglo-German Foundation for the study of Industrial Society, Apax Partners and the UK Department of Trade and Industry. The source data has been generously made available by Dun & Bradstreet UK Ltd. I would like to thank several individuals in these organisations for their support: Ray Cunningham at the Anglo-German Foundation, Peter Englander at Apax Partners and Gerard Buckley and Olivier Somenzi at Dun & Bradstreet UK.

Several entrepreneurs agreed to provide assistance during the pilot-testing of the questionnaire. The discussions with Brian Docherty, Mike Freeling, Tony Macedo and Anthony Dent provided an excellent "real life" test-bed for my ideas. In the interview phase after the survey, my conversations with 20 managing directors of high-tech start-ups were invaluable sources of inspiration that put my theoretical, literature-based knowledge of technology entrepreneurship into perspective. Given the constraints on their time, the generosity of spending up to three hours with a young researcher deserves my deepest thanks. My gratitude goes to – in random order - John Bloomfield, Gerald Rutherford, Andrew Skinn, Bruce Savage, Martin Rothman, Peter McGeehin, Mel White, Steve Kille, Stuart Penny, Tony Bickford, Julian Hilton, Scott Blackstone, Mark Goble, Peter McCulloch, Peter Brooks, Laurie Dickson, Alan Wyn-Davies, Simon Johnson, David Bailey, Alan Jones and Philip Godfrey.

During the last years, I benefited from a flexible working arrangement with Hewlett Packard's Business Alignment Team in Böblingen, Germany. I would like to thank my colleagues there, in particular Boris Kirn and John Wargin, for their support, for sharing their personal and professional experiences with me and for providing me with a healthy counterbalance to the life of a young academic.

My thanks go also to several members of the administrative staff of Warwick Business School. Cath Aubrey from the School's Finance Office steered the project calmly through the administrative cliffs of Senate House and kept the financial side running smoothly. My arrival at Warwick coincided with the arrival of Lesley Inness and later Jan Woodley who manage the administrative side of the WBS PhD Programme. PhD students have seen a lot of improvements of their working conditions over the last three years in terms of training and resources, and both Lesley and Jan (and Belinda March) deserve a lot of credit for this. As the focal point of the Marketing and Strategic Management Group, Sheila Frost soon became one of the most important persons to me at the Business School. Whether I desperately needed to speak to Robin or didn't know into which time zone Gordon had disappeared - I could always count on Sheila's help. These things matter a lot to a PhD student as they make life so much easier!

I also owe thanks to Solveig Nyvold and Matt Nichols, two MBA students at Warwick, who completed their dissertation on the internationalisation of venture capital backed start-ups just before my period of registration began. Although I never met them in person, I learned enormously from their work, which paved the way for my own contribution.

I would like to thank my thesis examiners, Professor David Storey from the University of Warwick and Professor Harry Sapienza from the University of South Carolina, for their constructive feed-back and valuable comments.

During the last years, I benefited immensely from the academic support given by my German research colleagues and my two supervisors here at Warwick. Andreas Fier and myself "hit it off" right from the start, which made him become a friend rather than a colleague (A rather intense working week in Portugal surely helped fostering that friendship). Georg Licht deserves enormous credits for supporting me and my research ideas. Ever since we first met, he gave me the impression of not having the slightest doubts about the positive outcome of the project. He also taught me a great deal about econometrics and empirical research on start-up companies. However busy Georg is, he somehow always seems to find time when you ask him about things such as the nature of the error term in Heckman selection models.

With my two supervisors, I had a relationship, both at the personal and academic level, that many PhD students can only dream of. Robin Wensley provided exceptional guidance throughout the overall process in his assured and calm way. I benefited from Robin's wealth of experience in supervising PhDs as he was always willing to share his thoughts on the process of doing a PhD and nature of research. I have to admit that, frequently, I only understood what he was trying to tell me long after he did actually tell me. But then again, it appears that I'm not the only one who has these experiences with Robin.

My greatest thanks go to Gordon Murray, my principle supervisor, who encouraged me throughout the last three years. He gave me the kind of support that many PhD students dream of, but few experience. Not only did Gordon always find time to discuss my ideas and listen to my worries (provided that I would find time to listen to him ...), but he actively reacted in his entrepreneurial way to make things happen, for example by sharing his network of contacts in order to get funding and access to entrepreneurs willing to test the questionnaire. This research is to a large extent the outcome of the combination of expertise, guidance and support given by these four individuals.

Finally, I could have never accomplished this project without the support from people that are close to me. Above all, over the last three and a half years, the members of the PhD programme at Warwick Business School, particularly the 1995/96 intake, have shared the ups and downs of the PhD process with me. Ianna and Gerrardo have spoiled me with fantastic Italian food and great discussions, especially during the first two years of the PhD when I stayed at Warwick. My thanks go also to Bitten and Martin ("the office mate from heaven"), Andreas for helping me with the mailings, Paula and Rob for being the perfect hosts (boy, what you guys taught me about Australian wine ...), Ruey-Lin for many challenging discussions on epistemology and Manuela for doing a good job at explaining the depths of my psyche to me.

In London, my flatmates during the last 2 ½ years, Bettina, Laure, Maria, Martina, Natascha, Mark and Freddy, our "pet" Keith (he fell asleep after proof-reading the first 3 pages of the introduction but saved himself through a timely intervention on the day of submission of the thesis) and the "extended family" (Christophe and Martine, Michael and Hyo-Yoon, Gis and Nada) created a pleasant habitat at Ivor Street and provided moral support - even though they probably more than once wondered why I did all that. During the last months in particular, Mark has been caring "like a mother", taking care of the essential tasks in the house. In addition, he went through the arduous task of proof-reading the thesis which substantially improved its quality.

Over the past three years, I somehow seemed to concentrate my expressions of frustration and excitement about the PhD process (...and there were many) on four good friends. I am indebted to Klaus, Mark, Christophe and Michael for never being tired of listening to me and for finding the right words to say so many times.

Finally, my parents helped me enormously during the time I spent in higher education. Knowing that they are there to support me wherever they can, helped me immensely in my decision to do a PhD and to complete it.

I only now realise that my acknowledgements are four pages long. Maybe it gives you an idea to what extent I'm grateful for the support of others in doing this work. To all of you, a big

"Thank you!"

Oliver Bürgel,
London, November 1999

Table of Contents

1.	**Introduction**	**1**
2.	**Literature Review**	**5**
2.1.	Technology-Based Start-ups / NTBFs	5
2.2.	Empirical Evidence on International Entrepreneurship	7
2.2.1.	The Internationalisation of Start-ups: Empirical Evidence from Case Studies	9
2.2.1.1.	The Studies	9
2.2.1.2.	Conclusions from the Review of the Case Studies	18
2.2.2.	The Internationalisation of Start-ups: Empirical Evidence from Quantitative Surveys	21
2.2.2.1.	The Studies	21
2.2.2.2.	Conclusions from the Review of the Quantitative Studies	27
2.2.3.	Conclusions from the Review of Research in International Entrepreneurship	30
2.3.	Theories of International Business	33
2.3.1.	Overview of Different Theories	33
2.3.2.	Internationalisation Process Theories and Stage Models	35
2.3.3.	Internalisation and Transaction Cost Economics	40
2.3.3.1.	Internalisation Theory	40
2.3.3.2.	Transaction Cost Economics	42
2.3.4.	Firm-Specific Advantages	47
2.3.4.1.	Monopolistic Advantage Theory	48
2.3.4.2.	Resources, Organisational Capabilities and Knowledge	49
2.3.5.	Conclusions from the Review of International Business Theories	53
3.	**Research Objective and Development of Hypotheses**	**57**
3.1.	Research Objective	57
3.2.	Research Hypotheses	60

3.2.1. Differences Between International Start-ups and Domestic Start-ups, the Degree of Internationalisation and Timing of Internationalisation 60
3.2.1.1. Operationalisation of Dependent Variables 60
3.2.1.2. Hypotheses 62
3.2.2. The Choice of Market Entry Mode 69
3.2.2.1. Operationalisation of the Dependent Variable 69
3.2.2.2. Hypotheses 71

4. Methodology 79
4.1. The Survey Instrument 79
4.2. Definition of High-Technology Start-ups 80
4.3. Identification of Data Sources: The Use of Credit Rating Data 82
4.4. The Primary Data Base 84
4.4.1. The Clean-up of Primary Data 85
4.4.2. Sampling Procedure 88
4.5. The Questionnaire 90
4.6. The Pilot Case Studies 91
4.7. Mailing and Response Pattern 91
4.8. Non-Response Analysis 93

5. Descriptive Data Analysis 95
5.1. Methodological Considerations 95
5.1.1. Calculation of Weights 95
5.1.2. Industry Groups 96
5.2. Descriptive Data Analysis: General Firm Characteristics 99
5.2.1. Firm Characteristics at Start-up 99
5.2.2. Firm Characteristics at the Time of the Survey 100
5.2.3. External Finance:
Venture Capital, Business Angels and Public Grants 102
5.2.4. Founders 104
5.2.5. Research and Development Activities 105
5.2.6. Product Characteristics 112
5.2.7. Growth Rates 116
5.2.8. Summary of the Descriptive Analysis of Firm Characteristics 120
5.3. Descriptive Data Analysis: International Activities 121
5.3.1. Prevalence of the Phenomenon 121
5.3.2. The Degree of Internationalisation 125
5.3.3. Entry Modes 128
5.3.4. Pattern of Market Selection 130

5.3.5.	International Production	131
5.3.6.	Growth and International Sales	131
5.3.7.	Motives, Triggers, Costs and Constraints	135
5.3.8.	Summary of the Descriptive Analysis of Internationalisation	139
6.	**Multivariate Data Analysis**	**141**
6.1.	Operationalisation of Independent Variables	141
6.2.	Differences Between International Start-ups and Domestic Start-ups, Degree of Internationalisation and Timing of Foreign Market Entry	145
6.2.1.	Differences Between International Start-ups and Domestic Start-ups	145
6.2.1.1.	Model Estimation	145
6.2.1.2.	Results	151
6.2.2.	The Degree of Internationalisation	154
6.2.2.1.	Methodological Considerations	154
6.2.2.2.	Model Estimation	155
6.2.2.3.	Results	160
6.2.3.	The Timing of Market Entry	163
6.2.3.1.	Methodological Considerations	163
6.2.3.2.	Model Estimation	164
6.2.3.3.	Results	165
6.2.4.	Discussion: Differences Between International Start-ups and Domestic Start-ups, Degree of Internationalisation and Timing of Foreign Market Entry	171
6.3.	The Choice of Market Entry Mode	177
6.3.1.	Model Estimation	177
6.3.2.	Results	180
6.3.3.	Discussion	182
7.	**Conclusions**	**187**
7.1.	Implications for the Field of International Entrepreneurship	188
7.2.	Theoretical Implications	189
7.3.	Areas for Further Research	192
7.4.	Managerial Implications	193
Appendix		**197**
List of Tables		**213**
List of Figures		**217**
Bibliography		**219**

1. Introduction

There are 17 million small and medium-sized enterprises (SMEs) in the European Union which play an important role in economic life. Within this subset, increasing recognition is being given to "new technology-based firms." [1] In the literature, different definitions have been put forward to describe the term new technology-based firm (Oakey et al 1988; Roberts 1991; Autio 1995; Storey and Tether 1998). Common denominators include that the activity is based on the exploitation of advanced technological know-how, the prior affiliation of founders with research establishments and the entrepreneurial character of the firm. Research studies in Europe, North America and the Pacific Rim have identified these firms' important contributions in new employment creation, export sales growth, product and process innovation and structural adjustment (e.g. Rothwell & Zegveld 1982; OECD 1986; Oakey et al 1988; Acs & Audretsch 1991; Roberts 1991; Coopers & Lybrand 1996).

While there is a growing body of literature on new technology-based firms that concentrates on strategic issues such as access to financial resources, growth processes and innovation behaviour (see Storey and Tether 1998, for a review), there has been relatively little research into the process by which young high-technology companies have internationalised. Research activity in the latter field has historically been strongly oriented towards large firms or, more rarely, towards "traditional transnational SMEs" in the manufacturing sector that often act as suppliers of bigger firms and are characterised by simple production technologies and low-technology products (United Nations 1993). Most of these studies conclude that export and co-operative arrangements rather than acquisitions or direct investment are the preferred forms for international engagements of SMEs. (United Nations 1993; Bamberger & Evers 1994). Frequently, the internationalisation process is a random development - often initiated by the move of a client abroad or an unsolicited order - rather than driven

---

[1] Throughout this thesis, the terms "new, technology-based firm" and "technology-based start-up" will be used interchangeably.

by long-term strategic considerations. These studies generally conclude that so-called stage models adequately explain the foreign activities of small firms and both size of the SME and its maturity are seen as explanatory variables (e.g. Bilkey 1978; Cavusgil 1980; Wagner 1995). Furthermore, the notion of "psychic distance" has been put forward to explain the locational choices of the internationalisation processes. Thus, SMEs should be more inclined to engage in cross-border activities with countries that are similar in cultural, economic and political terms. Studies in several countries as diverse as the US, Great Britain, Germany, Israel and South Africa have provided empirical evidence for this sequential internationalisation pattern of small traditional firms (Bilkey and Tesar 1982; Bamberger and Evers 1994; Calof and Viviers 1995; Chetty and Hamilton 1995). Even though these models have been found invalid in a number of cases (Turnbull 1987; Buckley et al 1988; Welch & Loustarinen 1988), they are still regarded as adequate to explain the behaviour of small firms at the beginning of their internationalisation (Johanson & Vahlne 1990).

There is evidence that the internationalisation pattern of start-up firms in high-technology sectors is not only different but potentially contradictory to the prevailing theoretical frameworks in the field of international business. These firms - labelled "infant multinationals" (Lindqvist 1991), "born globals" (McKinsey & Company 1993; Knight & Cavusgil 1996) and "international new ventures" (Oviatt & McDougall 1994) - have received an increasing amount of attention from researchers over the last couple of years. Despite being relatively young and small, these firms tend to internationalise from an early stage of their evolution (Lindqvist 1991; Bell 1995; Murray 1995). Some extreme cases are even international from inception and can perform different activities along the value chain in several different countries (Oviatt & McDougall 1994). It is remarkable that, despite their young age and their limited resources, the observed start-ups were operating in a relatively large number of different countries on different continents. In addition, some firms used entry modes ranging from simple export to the creation of subsidiaries simultaneously in different countries.

In the light of these findings, two influential contributors to the field of international entrepreneurship concluded that the emergence of these "born global firms" is at odds with the established body of theory in the area of international business (Oviatt and McDougall 1994). They further argued that the field of international business is in need of refined theoretical foundations to explain the emergence of these firms and the phenomenon of accelerated internationalisation. However, they also admit that existing knowledge is largely case study based and that there has been, to date, no systematic survey of the prevalence of internationally operating start-up firms in a given country (Oviatt and McDougall 1997).

The present dissertation will try to address this gap. It aims at applying theories from the field of international business to NTBFs in order to provide some explanation for the observed phenomenon of rapid internationalisation of high-tech start-ups. For the purpose of this study, high-tech start-ups will be defined as firms younger than ten years that operate in high-technology industries as defined by Butchart (1987). The different aspects of internationalisation that will be analysed are the decision to internationalise, the degree of internationalisation, the timing of internationalisation, the choice of market entry mode and the pattern of market selection. The research will attempt to meet three related objectives.

- First, it will establish the prevalence of internationally operating start-up firms in high-technology industries in the United Kingdom. To our knowledge, this is the first study that attempts to reach this objective.

- Second, it will systematically examine the dominant theories of the field of international business with regard to their relevance for internationally operating start-up firms. In doing so, we will assess whether the existence of international new ventures can be explained with these theories. We will also show that there has been little overlap between exploratory, case-study based work and quantitative research in international entrepreneurship. In order to advance this area of research, we will present a review of the existing published contributions and consolidate their results.

- Third, we will apply both the existing empirical and theoretical knowledge and develop a set of hypotheses regarding their internationalisation behaviour. We will collect a dataset of start-ups with international activities and a control group of domestic start-ups to test our research hypotheses.

In the following chapters, the rationale for these objectives and detailed research questions will be developed. The next chapter will present a review of the relevant literature required to discuss the phenomenon of international entrepreneurship. After that, the research questions and a set of testable hypotheses will be developed. We will then describe the methods used for obtaining the empirical dataset. After that, descriptive statistics and tests of the hypotheses in a multivariate setting will be presented. The dissertation closes with a discussion of the findings and suggestions for further research.

2. Literature Review

2.1. Technology-Based Start-ups / NTBFs

The surge of interest in new, technology-based firms is to a large extent motivated by the US experience. Firms like Hewlett-Packard, Intel, Microsoft, Genentech, Cisco Systems and more recently Yahoo, Netscape, America Online and Amazon.com have set examples of how firms can grow from small start-ups to global players that dominate their industries. They all based their activities on the exploitation of recent technological developments and produced a constant stream of hitherto unknown products and solutions. These firms are widely credited as creators of value-added, employment, innovation and as source of structural adjustment.

In the light of these experiences, European policy makers have put high expectations on the genesis, growth and economic impact of these firms. One of the earliest European studies was an Anglo-German comparison, carried out in 1977 by the consultancy Arthur D. Little. Besides coining the term "new technology-based firm", the study represented the first survey of the existing stock of this type of firm in Germany and the UK. However, the report was rather critical, emphasising that, in comparison with the US, both Germany and the UK were lagging behind in terms of formations of NTBFs and their contribution to the overall economy (Little 1977). In terms of policy contribution, this study has been instrumental in highlighting the lack of support infrastructures in the two countries. The picture painted ten years later was a more optimistic one. Another study funded by the Anglo-German Foundation set a further milestone by reporting a significant growth of the formation of high-tech start-ups in both countries, albeit with a more developed NTBF sector in the UK relative to the size of the economy. But like in the earlier Arthur D. Little study, this report came to the conclusion that the considerable gap between the US on the one side and the UK and Germany on the other persisted. It thus called for a realistic assessment of the phenomenon and highlighted the lack of public and private support mechanisms to strengthen this emerging sector of the economy.

Since then, academic studies have investigated issues such as creation, growth and survival rates of technology-based start-ups, regional concentration or "clusters" of NTBF activity, the background of the founders, the availability of finance and support infrastructures (for reviews see Autio 1997 and the special issue of Research Policy, November 1998). Yet, the actual performance of European new technology-based firms remains in striking contrast to the attention from policy makers, practitioners and academics alike. Today, it becomes increasingly evident that they have not managed to live up to their earlier promise as panacea for the economic ills of the "old world." After assessing the empirical knowledge in a study that involved researchers from all member states of the European Union, Storey and Tether concluded that, in the absence of dedicated support, "it is very likely that NTBFs will continue to frustrate the expectations of European policy makers who look enviously at the United States" (Storey and Tether 1998, p. 944).

A number of explanations have been put forward for explaining why few countries – Israel appears to be an exception – have been able to emulate the success of the United States. Above all, cultural issues and the attitude to entrepreneurship are a key factors to understand the differences. Other researchers have emphasised the role of tight-knit networks of business relations and support infrastructures to explain the formation of regional hot-spots of entrepreneurial activity (e.g. Florida and Kenney 1988; Saxenian 1991). A parallel stream of work has pointed out towards the dearth of finance for early stage financing in Europe. The late 1980s saw an influx of venture capital, particularly in the UK, but the subsequent crisis and decline in the mid 1990s (Murray 1995) resulted in a greater emphasis on the creation of attractive exit mechanisms such as second tier stock markets which had been absent so far.

The present research would like to add to the stream of research on European new, technology-based firms by developing a distinct argument. We argue that there has been virtually no systematic research into the process by which new, technology-based firms have internationalised. Yet, due to the limited size of the majority of national home markets, European start-ups with the aspiration and potential to achieve rapid growth will have to consider internationalisation at inception. Yet, international expansion and the ability to manage growth in several countries simultaneously adds an additional layer of complexity to the already considerable managerial challenges which the founders of NTBFs have to overcome. The broader question thus arises whether there is a systemic market failure, i.e. whether there is a situation in Europe where highly specialised, technology-based firms will have difficulties in growing beyond a certain threshold because their domestic markets are too small and the costs and problems of international expansion are prohibitive.

We would like to argue that, to date, this consideration has almost been completely absent in the agendas of researchers interested in European NTBFs. The available evidence on European internationally operating start-up firms is largely exploratory. To our knowledge, there is only one quantitative study that looked at these firms in a European setting (Lindqvist 1991). Similarly, the phenomenon has, until recently, received only limited attention in the US. This could be the case because the size of the national market is to a much lesser extent constraining the growth trajectories of American technology-based start-ups. A fresh impetus has been provided by entrepreneurship researchers interested in the growth strategies of new ventures. Yet, only over the past five years, there has been a significant increase of research that investigates the international activities of start-up firms.

Unfortunately, an assessment of whether or not European NTBFs are constrained in their growth trajectories by the limited size of their national home markets would go beyond the scope of the present research. Nevertheless, we would like to trigger a discussion and advocate that the managerial complexity of internationalisation has been overlooked by researchers interested in the growth of NTBFs. To shed light on those issues, we believe that the first step of a longer term research programme should determine to what extent the existing stock of NTBFs already engages in international activities. This is arguably best achieved at a national rather than European level. As a next step, it is important to identify the factors that impact on various aspects of internationalisation and subject them to empirical testing. In the next sections, we will therefore review the existing literature in international entrepreneurship and the theoretical contributions of international business theory in order to establish the current knowledge on internationally operating start-ups.

2.2. Empirical Evidence on International Entrepreneurship

During the last decade, the phenomenon of globalisation has received considerable attention and has shaped both the discourse and actions of managers, policy makers and academics. Research on the topic is rooted primarily in sociology, cultural studies, political science and economics. A common denominator is the definition of globalisation as a process in which the constraints of geography on social, cultural, political and economic arrangements recede (Waters 1995). One of the manifestations of a globalising world is the emergence of entrepreneurial start-ups that have an international outlook from inception. Coincidentally, over the last ten years, these firms have received increasing attention from entrepreneurship researchers. While there have been several exploratory studies in different countries conducted independently from each other, the recent increase of scholarly interest in internationally operating start-up companies emerged after the contributions of Oviatt and McDougall (1994). This section will summarise the most important findings of that research stream to date and highlight the implications for the present research. We will review a number of studies with regard to their methodological foundations and their content.

The studies have been identified after surveying the relevant journals of entrepreneurship and international business. In order to be included in the review, the papers had to deal with the international expansion of young, entrepreneurial firms.[2] The literature review sections of these papers were then screened for additional contributions to the field of international entrepreneurship. We acknowledge that there is a certain random element in this iterative procedure. Yet, there are a number of obstacles to a more systematic, keyword-based survey of computerised databases. First, a number of studies surveyed here appeared in journals that are not included in the standard databases such as the Social Science Citation Index or ABI Inform. Furthermore, as to be expected in a young field, the keywords "international entrepreneurship" or the combination of "international" and "entrepreneurship" and other variants produced only a limited number of studies. On the other hand, there is substantial support for the procedure chosen for the current literature review. During the recent conference on Globalization and Emerging Businesses in Montreal, October 1998, a number of recent papers on international entrepreneurship were presented. The literature review sections of those papers suggest that the studies reviewed here constitute a quite comprehensive overview of the "accepted" body of knowledge in international entrepreneurship at the time of the conference.

This iterative approach resulted in the identification of 11 empirical papers and one dissertation devoted to the topic. There have been six papers that are based on case studies (Jolly, Alahuhta and Jeannet 1992; McDougall, Shane and Oviatt 1994; Coviello and Munro 1995; Boter and Holmquist 1996; Murray 1996; Roberts and Senturia 1996) and four papers that are based on quantitative data collected either through a mail survey or content analysis of IPO prospectuses (McDougall 1989; McDougall and Oviatt 1996; Bloodgood, Almeida and Sapienza 1996; Reuber and Fischer 1997). Two authors used a triangulation method that involved case studies and a mail survey (Lindqvist 1991; Bell 1995). The contributions of these authors are therefore counted both in the case study and in the survey section of this review.

---

[2] Studies on exporting SMEs were thus not included in the review of international entrepreneurship studies. Nevertheless, we will refer to the rich body of export management research and SMEs in the following section that looks at international business theories.

2.2.1. The Internationalisation of Start-ups: Empirical Evidence from Case Studies

2.2.1.1. The Studies

Lindqvist (1991)

One of the earliest contributions to the international entrepreneurship literature was the doctoral dissertation of Maria Lindqvist (1991). The objective of her study was a closer examination of the internationalisation pattern and processes of young, technology-based Swedish firms. She carried out 15 cases studies in order to develop hypotheses for a subsequent mail survey. Lindqvist sees the key dimensions of the internationalisation process as being speed of market entry, pattern of market selection and choice of entry mode. A summary of her findings is reported below.

- **Speed** of internationalisation: Eight of the 15 firms were international almost immediately from inception and attributed this to the limited size of the home market. "International vision" of the top management team and previous international experience of key employees were all present among these the early internationalisers. A second group of firms took between two and four years to internationalise. The managers of these five firms attributed the time-lag mainly to the transition period required to transform the technological invention to commercially viable product. Two firms experienced a lag of five years between inception and first international sales. In this case, internationalisation has been initiated once the firm's activities switched from merely distributing products from foreign manufacturers to developing their own product ranges.

- Pattern of **market selection:** Countries that were entered rapidly included Scandinavian and continental European countries, the US, Japan and Australia. As companies commercialised technologically advanced products, most customers were found in industrialised countries. Some aspects of the market choice can be attributed by the perceived potential of the market. For example, firms sometimes entered the US before entering Norway. The initial choice frequently reflected an opportunistic behaviour that made use of contacts in various countries. Over time, however, market selection was more planned and involved evaluations of costs and benefits. Thus, a process of learning as predicted by behavioural theories has taken place.

- **Establishment form:** The main forms used included direct exports (9), independent representatives (12 local distributors, 2 local agents, 4 Swedish distributors), subsidiaries (8 wholly owned, 6 joint ventures) and licensing (3). Exporting was used by the majority of firms as initial entry form before the adoption of other forms. A certain relation with firm size was found here, as the smaller firms preferred entry modes that were less resource intensive. In markets with a high perceived potential, more resource-intensive entry forms such as subsidiaries and joint ventures have been chosen by the larger firms. Over time, direct exports became of limited importance for almost all of the firms. Only two firms relied exclusively on exports as their customers were a limited number of OEMs. Similarly some other firms relied on exporting as the main entry form for distant markets where it was difficult to find suitable distributors or where it was perceived as not viable to set up subsidiaries. The most important entry form was the use of local distributors as it proved to an effective way to provide product-related services such as installation, training and maintenance in foreign markets.

After analysing these case studies, Lindqvist concluded that there was considerable support for the internationalisation process perspective (Johanson and Vahlne 1977; 1990). Both the pattern of market selection and the choice and evolution of entry modes were characterised by learning processes that are expected by that theory. The main surprising feature was that the internationalisation process of the firms in her sample happened in an accelerated fashion. Note, however, that some of the firms included here were subsidiaries of large established firms. The firms were also up to 25 years old. Strictly speaking, one cannot include some of these firms as young independent start-ups. Still, the study produced substantive evidence that the internationalisation processes of young technology-based firms are proceeding in an accelerated fashion

Jolly, Alahuhta and Jeannet (1991)

Jolly, Alahuhta and Jeannet describe four high-technology start-up companies that challenged incumbent multinational firms. Not only did these companies sell their products across national boundaries, but they also performed different activities along the value chain in different countries. Jolly, Alahuhta and Jeannet identified a number of commonalties among these firms. They argue that the strategies of these four firms were based on a combination of the following features:

- All founders had international backgrounds from education and previous work experience and a "vision" to turn their businesses into globally operating firms.

- The firms operated in emerging industries such as computer peripherals and mobile telephony and offered standardised, high quality and innovative products that were targeted to growing market segments. All four firms rapidly introduced follow-up products that were developed and commercialised in parallel with the initial products.

- All firms chose to launch their products in key markets rather than in their home countries alone to build up volume. Lacking a global distribution infrastructure, all firms initially concentrated on development and manufacturing. They used strategic alliances with a limited number of key customers, mainly large OEMs, who incorporated the new components in their products. Having built up volume and being indirectly present in three continents allowed them to move into retail distribution soon after.

- None of these companies concentrated all their assets in one location. The companies entered foreign markets almost as soon as their products were ready for roll-out using entry modes that required direct investments. Rather than producing the products in their lead markets, they chose the lowest cost location for manufacturing. Two companies produced in two different countries with the objective of serving the entire world market from these locations.

- All firms have been structured as closely linked networks with actors meeting and communicating on a regular basis. These structures seemed to stem from the necessity to co-ordinate the different functional areas of the firms that are spread across different continents.

Jolly, Alahuhta and Jeannet conclude that the global orientation and organisation of these start-ups resembles those of strategic business units of established multinationals. It thus appears that these start-ups reacted boldly within a short window of opportunity in newly emerging industries. Due to their founders' insight of anticipating future demand for their products and their swift building up of a global manufacturing and distribution network, initially by using strategic alliances, they managed to establish a global presence before incumbent multinational firms decided to follow.

The article gives four highly interesting accounts of firms that grew extremely rapidly and built up international presence in several countries within few years. Unfortunately, Jolly, Alahuhta and Jeannet provide only a limited description of the internationalisation process as such. Nor do they report other critical issues, such as the financing of this rapid expansion. While these cases highlight a phenomenon that was hardly noticed by scholars and practitioners alike, the important question arises whether start-ups that perform different activities along the value chain on different continents are exotic outliers or whether we can observe a more general trend.

McDougall, Shane and Oviatt (1994)

McDougall, Shane and Oviatt's influential article is motivated by what they see as the increasing significance of "international new ventures" (INVs), a type of firms that they define as a "business organization that, from inception, seeks to derive significant competitive advantage from the use of resources and the sale of outputs in multiple countries" (p.470). They argue that firms of this type, which can be observed more and more frequently, represent a challenge for international business theory.

Altogether, McDougall, Shane and Oviatt report 24 case studies of international new ventures. Their article is based on two empirical sources. Twelve of these case studies were carried out by themselves. The remaining 12 case studies are compiled from conference papers and the above study of Jolly, Alahuhta and Jeannet (1992). Out of these 24 firms, 21 can be identified as high-technology firms, 3 are not attributable given the available information in the article. 17 (15 high-tech) firms originated from outside the US. Semi-structured interviews were conducted with the founders or Chief Financial Officers of these start-ups. In essence, they describe a number of cases where start-ups decided to build up international operations from the beginning. Over time, some of these firms evolved into mini-multinationals with manufacturing and sales activities spanning over different countries.

They contrast these findings with the prescriptions of the dominant theories of international business. They briefly review monopolistic advantage theory (Hymer 1976; Caves 1982), product life cycle theory (Vernon 1966), stage theories (Johanson and Vahlne 1977), oligopolistic reaction theory (Knickerbocker 1973) and internalisation theory (Buckley and Casson 1976).[3] They conclude that none of the reviewed theories is capable of explaining the formation of INVs. McDougall, Shane and Oviatt then provide their own explanation of why certain ventures internationalise form inception. Their explanation centres around three arguments.

The first argument focuses on the person of the entrepreneur. Following Kirzner's (1973) economic theory of entrepreneurship, they argue that markets are not in equilibrium and that there is no perfect availability of information. Entrepreneurs are people that are more alert to information about profitable resource combinations than other economic agents. The entrepreneur thus uses his superior knowledge or his anticipation of information asymmetries to combine resources in a profitable way. This alertness is often influenced by previous experiences. Consequently, McDougall, Shane and Oviatt argue that founders of INVs are more alert to the possibilities of combining resources from different national markets because of the competencies that they have developed in earlier activities.

Their second argument tries to explain why these start-ups *can* compete internationally. They argue that over time, inertia permeates organisations, and that inertia is promoted by structural impediments to change, stakeholder demands, perceptual biases of domestic managers, location of power in organisations and market stickiness when it comes to the reorganisation of economic relationships. International entrepreneurs avoid this path dependence and create firms that, from inception, incorporate routines and organisational capabilities which enable them to serve a global market place. Thus they

---

[3] A detailed review of these theories will be presented in the next chapter.

overcome the cost and information disadvantages traditionally associated with international business environments.

The third part of their argument investigates the structural form of the international activities of these ventures. Since the process of founding a firm demands sufficient resources within a short period of time to sustain the initial negative cash-flows, international entrepreneurs have less discretion to invest in assets located in foreign countries. The entrepreneurs interviewed in their case studies rather relied on hybrid or network-type structures of governance or control assets that they do not own.

McDougall, Shane and Oviatt's seminal contribution produced a series of rich insights into why start-ups can compete internationally. Yet, their paper can also be criticised on two grounds. First, their review of international business theories is somewhat selective. While they summarise the initial core statement of the theories, they do not take their subsequent developments into account. In addition, it might be argued that they only selectively quote the proponents of these theories in order to support their own argument. An example from their criticism of monopolistic advantage theory will illustrate the point. McDougall, Oviatt and Shane argue that

> "the tradition of monopolistic advantage theory has been to argue that a firm will engage in foreign investment *after* some monopolistic advantage has been developed and exploited in the home country (e.g., Buckley and Casson 1976). By extending its mature operations to foreign countries, the advantaged MNE can exploit the *already developed asset* at a low marginal cost" (McDougall, Shane and Oviatt 1994, p.474; italics in original).

We would argue that this a too narrow interpretation of the monopolistic advantage theory since it ignores its key feature, namely the notion that firms can offset additional costs caused by international operations through firm-specific assets (Hymer 1976). It is the deployment of these assets which leads to rent-generating differentiation rather than the timing of that deployment or the sequence of events which is the defining feature of monopolistic advantage theory.[4] This approach could seriously weaken McDougall, Shane and Oviatt's endeavour. On the one side, they provide compelling evidence that the emergence of international new ventures fits uneasily into the theories of international business. On the other hand, their theoretical discussion appears too selective and does not quite lead to an acceptance of the charge that the established body of theory in international business fails to explain the emergence of INVs.

---

[4] Note that a more thorough discussion of these theories and their application to international start-ups will be undertaken in the following chapter. We will argue there that the formation of international new ventures per se is not inconsistent with both internalisation and monopolistic advantage theory (see also section 2.3.).

Second, McDougall, Shane and Oviatt provide no detailed tabulated information that demonstrates the extent to which their three arguments are consistent with their 24 case studies. Therefore, despite providing intuitively plausible and theoretically sound rationales for the existence of international new ventures, the paper can be criticised on methodological grounds. Even so, this is a small criticism to make, given the paper's rich insights and contribution to theory development.

Coviello and Munro (1995)

Coviello and Munro applied a network perspective to examine international activities of New Zealand software firms. To this end, they carried out four detailed case studies in combination with a short questionnaire sent to 25 firms. They were interested in finding out how network relationships impact on international market development and marketing related activities. Coviello and Munro report that the behaviour of the four case studies substantially departs from the logic of the internationalisation process model (Johanson and Vahlne 1977). This may be a function of the highly competitive software market which is usually characterised by short product life cycles and the limited demand in the New Zealand home market. Coviello and Munro argue that the firms could enter several markets in rapid succession because they associated themselves with existing networks lead by powerful players. At the same time, the relationships developed also constrained their internationalisation efforts.

Though they were initially the focal firms in their networks, the role of these firms changed over time as their relationships with local dealers and distributors lead to unsatisfactory international market development. Rapid overseas growth (annual mean of 83%) was experienced after the firms associated themselves with powerful multinational players. Today, three of the four firms have been acquired by these larger partners. When looking at the evolution of marketing activities over time, the dataset indicates that activities involving product development, modification and technology decisions were to a large extent carried out by the software firms. As expected, activities that were closer to the end customers were carried out by relationship partners.

Like other contributors to the field of international entrepreneurship, Coviello and Munro report firm behaviour that is seemingly at odds with the logic of established internationalisation theories. Their contribution is highly descriptive and demonstrates how the interactions of software firms with their network partners influenced the internationalisation process. Overall, they see network models as additional perspective on internationalisation processes of firms.

Boter and Holmquist (1996)

Boter and Holmquist carried out six case studies in order to investigate the impact of industry influences on the internationalisation processes in small firms. To this end they looked at "innovative" versus "conventional" firms, one of each coming from Norway, Sweden and Finland. Conventional firms were here described as operating in mature industries (mechanical engineering, caravans, metal construction) and using an established technologies. Two of these firms were established SMEs. The "innovative" firms operated in the fields of radar technology, medical instruments and optical equipment. They were between 10 and 15 years old.

All conventional firms had a very hierarchical organisation with a high degree of formalisation. Exports were between 5% and 30% of all sales and were directed mainly to the neighbouring countries. Their culture could be classified as production-oriented and their technological focus rested on the gradual improvements of existing products using established technologies. Conventional firms either appeared to be constrained by the "industry rules" (producing capital goods that demand far-reaching investments in a market organisation for retail dealers, customer finance, service and maintenance) or were part of a larger supplier-buyer network. Thus they were part of a "tightly coupled business system."

On the other hand, all innovative companies had well-developed links with other knowledge-intensive organisations (universities, other firms), highly educated staff that worked together in a project organisation, and a very high export share of turnover. In all cases, only between 5% and 10% of their revenues were generated in their home market. Export markets covered all strong economic areas of the world. Innovative companies were free to follow any route to internationalisation, except for constraints stemming from their technology. The product development process involved close contacts with organisations at the technological core of the industry, irrespective of their location. The search for new commercial breakthroughs, new technologies, new products and partners is a transnational process that involved organisations operating on different continents. They were thus part of a "loosely coupled" business system which was made up of independent free-standing actors. The newness of the technology seemed to be a relevant indicator for how far these firms were able to depart from conventional industry wisdom.

A major finding was that no important differences between the firms were found that could be attributed to their nationality. However, there were marked differences between the two different groups of firms. This suggests the presence of an industry-specific entrepreneurial high-tech culture that transcends national borders. What is not clearly developed in this article is how the differences between the two groups affected on the internationalisation process or pattern. Though it remains a very insightful account of why and how the two groups differ, the study is marked by the absence of hypotheses about how these differences affect internationalisation behaviour.

Murray (1996)

Murray looked at successfully-exited venture capital backed companies that received external funding in the early stages of their evolution. Internationalisation is not the main focus of this paper but the account of the early years of these firms contains some interesting findings. Out of the six companies examined in the case studies, five recorded international sales within two years after formation. These firms respectively developed products in the areas of medical technology, laser-based rapid prototyping, integrated circuit testing, inkjet printing and biotechnology.

A common denominator of these firms is that their founders saw their industry as being independent of national boundaries. The market potential for different countries was assessed at inception and products were launched internationally. Without exception, the markets into which the products were launched were large and growing. In addition, their products required limited or no adjustments for cross-border commercialisation. Competition was also international. All major rivals of these firms were based in foreign countries and equally appeared to serve the world markets from their home-base. A particular feature of the founders of these firms is that, with the exception of the biotechnology company, all appeared to have some sort of international experience. The technological specialists all demonstrated a degree of innovative excellence, which made them known among their peers at an international level. Without exception, the professional managers previously worked in larger firms and had business experience in several countries. This resulted in a high degree of commercial awareness at an international level and knowledge of foreign partners.

Thus, one can say that these start-ups had an international outlook right from inception. This "international" mindset can, on the one hand, be interpreted as a "normal" feature in these high-tech industries. On the other hand, Murray argues that this attitude is closely related to the presence of the venture capitalists. In order to achieve their target internal rate of return, the VCs usually back a tiny minority of exceptional companies that feature aggressive growth trajectories in their business plans. Still, while the aggressive growth imperatives imposed by the venture capitalists automatically required international expansion, particular competencies of the founders seemed to have helped successful expansion.

Roberts and Senturia (1996)

Roberts and Senturia's study was motivated by exploring the internationalisation performance of early internationalisers. They argue that internationalisation is influenced by an "opportunity space" which is in turn determined by the condition of a particular product and its market, but not by its product life cycle. In addition, as many authors have done before, they link internationalisation to the attitudes, commitment and responsiveness of senior managers towards global opportunities. In order to find further support for their propositions, they carried out interviews with senior employees of the target companies, a convenience sample of 19 Massachusetts-based computer manufactures and software companies. The firms were between 5 and 25 years old. Half of these firms started their international involvement within one year of the domestic product launch. Today, 52% of their turnover is generated through international sales. Like in the other case studies, a sub-set of firms decided to move parts of their manufacturing abroad. The majority of firms, however, saw internationalisation almost exclusively in terms of commercialisation. Roberts and Senturia's findings can be summarised as follows.

- **Management:** Virtually none of the companies had internationally experienced staff at formation. However, among the firms that considered global markets as important from inception, usually at least one member of the management team had prior work experience in a company that was exposed to foreign markets. The management of these firms - as opposed to the others - felt comfortable from inception with the idea of overseas expansion.

- **Entry Modes:** Most companies engaged in some form of foreign activity within two years of their birth. The expansion patters ranged from a merely supporting overseas markets covered by distributors to simultaneous product launch in major European and Asian markets. The most popular entry mode was through local distributors followed by setting up local sales office. None of the 12 companies that now operate sales offices used that operating mode for their first entry. After having reached a certain threshold of international sales, they started supporting local staff or acquired their local distributor. The main motive behind making this step appeared to be the desire to internalise the local/regional marketing, distribution and support activities carried out by their partners. Roberts and Senturia observe the tendency for international activities to become configured in a way that resembled the domestic business model. In all cases, this lead to a substantial increase in their non-domestic revenues. Five of the 19 companies entered their international activities by reactively serving and supporting foreign markets. This move has usually been triggered by the initiative of a foreign distributor. These firms were characterised by relatively low levels of non-domestic revenue.

- **Internationalisation Performance:** Roberts and Senturia operationalise performance through the measurement of the proportion of non-domestic revenues. As expected, a high share of none-domestic revenues was generated quicker among those firms that that expressed early interest in international expansion as opposed to firms with a domestic focus. In addition, companies that progressed to more resource intensive modes saw sudden increases in their international sales. The least successful internationalisers had products that required regulatory approval in every country, technical modifications and extensive support arrangements. A further finding is that successful globalisation seems to be related to how quickly a company can create a foreign structure that resembles the domestic business model. In this context, they note that the use of distributors appeared to retard quick international expansion. The adoption of technological standards was an additional success factor for internationalisation. Roberts and Senturia argue that a standard or an established technology platform is a way to increase the legitimacy of small and young firms and to reduce information asymmetries. In addition, these firms did not have to rely on local distributors. Finally, companies that successfully entered foreign markets from an early stage on *did not* adapt their products to local markets. Localised or tailor-made products were only introduced at a later stage - accordingly to Roberts and Senturia mainly with the aim of achieving deeper market penetration and/or rising the entry barriers for their competitors.

In essence, like all the previous studies, Roberts and Senturia observed young high-tech firms that made substantial commitments to international activities from a very early stage of their existence. While, at a superficial level, this seems to be at odds with stage models or internationalisation process theories, Roberts and Senturia provide evidence that firms decided to switch to the most resource-intensive modes only after a certain experience or learning threshold was reached. While they conclude that the behaviour of the firms in their sample is inconsistent with established theory, the evidence they produce partly suggests otherwise. Nonetheless, like the findings of the other studies above, this does suggest that internationalisation processes do occur in accelerated fashion.

2.2.1.2. Conclusions from the Review of the Case Studies

A number of issues emerge from the discussion of these case studies. Table 1 gives an overview of the reviewed case studies. One can observe a number of commonalties. Above all, it was striking that every sample was made up of firms operating in technology- or knowledge-intensive industries. While this may simply reflect the authors' research and sampling preferences, the choice does suggest that the phenomenon of international entrepreneurship is particularly pertinent in high-technology industries.

Empirical Evidence on International Entrepreneurship   19

Table 1: Overview of Case Studies in International Entrepreneurship

Authors	Lindqvist	Jolly, Alahuhta and Jeannet	McDougall, Shane and Oviatt	Bell	Coviello & Munro	Boter & Holmquist	Murray	Roberts & Senturia
Year published	1991	1992	1994	1995	1995	1996	1996	1996
Number of Cases / Interviews	15	4	24 (12 indirectly from secondary sources)	24	4	3 "innovative", 3 "conventional"	6	19
Industry	Various High-Tech	IT/Com. hardware	Various industries, mainly technology intensive	Software	Software	Convenience	Various High-Tech	IT hardware and software
Sampling Criteria	Export directory	n.a	Convenience, n.a.	selected after questionnaire analysis	Convenience	Convenience	Successful VC investment and exit	Convenience, Massachusetts-based
International Sales as part of sampling criteria	yes	yes	yes	yes	yes	no	no	yes
Control group	no	no	no	no	no	yes, matched pair	no	no
Firm Age	6-25 years	<= 8 years	n.a	n.a.	10-15	10-15 *	n.a.	n.a.
Firm Size	7-135 employees	n.a.	n.a	n.a.	25-250	8-180	n.a.	n.a.
Focus	internationalisation process	start-ups competing against multinationals	review / theory development	internationalisation process	impact of network relationships on internationalisation	comparison of innovative and conventional firms	Characteristics of successful early stage technology VC financed firms	internationalisation process
Explicit Focus on international new ventures	no	yes	yes	no	yes	no	no	no
Discussion of International Business Theories	internationalisation process theory and stage models, internalisation theory	no	stage models of internationalisation, internalisation, oligopolistic reaction, product life cycle, monopolistic advantage	stage models	process models, networking theories	behavioural approaches to internationalisation	no	process and product life cycle models
Key findings	Evidence of rapid internationalisation with strong resource, but stronger commitment form larger and older firms	Reports the case of four small start-ups that became global players, they now perform different activities of their value chain in different countries	Established theories of international business fail to explain the formation of international new ventures	Stage models cannot account for foreign market selection and entry mode	"Random" involvement in foreign markets can be attributed to network of contacts	internationalisation should be understood in industry context, all innovative companies were more proactive internationalisers	international experience of founder, international and industry experience of key managers	More rapid and bolder resource commitment than expected by international business theories, but incremental pattern
Other findings	strongest commitment in firms with executives with international and industry experience	international vision, standardised products, innovative products based on industry shift, speed, follow-up products	background of the entrepreneur, his international vision and network are important determinants	product standardisation	Heavy reliance on network relationships for marketing related activities	concentrated product scope, background of managers	deliberate targeting of large and growing US market, international competition, complacency of incumbent large firms	standardisation, founders' international experience, higher commitment leads to higher foreign sales, replication of domestic business model
Issues	inclusion of corporate subsidiaries	no account of methodology	discussion of international business theories	no account of methodology		conventional firms are established SMEs rather than start-ups	no explicit focus on INVs	selective review of international business theories

* innovative firms only

All authors reported bold and proactive moves into foreign markets that are seemingly at odds with the fact that the firms in question were young start-up businesses. These firms initiated international activities almost from inception and entered several markets simultaneously in order to launch their products. A number of factors that are likely to facilitate this process have repeatedly been identified by the researchers. The internationally operating start-ups have been founded by individuals with extensive international and industry experience (Lindqvist 1991; Jolly, Alahuhta and Jeannet 1992; McDougall, Shane and Oviatt 1994; Murray 1996 Roberts and Senturia 1996). Furthermore, the founders had what researchers called "international vision" (Jolly, Alahuhta and Jeannet 1992; McDougall, Shane and Oviatt 1994; Roberts and Senturia 1996), i.e. the drive to compete with the products in lead markets across the globe, irrespective of their home countries. Rapid internationalisation was also associated with standardised products and products incorporating leading-edge technology (Jolly, Alahuhta and Jeannet 1992; Boter and Holmquist 1996; Murray 1996; Roberts and Senturia 1996). The latter suggests that a high degree of technological differentiation is met by a certain demand regardless of national boundaries.

In terms of market entry modes, a minority of the start-ups used arrangements that required direct investment. However, the most popular entry modes were direct exporting and foreign sales via third parties such as agents and foreign distributors. Activities closer to the product and technological core were thus carried out by the start-ups whereas activities closer to the end customer, such as installation, training and maintenance were handled by local partners. While the involvement of third parties lead to obvious advantages, i.e. the pooling of resources and skills, it did not always lead to satisfactory results in terms of market development (Coviello and Munro 1995; Roberts and Senturia 1996).

When looking at the studies, an additional and quite remarkable feature becomes apparent. With the exception of Lindqvist (1991) and McDougall, Shane and Oviatt (1994), none of the authors carried out a systematic review of international business theories in order to explain the phenomenon at hand. Admittedly, all these studies had an exploratory focus. In addition, extreme cases are included on purpose to highlight the limits of the existing theoretical frameworks (McDougall, Shane and Oviatt 1994). However, it does appear that the available theoretical apparatus to explain the phenomenon has not been used to its full extent. Thus, while a number of authors argue that their results cannot be accommodated by traditional international business theories, the evidence they produce could also suggest that firms actually internationalise in an accelerated fashion, but in accordance with theory (Lindqvist 1991; Roberts and Senturia 1996). A more systematic application of international business theories to that phenomenon therefore does seem to be warranted. We will now review the quantitative studies at hand and report how their results fit into the picture from the case studies.

2.2.2. The Internationalisation of Start-ups: Empirical Evidence from Quantitative Surveys

2.2.2.1. The Studies

McDougall (1989)

McDougall's 1989 paper is one of the earliest quantitative studies in the field of international entrepreneurship. Her work was motivated by the lack of research on how entrepreneurial companies compete internationally. As a starting point, she developed an early working definition of international new ventures which "see their operating domain as international from inception of the firm's operation" (McDougall 1989, p.388). She argued that international new ventures should be distinguishable from domestic new ventures based on their strategic orientation. Her mail survey to 2550 firms in the computer and communications hardware industries generated 250 valid responses. These firms were then grouped into two classes according to their international sales. Domestic new ventures (90 firms) did not have any international sales. Firms were classified as international new ventures (98 firms) if their international sales exceeded 5% of turnover.

In essence, McDougall's results suggest that the strategy and perceived industry structure profiles of the domestic firms differ significantly from the international ones. The strategy content variables contributed more to these differences than the perceived industry structure variables. The variable that had the highest discriminatory power was related to the marketing and distribution strategy of these firms. Rather than being niche providers, international new ventures seemed to serve customers in numerous different segments.

Overall, the paper does not analyse the international activities of these firms in more detail. It gives no account on key indicators such as the size of the firms, entry modes used, timing of market entry or the distribution of the share of non-domestic revenues. The lack of information on the latter makes the chosen threshold of 5% international sales for international new ventures appear somewhat arbitrary. The paper does, however, provide evidence that a quite a substantial proportion of new ventures in the chosen industries compete internationally. As such, it is one of the first statements highlighting the emergence of international start-ups

Lindqvist (1991)

As part of her dissertation, Lindqvist carried out a mail survey in order to test the propositions derived from her case study work with regard to the speed of market entry, the pattern of market selection and the choice of entry mode (see also the preceding section). Firms were identified using both export and industry directories. The mail survey resulted in a sample of 95 firms with international activities for which usable questionnaires were obtained. On average, these firms were 12 years old and employed 56 employees.[5] Today, the non-domestic revenue of these firms amounts to 60% of total turnover. Lindqvist's findings can be summarised as follows:

- **Speed of market entry:** 44% of the firms entered their first foreign market during their first or second year of operation. 78% of the firms initiated international activities within five years. However, once international activities had been initiated, the speed of foreign market commitment differed markedly with the time required to enter five foreign markets ranging from 0 to 17 years. The multivariate analysis revealed that the speed of market entry was influenced by the following factors. Firms entered their first foreign market more quickly when their management had previous international experience. Firms that characterised their products as being very innovative were older when they entered foreign markets for the first time, but quicker at entering five markets. This suggests that innovative products require more time to develop. Subsequently, they are then launched simultaneously in several markets. Structural factors such as firm size and R&D intensity did not have a significant influence on the timing of market entry.

- **Pattern of market selection:** On average, the firms in Lindqvist's sample entered six foreign markets. When looking at the markets entered, it became apparent that the firms followed a relatively traditional pattern. The majority of entries (both initial entries and total entries today) were made into relatively close Scandinavian and Western European countries. In many cases, there has not been a sequential pattern of market entry, but rather a pattern where firms entered "clusters" of markets simultaneously.

- **Foreign entry modes:** Foreign agents and distributors were the most popular entry modes among the firms in Lindqvist's sample. They were used by 87 % of the firms. Direct exports were used by 68 %, subsidiaries by 44 % and licensing by 11 % of the firms. This also shows that the majority of firms used several entry modes at the time. Subsidiaries were most common in large markets such as the US, the UK and Germany. Note also that these firms were quite old and had extensive experience before establishing subsidiaries. Most subsidiaries performed sales and after sales tasks rather than production activities.

Lindqvist concluded that there are a number of results that lend support to the theoretical prescriptions of the internationalisation process model (Johanson and

---

[5] Firms that were up to 25 years old were included in the survey. Note that this would be inconsistent with definition of a young start-up in the majority of US studies (Oviatt and McDougall 1997).

Vahlne 1977). While the majority of firms seemed to follow a traditional, albeit accelerated pattern, there is an important minority of firms whose internationalisation behaviour deviated. Furthermore, the bivariate and multivariate regressions did not reveal any structural, firm-specific variables such as firm size, age or R&D intensity that had an unanimous effect on the different dimensions of internationalisation. This suggests that internationalisation could actually be understood as a threshold. Once firms have internationalised, the variable traditionally associated with that decision can not explain subsequent internationalisation behaviour.

Bell (1995)

Bell's article reviewed the discussion of the appropriateness of stage theories with regard to the internationalisation of business firms. The proposition that internationalisation proceeds in an incremental way is tested with observations of small software firms from Ireland, Finland and Norway. These countries have been chosen because of the limited size of their home markets, the resulting dependence on export markets and the fact that they are relatively isolated from their target export markets. Using a triangulation approach, the author first conducted a survey which leads to the collection of data from 98 firms, 88 of which were exporting at the time of the survey. Subsequently, he chose a sub-sample of 24 firms to examine the result of the survey in more detail. The results can be summarised as follows:

- **Market selection:** Some software firms entered foreign markets before selling into their home market. The survey data seemed to support the "psychic distance" concept, as the majority of firms chose countries that were geographically and culturally close for their initial market entries. However, an important minority of firms chose distant countries for their first market entry. The case studies revealed a number of explanations for this unusual behaviour. These consisted of following an existing client abroad, of receiving unsolicited orders, of strategies that targeted a specific sector for their products irrespectively of the country of destination and of general trends in the computer industry. The latter stem from the fact that the computer industry seems to be concentrated in a few countries and that presence in these countries was judged as strategic necessity by the respondents.
- **Entry Modes:** When looking at entry modes, the survey revealed that 70% of overseas transactions have been conducted through direct exports or exports using agents and distributors. Firms that commercialised bespoke or semi-bespoke products usually did not involve intermediaries. Firms that sold standard, "off-the-shelf" products were more likely to use intermediaries. Few firms engaged in foreign direct investment. No subsidiary carried out production or research and development activities, but this may reflect the peculiarities of the software industry. The case studies indicated that direct

contacts with the clients (i.e. not involving intermediaries) were chosen especially when the support in terms of consultancy, systems design, customisation, configuration, installation, training, up-grading and after sales requirements was needed. Due to the short expected life cycles (two to three years), direct exporting was perceived by the interview partners as the quickest way to get access to international markets. This was especially the case for firms that offered highly specialised niche products whose sales would not be able to generate high revenues in any given national market over a long period. Most firms did not change their initial entry mode over time.

Bell stated that neither firm age nor size were significantly related to the decision to internationalise as firms of all size and age groups were found to engage in cross-border activities. Bell thus concluded that his data represents further evidence that the prescriptions of the internationalisation process model (Johanson and Vahlne 1977; 1990) do not correspond to the observed internationalisation pattern of his sample. In the present case, Bell argued that industry specific factors seem to contribute more to an understanding of the rapid internationalisation. However, Bell's study has a number of shortcomings. First, he did not provide any data on firm age or critical issues such as timing of market entry. Second, he merely described his dataset instead of testing hypotheses on the internationalisation behaviour. Third, he gave no account of the selection criteria for his case studies. If these are mainly composed of the most extreme internationalisers, then the claim that his data does not correspond to the behaviour predicted by process models is not remarkable. In the absence of that information, the study has to face the criticism that there is a certain incongruence of investigative method and conclusion. Thus, this study mainly highlights the phenomenon and provides qualitative evidence from interviews on the export decision, entry modes, location and subsequent evolution of international activities.

McDougall and Oviatt (1996)

This project is a follow-up study of McDougall's (1989) earlier study on the difference between international new ventures and domestic new ventures in the information technology and communications hardware industries. Both authors were concerned with the performance implications of internationalisation. They point out that most studies that investigated the impact of internationalisation on performance are based on cross-sectional datasets. In order to examine performance implications over time, they recontacted the respondents of McDougall's earlier study reviewed above. Usable questionnaires were received from 62 firms.

McDougall and Oviatt's data suggests that ventures with higher levels of international sales have a higher level of performance in the subsequent period when considering relative market share as measure. However, this relationship was insignificant when taking return on investment as performance indicator. The results suggest that, although the more international firms have been able to increase their market share over time, this did not translate into higher profitability. McDougall and Oviatt's analysis also reveals that firms that increased their internationalisation had a high association between changes in their strategy and their performance level. However, the pattern of strategic change is not consistent. The inability to provide consistent indications of change is explained by the small sample size due to low response of follow-up and the short period between initial enquiry and follow-up.

As in McDougall's earlier study, this article less concerned with the internationalisation pattern and processes rather than with general performance issues. In that respect, it raises the important point that, although many observers recommend internationalisation as a performance enhancing strategy, this may not automatically lead to higher profitability.

Bloodgood, Sapienza and Almeida (1996)

Bloodgood, Sapienza and Almeida examine the strategic and structural characteristics of internationally operating new high-technology ventures at the time of their initial public offering (IPO) and the impact of internationalisation on performance two years after the IPO. Drawing on the resource-based view of the firm, they argue that internationalisation is a function of top management's international exposure, sources of competitive advantage, innovation and firms size. Their sample consists of 61 venture capital-backed firms that were five years old or younger at the time of their 1991 IPO. Information was gathered by analysing the content of IPO prospectuses. The firms came from several different industries. On average, they had sales of US $79 million (median US $13 million) and employed 1668 people (median 171). The dataset also contains one firm with 47,000 employees and a turnover of US $660 million which probably accounts for most of the differences between mean and median. Bloodgood, Almeida and Sapienza develop hypotheses and operationalise their measures. Internationalisation is measured using Porter's (1985) value chain concept. Accordingly, a firm's activities were divided into inbound logistics, operations, outbound logistics, marketing and sales and service. The researchers then screened the IPO prospectuses for international activities and assigned scores depending on how many of those five elements were performed abroad. Performance is operationalised using sales growth and income before interest and taxes. R&D expenditure as a percentage of total expenditure was used as a measure for innovation. Control variables include leverage, industry growth rate and industry profitability.

Their regression results can be summarised as follows. A positive relationship was found between internationalisation and the number of directors with previous international work experience. International education of top management did not have a significant impact. The hypothesis that internationalisation was positively related to a low cost strategy could not be supported. Pursuing a product rather than a marketing differentiation strategy lead to higher internationalisation scores. As opposed to the positive hypothesised relationship, the measure innovation turned out to be negatively related to internationalisation, albeit only at a marginally significant level. Firm size (employees) had a positive impact on internationalisation. With regard to performance, the regressions produced mixed evidence. Income was affected positively by internationalisation, but negatively by innovation. Sales growth was not affected by the degree of internationalisation at the starting period. It was, however, positively affected by a low cost strategy and a product differentiation strategy, innovation and firm size. No significant relationships were found for the remaining variables. Altogether, the impact of the independent variables on internationalisation and the two performance variables is not uniform. Furthermore, internationalisation was positively related to income, but was not related to sales growth. The lack of a significant increase in sales among the more international firms can, according to the researchers, be attributed to the fact that those firms were already the largest in absolute terms at the time of the IPO. This could also mean that most successful firms were also the best at internationalising their business activities.

Bloodgood, Almeida and Sapienza mention two issues - their exclusive inclusion of US ventures and their cross-industry sampling - as primary limitations of their study. Yet, there are at least two additional points that also merit discussion. The first point is related to their sampling strategy. All firms included in this study are venture capital backed firms that have staged an IPO. The sample is thus composed of a particular type of highly successful firms - "new high potential ventures" in the terms of the authors, which, compared to the total population of start-ups of similar age, can almost be regarded as outliers or exceptions. It is therefore unclear, whether or not the results apply to other samples of internationally operating start-ups.

The second point is related to the chosen measure of internationalisation. There is a certain literature concerned with measuring the degree of internationalisation of the firm which suggest that the most frequently used and arguably most appropriate measure is the share of non-domestic revenue (Sullivan 1994, Ramaswamy, Kroeck and Renforth 1996). The operationalisation chosen by Bloodgood, Almeida and Sapienza of using Porter's value chain is not without danger. A firm that manufactures and performs inbound logistics abroad but sells domestically will get a score identical to that of a firm with a foreign sales and service subsidiary. Yet, the latter firm may generate a substantial part of its revenues from foreign sales whereas the former doesn't. Therefore, despite the identical score, the strategy and structure profiles may be quite different. The fact that some of the empirical relationships do not correspond to the hypothesised relationships may be a side-effect of the measure of internationalisation used. Finally, despite the fact that higher internationalisation leads to higher sales, it may not be desirable for a company to perform all activities along the value chain abroad. Given the prominence of Silicon Valley for the development and manufacturing of leading edge information technology, it might not be sensible for a US venture to relocate these activities abroad.

Therefore, while the overall argument of the study is convincing, the results should be interpreted in the light of the peculiar sample and the operationalisation of the concept of internationalisation. Nonetheless, this one of the few studies that discusses several international business theories in order to derive variables and test their impact on the degree of internationalisation of a firm.

Reuber and Fischer (1997)

Reuber and Fischer's article examines the relationship between the international experience of management teams of Canadian software firms and their degree of internationalisation. Their sample includes 49 cases. The firms were on average 11 years old and employed 41 people. On average, international activities were initiated after five years. Today, 88% of software firms have international sales (71% outside North America). The mean share of non-domestic revenue amounts to 54%.

An interesting feature of Reuber and Fischer's work is their indirect modelling of the influence of international experience on the degree of internationalisation. Accordingly, international experience is expected to influence two mediator variables, the use of foreign strategic partners and delay (time lag) in initiating foreign sales after start-up. In essence, their data does suggest that international experience leads to a shorter delay of internationalisation and to a greater number of alliances. Both these factors, in turn, had a significant impact on the degree of internationalisation. In addition, both firm age and firm size were not significantly related to the degree of internationalisation. Overall, the article is very focussed and contains an insightful discussion on the measurement of the degree of internationalisation.

2.2.2.2. Conclusions from the Review of the Quantitative Studies

During the review of these quantitative studies, it became clear that there was no unifying agenda guiding these research projects. Consequently, the majority of the results are complementary rather than conflicting. While some studies were concerned with performance issues, others had a defined focus on internationalisation behaviour. Table 2 gives an overview of common elements of the studies.

Despite the different objectives of the above studies, it is possible to identify a number of common denominators. Above all, three of the six studies have confirmed the influence of top management's international experience on internationalisation behaviour (Lindqvist 1991; Bloodgood, Almeida and Sapienza 1996; Reuber and Fischer 1996). Those results corroborate the findings of the case studies as they largely indicate that this experience facilitates internationalisation processes and leads to a higher the degree of internationalisation of a firm. Furthermore, in their conclusions, the authors of two studies also argue that the internationalisation behaviour of the firms is influenced by industry-specific factors (McDougall 1989; Bell 1996).

There is relatively little information given on the structural forms that the international activities of these firms take. Thus, while all papers based on case studies contain some cases that internationalised rapidly into several markets using resource-intensive entry strategies, there is, with the exception of Lindqvist (1991), no quantitative study that investigates the prevalence of this behaviour with a larger sample of firms. The authors do not provide any information on the entry modes used.

The review of these studies revealed an additional feature that merits consideration. With the exception of McDougall (1989) and McDougall and Oviatt (1986), none of the studies intentionally compares international start-ups with domestic start-ups. In these two studies, the two groups of firms are compared in order to identify differences in their strategy and structure pattern. Possible factors that could cause internationalisation in the first place and differences in their internationalisation behaviour are not examined. The studies of Bloodgood, Almeida and Sapienza (1996) and Reuber and Fischer (1997) do contain a number of firms without international activities. However, these firms are not used as a control group. Rather, internationalisation is regarded as a continuum (reaching from 0 to 1 or from 0 to 100) and no particular attention is devoted to the non-internationalising firms.[6] The remaining two studies sampled only internationalisers.

A further observation relates to the theoretical core of the papers. With the exception of Lindqvist (1991) and Bloodgood, Almeida and Sapienza (1996), none of the studies is discussing different theories of international business in their literature review. This became apparent, as several studies criticised internationalisation process theory and stage models. Yet, these are not the only theories of international business that could be applied to the case of international start-ups. To date, it has not been tested whether different theories of international business can account between the differences of internationalisers and non-internationalisers.

---

[6] Note that the notion of internationalisation as continuum would be disputed by those scholars that see internationalisation as "organisational innovation" for a firm (see Andersen 1993 for a review).

Empirical Evidence on International Entrepreneurship 29

Table 2: Overview of Quantitative Studies in International Entrepreneurship

Authors	McDougall	Lindqvist	Bell	McDougall & Oviatt	Bloodgood, Almeida & Sapienza	Reuber & Fischer
Year published	1989	1991	1995	1996	1996	1997
Number of firms	188	95	98	62	61	49
Industry	IT/Comm. Hardware	Various High-Tech	Software	IT/Comm. Hardware	Various Services and High-Tech	Software
Sampling criteria	Dun & Bradstreet	Export Directory	n.a.	Inclusion in McDougall (1989)	IPO	Industry directory
International sales as sampling criteria	no	yes	n.a.	no	no	no
Control group	yes	no	no	yes	not explicitly	not explicitly
Mean firm age	n.a.	12	n.a.	4	less than 5 years at time of IPO	11
Mean firm size	n.a.	56	n.a.	22.6	1668	41
Focus	Strategy and industry profile	Internationalisation Process	Internationalisation Process	Performance	Determinants of internationalisation and performance	Degree of internationalisation
Explicit focus on international new ventures	yes	no	no	yes	yes (?)	no
Discussion of international business theories	no	internationalisation process theory and stage models, internationalisation theory	internationalisation process theory and stage models	no	internationalisation process model, monopolistic advantage	process model
Key findings	domestic and international ventures differ in terms of industry and strategy profile, notion that INVs are different	observed rapid internationalisation, but market selection and entry modes in line with internationalisation process theory	Stage models cannot account for foreign market selection and entry mode	international new ventures have higher levels of market share, but not ROI. Increased international sales only lead to increased performance when accompanied by strategic change	international work experience of managers, product differentiation and firm size are positively related to internationalisation level and internationalisation at IPO is positively related to earnings 2 years later	international experience of management, mediator effect of internationalisation behaviour which in turn positively influences the firm's degree of internationalisation
Issues		some old SMEs and corporate subsidiaries included	no account of methodology		firm size, sample of very successful firms, measure of internationalisation	

The final point emerging from the discussion is related the prevalence of the phenomenon. The only study using a random sampling procedure within the chosen industries is the initial study of McDougall (1989). The share of firms with international activities identified suggests that, in the absence of non-response bias, about half of the US start-ups that manufacture information technology and communications hardware equipment have generated revenues from international sales, albeit at a low level. All other studies use non-random sampling procedures. The study of Bloodgood, Almeida and Sapienza (1996) only includes data on exceptionally successful firms. All other studies are based on export directories. As a result, there is, to date, no reliable information on the prevalence of the phenomenon of international entrepreneurship in industrialised economies.

To conclude, the lack of overlap between the exploratory case studies and the quantitative studies was striking. There are a number of issues that have been raised by the case studies which have not been subject to empirical testing so far. The only point where the results of these studies converge is the international experience of the top management of these firms. A reason for this apparent lack of overlap could be the simultaneous timing of these studies. In any case, it shows that, in this relatively young area of academic activity, plenty of issues have yet to be researched.

2.2.3. Conclusions from the Review of Research in International Entrepreneurship

The main results of the review of the empirical research papers in international entrepreneurship can be summarised under four broad headings.

First, there is relatively little overlap between the case study based research and the studies based on mail survey data. With the exception of Lindqvist (1991) who uses a triangulation approach, the quantitative studies surveyed incorporate few research hypotheses derived from a review of qualitative studies in international entrepreneurship. As mentioned already above, this could be a result of the simultaneous timing of these studies and the fact that even some of the quantitative studies were exploratory in focus. Therefore, it does not come as a surprise that there is little common ground between these two groups of studies aside from the largely undisputed influence of top management's international experience on the start-ups internationalisation behaviour.[7] Yet, there are a number of additional propositions derived from the case studies that merit further testing.

---

[7] Bloodgood, Almeida and Sapienza (1996) found that international schooling had no significant effect on the degree of internationalisation of the firms in their sample. International work experience, however, was positively related at a significant level.

Second, with the exception of McDougall (1989) and McDougall and Oviatt (1996), none of the studies has tried to identify differences between internationalising and non-internationalising firms. Although, McDougall (1989) and McDougall and Oviatt (1996) are concerned with strategy and structure profiles and performance issues, they do not investigate the pattern of internationalisation of the firms in their sample. Consequently, it is currently unknown whether the case study findings, which are largely based on convenience samples, can be replicated using large samples, let alone whether they can discriminate between international and domestic start-ups. Thus, a test of these propositions should involve a control group of non-internationalisers.

Third, an interesting feature of all reviewed papers on the internationalisation of start-ups is that nearly all firms were operating in high-technology sectors. Not a single study focused on low technology firms. This raises the question of whether there is anything particular about technology-intensive firms that makes them engage in cross-border operations earlier than other firms. In the context of small firms in general, this notion of a systematic difference received some support in the past from a survey that reported that high-technology SMEs were more likely to engage in international activities than low-technology SMEs (Small Business Research Centre 1992). A number of points, such as increasing cost of research and development, shorter life-cycles for technology and the convergence of demand pattern for technology-intensive goods across countries, can be identified that speak in favour of high-technology being a special case. Accordingly, various operationalisations of technology-intensity at industry level have been shown to be important determinant of the increase of flow of goods across national borders (Franko 1989, Kobrin 1991). Technological change, the same factor that provided the initial opportunity for a start-up to respond to demand irrespective of national borders, can also represent its biggest threat. A one-product start-up faces the danger of obsolescence as soon as technological evolution moves on. This means that a start-up competing in a narrow market niche may have no choice but to venture abroad from an early stage in order to generate revenues to pay back the initial development costs and to finance ongoing development. But how many of these firms are there? How realistic is the assumption that a start-ups can compete internationally? Evidence on these questions remains scarce as there is, to date, no study that systematically surveys internationally operating start-ups in a particular country.

A final issue became apparent after the review of the empirical studies. In their influential 1994 paper, based on a discussion of international business theories and 24 case studies of international new ventures, McDougall, Shane and Oviatt make the following claim:

> "Neither monopolistic advantage theory, product cycle theory, stage theory of internationalization, oligopolistic reaction theory, nor internalization theory can explain the formation process of INVs. These theories fail because they assume that firms that firms have become international long after they have been formed, and

they therefore highlight large, mature firms" (McDougall, Shane and Oviatt 1994, p.469-470).

However, the majority of subsequent studies published to date have not applied all existing international business theories to the study of these firms. While several authors have echoed these criticisms (e.g. Knight and Cavusgil 1996) and argued that existing international business theories fail to explain the behaviour of international start-ups, the majority of them discuss one or at best two of the theoretical frameworks available to explain internationalisation (Bell 1995; Coviello and Munro 1995; Roberts and Senturia 1996). Notable exceptions include Lindqvist (1991) and Bloodgood, Almeida and Sapienza (1996). Note however, Lindqvist's research includes firms that are up to 25 years old in her sample. These firms fall outside the definition conventionally used in order to operationalise "new ventures" (Oviatt and McDougall 1997). The firms in the sample of Bloodgood, Almeida and Sapienza are highly successful ventures that staged an IPO which raises issues of how representative that sample is. Furthermore, their research focus was not on testing different international business theories. The questions thus remains whether there is a need for a new theory or whether the phenomenon can be explained with existing theoretical frameworks of the field of international business. As we already pointed out during the above review of McDougall, Shane and Oviatt's 1994 paper, we have some doubts as to whether the international business theories reviewed there are interpreted in the spirit of their original proponents. For McDougall, Shane and Oviatt's argument to become accepted by a broader community of international business scholars, a more systematic discussion and application of international business theories to the phenomenon of international start-ups is required.

While we sympathise with the claim that refined theoretical foundations are required to explain the emergence of that peculiar type of firm that is international at inception, we believe that the established theories of international business can still inform us in explaining the larger phenomenon of start-ups that initiate international activities during their first years of operation. To this end, we will undertake a task largely absent in the work of international entrepreneurship researchers: we will review the dominant theories of the field of international business and discuss their application to technology-based start-ups.

2.3. Theories of International Business

2.3.1. Overview of Different Theories

The term international business has become the common denominator for a highly eclectic array of research areas including disciplines such as economics, management, marketing, organisational behaviour, social psychology, industrial relations, finance and accounting to name only a few. The literature most relevant for this research investigates the internationalisation of the firm. Most scholars of internationalisation have focused on a number of core questions. In essence, these are:

- Why do firms compete abroad?
- Which firms go abroad?
- What structural forms do their international activities take?
- Which foreign markets do they chose?
- How fast do they enter different markets over time?
- Why can some firms compete in foreign settings despite the obvious disadvantages whereas others choose to stay in their domestic environment?

These different questions have been addressed through various theoretical and empirical approaches. Among the theories of internationalisation, one can make a distinction between research that, on the one side, uses the concepts and tools of economic analysis and research that stems from a more behavioural perspective on the other. The former has mainly been built around the notions of monopolistic advantage, oligopolistic behaviour, product life cycles, transaction costs and market failure. The latter consists mainly of internationalisation process models, stage theories and network theories of international business. More recently, the resource-based and organisational capability perspectives, which draw on both economic and behavioural concepts, have been applied to international business.

When looking at these theories and their empirical application, it appears that some of them provide only limited insights into the internationalisation processes of small, entrepreneurial start-ups. For example, oligopolistic behaviour theory has been developed to explain the actions of large multinational firms that compete on a global scale against a limited number of multinational rivals. It provides a theoretical explanation for the competitive interaction of these firms with their rivals (Knickerbocker 1973). While certainly relevant when looking at established multinationals, it is doubtful whether the "global oligopoly" assumption can be applied to the objects of the present research.

Similarly, product life cycle will probably be ill-suited to investigate the international activities of start-ups as it is mainly concerned with the location of international production of large mature firms. It was originally aimed at providing an explanation for the failure of the neo-classical theory of comparative advantage to predict the pattern of international trade and production. In its various forms (Vernon 1966; Vernon 1979) it distinguishes between several stages in the life cycle of a product. Its main argument is that a product's life cycle stage will determine the geographical pattern of its production. At every stage, the different competitive context, which is usually expected to follow some sort of commoditisation logic, forces the firm to reduce the product's price. Over time, this requires different factor inputs. Firms are then expected to locate to those countries where these production factors are cheapest.

While there is no "network theory of internationalisation" as such in the field of international business, network theories have become increasingly popular with researchers of interested in the internationalisation pattern of firms (Johanson and Mattson 1993; Coviello and Munro 1995; Blankenburg Holm, Eriksson and Johanson 1996; Welch and Welch 1996). Networks are at the same time an antecedent and outcome (Welch and Welch 1996) of internationalisation. The network perspective is a serious contender for inclusion and has in the past been applied to study the interactions of high-tech start-ups with their environment (e.g. Coviello and Munro 1995; Yli-Renko and Autio 1998). However, we would like to argue that there are a number of problems associated with that approach. Besides the problem of operationalisation (Borch and Arthur 1995), the approach arguably lacks normative and discriminative power when applied to internationalisation. The majority of international activities take place between business firms and contain therefore some relational element. At the same time, it is not clear to what extent this relational element *triggered* internationalisation, as it is virtually impossible to obtain networking variables on those firms that have not internationalised. Furthermore, case studies show that there are firms, whose *initial* internationalisation decisions cannot be accounted for by network arguments (Bell 1995). It therefore does not come as a surprise that empirical tests on the impact of networks on organisational outcomes take both networks and international activities as given variables (e.g. Coviello and Munro 1995; Blankenburg Holm, Eriksson and Johanson 1996). Note, however, that this is not to deny the premise on which many networking studies are based, i.e. that economic analysis has an undersocialised view of the world which ignores that most transactions are embedded in a context of social relations (Granovetter 1985). The impact of social control and trust as determinants of organisational outcomes is also undisputed. Furthermore, there have been important insights emerging from studies that interpreted networks as mechanisms for resource leveraging (Yli-Renko and Autio 1998) or reported that the quality and frequency of a firm's interactions with its environment affects its approach to internationalisation (Johanson and Mattson 1993). Still, the approach arguably lacks power to *predict* the answers of the above-mentioned core questions in international business. It is therefore probably best applied to studies that compare the impact of different network characteristics on organisational outcomes or to case studies concerned with the overall evolution and pattern of international activities over time, after internationalisation has been initiated.

We would therefore like to argue that the above approaches provide only limited insights when applied to the present research objective, the internationalisation of high-tech start-ups.[8] The literature review will thus concentrate mainly on internationalisation process theories, transaction-cost theory, monopolistic advantage and resource-based perspectives. Their core elements, criticisms and implications for high-tech start-ups are discussed in the following sections.

2.3.2. Internationalisation Process Theories and Stage Models

Theoretical Core

Besides those theories of international business that are based on the concepts and tools of economic analysis, models which are strongly influenced by the behavioural theory of the firm developed by Cyert and March (1963) have become influential in explaining cross-border operations of firms. One of the earliest contributions can be found in the work of Aharoni (1966). In his study of 38 US firms, he found several factors that influence the internationalisation decision, the most important being an international outlook of higher executives. Once the decision to internationalise had been taken, the pattern of foreign activities followed a learning process during which international operations where gradually scaled up.

These results served as starting point for a number of Swedish researchers at Uppsala University in the 1970s whose case studies led to the development of a more general model of the internationalisation of the firm (Johanson and Wiedersheim-Paul 1975; Johanson and Vahlne 1977). One of the earliest manifestations of their work became the concept of "economic distance" which in itself consists of the two factors "physical distance" and "psychic distance."[9] They showed that economic distance influenced the geographical choice of market entry and that the firms in their sample initiated their operations in countries that were

---

[8] As the above discussion has shown, this does, strictly speaking, not apply to networking theories. However, the methods required for their application are probably incompatible with the main objective of the present study.

[9] The concept has its origins in context of international trade. Introduced by Burenstam-Linder (1961), it was used to explain why most trade takes place between countries with relatively similarly factor endowments despite contrary predictions derived from the principle of comparative advantage. In the management literature, the terms economic distance and psychic distance are frequently used interchangeably.

relatively close. Once the entry decision had been taken, the pattern of the foreign activities followed an "establishment chain" (Johanson and Wiedersheim-Paul 1975) where firms successively extended their involvement in foreign markets over the years from no regular exports up to foreign production.

The mechanism behind this increasing involvement was introduced in an influential article by Johanson and Vahlne (Johanson and Vahlne 1977). They argued that the establishment chain is the result of a circular learning process which starts after the decision to venture abroad has been taken. They see internationalisation as a "process of incremental adjustment to changing conditions of the firm and the market" (Johanson and Vahlne 1977, p.26). A basic assumption - like in the economic approaches described above - is that firms have to deal with costs and uncertainties when entering a foreign environment. These are caused by the different business culture, language, market structures, to name only a few. According to Johanson and Vahlne, firms overcome these disadvantages by gaining direct experiential knowledge of foreign markets over time.

They propose a dynamic model consisting of change and state aspects where the outcome of one decision feeds back as input into the next decision. They argue that the initial decision to commit resources to the commercialisation of products abroad over time leads to a better knowledge of the foreign environment. This knowledge, derived from the current international activities, feeds back on the decision to commit resources for future activities and leads, over time, to a steady increase of commitment to the foreign market (Johanson and Vahlne 1977). In their own words "market knowledge and market commitment affect both commitment decisions and the way current decisions are performed - and these, in turn, change market knowledge and commitment" (Johanson and Vahlne 1990, p.12).

According to this view, a firm starts its internationalisation by venturing into those markets with the lowest perceived uncertainty (or lowest economic distance). Arrangements that require relatively few resources, such as exporting, will be the preferred entry modes. Better knowledge is acquired over time through operating in that market and thereby uncertainties and information costs present prior to the initial investment decrease. Based on the new knowledge, the firm might now reassess its position and increase its involvement in the foreign environment.[10] It follows then that internationalisation proceeds along a dynamic feedback logic where the initial involvement reduces uncertainty which may then lead to an increasing commitment and a scaling up of the foreign operations towards more resource-intensive modes. Furthermore, the knowledge acquired during the first foreign market entry influences the choice and entry mode of subsequent market

---

[10] Others have pointed out that better knowledge might equally lead to a reduction of commitment (see Dalli 1994, Calof and Beamish 1995).

entries. Employees involved in the internationalisation process will, due to their greater knowledge of foreign markets, perceive better opportunities and promote solutions to exploit them. Therefore, Johanson and Vahlne argue that the internationalisation proceeds irrespective of whether strategic decisions are taken by management (Johanson and Vahlne 1990). The quasi-deterministic nature is thus an additional feature of their model.

In a more recent restatement of their model, Johanson & Vahlne (1990) identify three exceptions to the assertion of incremental involvement in small steps. First, big firms with a large resource base can be expected to make larger internationalisation steps. Second, relevant market knowledge can be gained by means other than first-hand market experience when market conditions are stable and homogeneous. In this case, firms may also internationalise faster and in larger steps. Third, firms may generalise experience gained from other markets with similar conditions. Thus, the process of increasing commitment may not have an identical pattern in all countries.

Critical Comments

Johanson and Vahlne's work provided the basis for extensive empirical research from numerous scholars in different countries. Known under the heading "stage models" of internationalisation, they support the view of internationalisation as incremental process (Bilkey and Tesar 1977; Bilkey 1978; Cavusgil 1980; Reid 1981; Wortzel and Wortzel 1981; Czinkota 1982; Barrett and Wilkinson 1985; Lim, Sharkey and Kim 1991; Moon and Lee 1991; Rao and Naidu 1992; Crick 1995). All studies argued that internationalisation behaviour is best represented by invoking distinct stages reaching from no foreign involvement to foreign direct investment. The methodological foundations of these empirical studies using the concept have frequently been subject to strong criticism (Turnbull 1987, see also Andersen 1993; Leonidou and Katsikeas 1996 for reviews). Critics point out that stage models are tautological (Andersen 1993). Instead of reflecting increasing commitment to internationalisation, the different stages are direct results of the classification criteria used by the researchers. Their arbitrary definition makes it difficult to delimit the stages. In addition, all studies have been derived from cross-sectional samples which makes it impossible to analyse the temporal and causal logic behind the internationalisation process. Thus, the question of whether firms' action is as deterministic as claimed by Johanson and Vahlne, i.e. whether firms really move from stage to stage until they produce abroad, and the influencing factors behind the moves remains contested. Furthermore, factors that lead to the initiation of the internationalisation process in the first place and reasons why firms can operate in foreign environments despite obvious cost disadvantages against host country competitors are not examined in detail. Finally, critics have pointed out that stage models are purely descriptive. As opposed to

Johanson and Vahlne's original mechanism, they lack explanatory power as they fail to develop a mechanism for the transition between stages.

Note that the process view of Johanson and Vahlne does not explicitly expect *distinct stages* of internationalisation (Johanson and Vahlne 1990). However, the establishment chain and the pattern of firms entering markets with successively greater psychic distance over time are seen as "possible indicators" for the existence of the process as outlined above (Johanson and Vahlne 1990). Besides the methodological problems associated with the empirical test of Johanson and Vahlne's mechanism of internationalisation, its theoretical core and behavioural assumptions have been subject to criticism. The emphasis on experience as a principal independent variable and the quasi-deterministic nature of the internationalisation process, irrespectively of whether strategic action in that direction are taken by its management, is difficult to reconcile with strategic management theories based on micro-economic frameworks. Furthermore, none of the three exceptions to the incremental logic mentioned by Johanson & Vahlne (1990) applies, that would explain the rapid internationalisation of small, young firms that operates in fast changing, unstable high-technology markets and that have no prior experience in international environments (McDougall, Shane and Oviatt 1994; Oviatt & McDougall 1994). Finally, as better knowledge may not always lead to *increasing* commitment, the notion of *more appropriate* commitment, after a consideration of the firms resources and its strategic orientation, is more appealing. This would reconcile the theory with observations of small firms that enter and leave foreign markets in a flexible manner and make the model less deterministic (Dalli 1994; Welch and Welch 1996). The combined criticism has lead one observer to conclude that "the use of only one explanatory variable (experiential knowledge) is not likely to provide a sufficient explanation for a firm's choice of entry mode" (Andersen 1997, p.32; parentheses in original).

Despite these criticisms, elements of the original approach of Johanson and Vahlne have recently been 'rediscovered' by scholars interested in the management of multinational firms (Madhok 1997). The focus on experience and learning in the process model bears a certain resemblance to knowledge-based, resource-based and organisational capability approaches that see the development and deployment of capabilities as the key sources of competitive advantage (see for example Barney 1991; Peteraf 1993; Grant 1996; Teece, Pisano and Shuen 1997). While it is accepted that internationalisation may not proceed in distinct stages, the basic logic behind the internationalisation process developed by Johanson and Vahlne is arguably still a powerful model of the dynamics within the internationalising firm (Melin 1992). The emphasis has thus shifted away from using it to predict the structural and geographical pattern of international operations to seeing it as a model of knowledge accumulation in multinational companies.

Implications for Technology-Based Start-ups

The process perspective is widely believed to be of relevance during the early stages of internationalisation of small firms (Andersen 1993). It should therefore lend itself to the analysis of the determinants of international activities of start-up firms. According to this view, one would expect a young and small firm to adopt a rather cautious attitude towards rapid early internationalisation. One would expect these firms to be orientated towards the domestic market until a certain degree of market penetration is reached. After a certain time, probably when the perceived growth potential in the home market has been realised, the adolescent firm might then turn its attention towards expanding into foreign markets. Note that it may be inappropriate at this stage to still speak of a young "start-up." Note also that in the case of highly specialised technology, the domestic demand can be very limited so that the firm will consider internationalisation at a very young age. Markets which are close to the home market in terms of geographical and psychic distance would be considered for initial market entry. An incremental pattern of increasing resource commitment to foreign operations, determined by the experienced gained over time at every stage, might then turn the firm into an international player. According to the circular process logic, the increased market knowledge would cause an evolution of the cross-border activities. Given the resource constraints of the majority of start-ups, one would expect them to start cross-border activities using entry modes that require the lowest degree of resource commitment. Initially, this entry mode is likely to be (reactive) direct exporting. Upon assessment of the foreign market potential, the young firm would over time be expected to opt for a more proactive market coverage, e.g. through the use of sales intermediaries. Given sufficient growth potential through international expansion, the firm would later set up its own sales and production facilities and finally become a fully fledged multinational co-ordinating activities along the value chain in different countries. Note that the process logic does not give any indication on the expected duration of use of each operating mode. Therefore, the use of resource-intensive entry modes by start-ups would, strictly speaking, not be incompatible with this theory. One would, however, expect that the start-up initiated international sales using a low commitment entry modes prior to switching to the current resource-intensive entry mode. Given that the defining element of start-ups is their young age, it is thus very unlikely - though not impossible - to observe start-ups that operate in foreign markets using resource-intensive operating modes.

Given the evidence of start-ups that compete in a number of countries using entry modes of various levels of resource commitment, Oviatt and McDougall (1994) concluded that Johanson and Vahlne's model fails to explain the phenomenon of international entrepreneurship. However, the empirical evidence to date is largely case based. A more systematic survey should be undertaken in order to assess the prevalence of the phenomenon of international new ventures.

2.3.3. Internalisation and Transaction Cost Economics

Besides the internationalisation process perspective which is rooted in the behavioural tradition, concepts of the field of economics have been used to analyse the determinants of entry modes. The main approaches within the latter tradition are represented by transaction cost economics (TCE) and the related concept of internalisation. According to internalisation theory, which is the main theoretical lens for explaining the establishment of wholly owned subsidiaries by multinational corporations (Madhok 1997), the international growth of a company is achieved through the displacement of markets that operate in a less efficient way than firms. In transaction cost economics, the emphasis is placed on finding the most efficient institutional or contractual arrangement for economic transactions (Williamson 1985). Both approaches can be traced back to Coase's (1937) seminal treatment of the question of why firms exist. Applied to international business, they have become an explanation of why firms set up foreign operations (hierarchies) instead of engaging in cross-border trade (markets).

2.3.3.1. Internalisation Theory

Theoretical Core

Internalisation theory has been developed to explain why firms set up wholly owned facilities in foreign countries as opposed to engaging in cross-border trading relationships. Using Coase's early analysis of transaction costs, it is based on two premises. First, firms choose the lowest cost location for performing activities along their value chain. Second, firms grow through internalising markets until the costs of doing so outweigh the potential benefits (Buckley and Casson 1976). Generally speaking, a firm is a mechanism to replace market transactions with internal transactions. In international markets, transactions can take place between firms (via direct exporting, licensing or through intermediaries) or involve setting up wholly-owned facilities (production and/or distribution) in the respective host countries. There may be particular market imperfections associated with cross-border activities such as difficulties with regard to the valuation of products and patents or governance costs arising from dealing with agents and distributors, to name only a few. "Internalising" cross-border markets by setting up subsidiaries may then lead to a more efficient allocation of resources than conducting transactions between firms at arms-length (Buckley and Casson 1976). Firms thereby obtain the opportunity to earn higher rents and thus offset the costs associated with doing business abroad. For the host country, this can mean that product markets can be created where none existed before due to a lack of supply.

One of the main characteristics of this approach is that returns are not seen primarily as a result of market power (or any collusionary practice) but rather as a result of increased internal efficiency and better resource allocation due to internalisation of external economies or diseconomies. Note, however, that the emphasis here is on better resource allocation, and not necessarily market-perfecting behaviour, as the firm may, after its entry in a foreign market, erect barriers to entry for other firms or invest in other forms of rent seeking and isolating behaviour (Buckley 1990). Internalisation theory, by implying market failure, is mainly an attempt to explain foreign direct investment as an operating mode of international business. In that case, the international growth of a company is achieved through the displacement of cross-border markets, which operate in a less efficient way than cross-border hierarchies.

Critical Comments

A number of criticisms have been put forward against the internalisation model. First, internalisation is a fairly static concept that compares given alternatives at a given time. It even takes international activities as given and - without the inclusion of specific propositions - offers no answer for the questions on how the pattern of international activities evolves over time. Even its proponents admit that the original theory can only allow for comparative static choices (Buckley 1993b). Second, it does not incorporate all strategic alternatives available to firms. Its most recent reformulation has put the emphasis on firms entering foreign markets for the first time (Buckley and Casson 1998). Yet, it is surprising to notice that, even in this extension, the entry mode of "direct exporting to end customers," a frequently used initial entry mode in industrial markets, is absent. Third, the approach treats all different costs associated with international expansion as given. Its normative value appears to be somewhat limited as assumed cost types such as "Cost of building trust of acquiring knowledge through wholly owned distribution" or "Additional transaction cost incurred in using an external market for the wholesale market" (Buckley and Casson 1998, p. 544) are difficult to estimate *ex-ante* for a managerial decision maker. Furthermore, it does not incorporate any notion of switching or adjustment costs between different approaches over time. It therefore remains a static approach. A related criticism is the failure of the concept to incorporate managerial aspects in its decision rules. Set in a neo-classical world in which information on the environment is widely available, the "invisible hand of the market does practically all the management required" (Buckley 1993b, p. 201). Thus, a dilemma becomes apparent: While on the one hand, internalisation is explicitly seen a source of above average rents, it ignores managerial or competitive action as equal sources on the other. It has therefore been criticised for lacking managerial relevance as it relegates management to a "ceteris paribus" condition. Still, it is widely accepted as powerful explanation for the international growth of firms (Cantwell 1991).

2.3.3.2. Transaction Cost Economics

Theoretical Core

The version of transaction cost economics (TCE) best known to a wider audience of scholars has been developed by Oliver Williamson (for example Williamson 1981; Williamson 1985).[11] While this theory is closely related to the concept of internalisation, one should note a number of differences which impact on their prescriptions with regard to internationalisation. In TCE, the emphasis is placed on finding the most efficient institutional or contractual arrangement - or 'governance mechanism' in the jargon of TCE - for economic transactions. Like internalisation, the logic of TCE would argue that, under certain conditions, a transaction carried out within a hierarchy can represent a more efficient arrangement than a market-based contractual arrangement like exporting or licensing. The crucial difference is that, according to TCE, efficient transactions may also be of an *external* kind without necessarily exercising any ownership rights (Cantwell 1991). This may be the case when a firm is in a position of controlling a network of production or income-generating assets. Thus, transaction cost theory can be seen as a more general theory defining the boundaries of the firm.

Compared to internalisation which implies market failure by default, TCE is more concerned with the behavioural conditions that give rise to transaction costs. In essence, TCE makes the behavioural assumptions of bounded rationality and self interest which may lead actors to behave opportunistically. Safeguarding against these risks when dealing with a partner as opposed to carrying out the transaction within a hierarchy gives rise to transaction costs (Williamson 1985). Situations where bounded rationality and self interest are particularly problematic arise in the presence of asset specificity and uncertainty or information asymmetries (Williamson 1985; Anderson & Gatignon 1986). Asset specificity occurs when one party of the transaction has to invest into co-specialised assets to make the relationship work (Teece 1986). This party can subsequently be taken hostage by the other contracting party due to the sunk costs involved in the arrangement. Contracts can be devised to minimise the risk of shirking of one of the parties. Yet, the notion of the 'incomplete contract dilemma' (Klein, Crawford and Alchian 1978) holds that it is unrealistic to specify a situation entirely. Furthermore, the costs of devising the contracts, monitoring and enforcing them may be prohibitive for both parties. TCE theorists argue that, in the presence of these conditions, it is more efficient to carry out economic activity within a hierarchy rather than to deal

---

[11] Note that there are transaction cost theories other than Williamson's approach that incorporate different assumptions (see for example North 1990). However, it is Williamson's approach that has been most frequently applied to the management area (Goshal and Moran 1996).

with a partner. In essence, the firm's advantage over markets lie in its ability to set incentives, monitor, settle disputes and refine rewards (Mahoney 1992).

The theory has in the past two decades been widely used and represents one of the key theoretical frameworks in organisation economics (Conner 1991; Mahoney 1992). In a domestic setting, it has been applied to examine diverse topics such as make or buy decisions, the degree of vertical integration (e.g. Monteverde and Teece 1982, Walker and Poppo 1991), distributor management (e.g. John and Weitz 1988; Heide and John 1994), and strategic alliances and joint ventures (e.g. Hennart 1988; Robertson and Gatignon 1998). In the field of international business, TCE has been most successfully applied to the study of entry modes chosen by multinational corporations (Gatignon & Anderson 1988), service firms (Erramilli & Rao 1993) and the study of international joint ventures (Hennart, 1990). Entry decisions that were not aimed at establishing foreign production facilities but at the commercialisation of goods and services have been analysed within the field of international marketing. Here, this framework has been used to study the degree of channel integration in foreign markets (Klein et al 1990; Aulakh & Kotabe 1997).

Critical Comments

In recent years, the transaction cost framework has increasingly been subject to criticism from scholars (see for example Granovetter 1985; Goshal & Moran 1996; Kogut & Zander 1996; Madhok 1996). The majority of criticisms are concerned with the behavioural assumptions that are part of transaction cost theory. While some argue that TCE provides an accurate, but rarely a complete picture of the determinants of organisational outcomes (Conner and Prahalad 1996), there are others that go as far as seeing the logic of TCE as counterproductive for good management practice (Goshal and Moran 1996; Moran and Goshal 1996).

TCE has been criticised for its "undersocialised" view of economic relations. In his classic article, Granovetter (1985) argues that economic actions are embedded in a network of social relations. Social control and trust act as natural safeguards against opportunism thus making certain prescriptions of TCE with regard to the design of governance mechanisms redundant. Goshal and Moran (1996) and Moran and Goshal (1996) make two related points. First, they review a number of empirical papers that apply TCE and argue that the assumption of opportunism is not required in order to predict particular outcomes. Second, they argue that the assumption of opportunism becomes a self-fulfilling prophecy when accepted for normative purposes. They subsequently expose the mechanism behind this circular logic. Increased control and monitoring mechanisms have been shown in empirical studies of occupational psychology to lead to lower identification of individuals with organisational entities. Lack of identification, on the other hand, has been shown to increase the risk of opportunistic behaviour. Therefore, the preemptive design of governance mechanisms - a rational managerial decision within a "Williamson hierarchy" given that TCE assumes opportunism by default - is likely to provoke opportunistic behaviour. While not necessarily present in the first place, this occurrence of opportunism results in an ex post justification of the governance mechanism. Hence Goshal and Moran (1996) argue that the normative implications of TCE adversely affect organisational performance.

Criticism has also been voiced by those scholars that developed knowledge-based explanations of why firms exist (Kogut and Zander 1996; Prahalad and Conner 1996). Kogut and Zander have argued that firm boundaries are more likely to be determined by "the costs of communication, co-ordination, and new combinations, not those of transactions" (Kogut and Zander 1996, p.503). TCE therefore lends insufficient attention to other factors, such as identity and learning effects, that have an impact on organisational modes. Both Prahalad and Conner (1996) and Madhok (1996) have argued that the emphasis of TCE on economising on transaction costs in order to maximise rent ignores an analysis of the creation of value in the first place. The managerial relevance beyond the truism that "transaction costs should be minimised, all other things being equal" is therefore doubted. A related criticism is triggered by the emergence of co-operative strategies, both domestically and internationally. The upsurge of alliances and hybrid strategies would be considered sub-optimal according to the TCE perspective. Yet, the empirical evidence available shows that firms increasingly engage in such strategies and apparently do so with success (Kogut 1988, Madhok 1997, Gulati 1997). Madhok argues that theoretical approaches need to incorporate motivations other than economising on transaction costs (i.e. the generation or exploitation of capabilities and resources) in order to align theory with managerial practice (Madhok 1997).

A final criticism of both TCE and the internalisation framework is closely related to the research objects of the present study. Both internalisation and TCE are comparative static concepts which have been developed with large mature organisations in mind. Both make the implicit assumption that firms can freely choose between the different entry and operating modes. Constraining factors assumed by other theories of organisational economics, such as path dependency (Madhok 1997), learning effects (Kogut and Zander 1996) and resource endowments of firms (e.g. Barney 1991) are absent from the analysis. Both internalisation and TCE treat learning costs as "cost of information." Both are seen as exogenous to the firm and are treated as given variables (Buckley and Casson 1998). Resource endowment is of even more critical importance in the case of technology-based start-ups. Arguably, the latter is a critical constraint on organisational outcomes and largely reduces the scope of different modes available for consideration. In fairness, it has to be acknowledged that the most recent extension of the internalisation approach (Buckley and Casson 1998) does advance a more sophisticated argument which in principle is compatible with the limited resource endowments of start-ups. However, given that all cost types that can occur in international transactions are treated as given, the implications of the approach for firms that operate on a constrained resource base remain unclear.

Implications for Technology-Based Start-ups

Despite the criticism, the transaction cost approach promises to be valuable when applied to the international activities of firms operating in high-technology sectors. Even its critics acknowledge its value when applied to positive rather than normative analysis (Goshal and Moran 1996) since the empirical applications of transaction cost-based approaches usually do not require the notion of opportunism.[12] However, the other two conditions that give rise to high transaction costs - asset specificity and information asymmetries - are of particular relevance in high-technology industries. Furthermore, in his discussion of factors influencing governance mechanisms, Williamson (1991) identified two additional issues related to technological innovation: the problem of appropriability of rents and responsiveness.

In high-tech industries, it may be difficult to establish the true value of products and solutions given information asymmetries between buyer and seller. For example, an industrial buyer of a complex piece of software will frequently not be in a position to assess the benefit of the solution to his business before its installation. Consequently, prices may fail to reduce each party's bounded rationality. Given this inability to assess the true value of the intangible technology content of a product, a firm might not be able to appropriate the potential returns from commercialising a new technology through arms-length transactions (Magee 1977; Teece 1977; Teece 1983). Furthermore, if extensive consultation efforts are required to persuade potential buyers of the merits of a high-technology product, the degree of asset specificity can be expected to be high. Note that the direct transaction costs required during the entire sales transaction will also be substantial. In that situation, the governance problems and costs of using intermediaries are expected to be higher relative to those of setting up own sales subsidiaries in foreign countries. In accordance with these theoretical prescriptions, a positive relationship between technological innovation and

---

[12] A short example on the manufacturer-distributor relationship illustrates this point. Without assuming opportunism of either parties, it can be expected that the sunk costs to build up a commercial relationship and to train the local distributor's sales and support staff represent a financial risk that both parties will seek to minimise. These costs may be higher in the case of technologically advanced products. From the distributor's point of view, the trade-off between the product's potential to add value to his portfolio on the one side, and the asset specificity and risk of taking on an unproven solution from a unknown young start-up company on the other ("Will it fulfil its potential?"), is more likely to determine the terms of the collaboration. Asset specificity and uncertainty rather than opportunism thus produce a situation that will - according to the TCE logic - require sophisticated governance mechanisms.

vertical integration has been shown empirically (Armour and Teece 1980; Teece 1986). Hence, according to this logic, hybrid arrangements involving parties other than manufacturer and end-customer should be avoided. Depending on the frequency of the transaction and the amount of service content to be provided locally, a high-technology firm would then be expected either to export directly or to build up a wholly owned distribution facility.[13] Note that this implication is in stark contrast with the internationalisation process logic which sees first-hand experiential knowledge as a determinant of the entry mode choice.

At this point, an issue of particular relevance to start-up firms arises. The theory suggest that there may be situations, where a very innovative start-up companies operating at the forefront of technological developments can only appropriate rents for their activities through setting up subsidiaries in foreign countries instead of exporting. Furthermore, transaction frequency and the pre- and after-sales service requirements may require local presence instead of arms-length exporting. Yet, the average start-up will rarely have the financial resources to set up a wholly-owned foreign subsidiary. As a result, we end up with a dilemma where, on the one hand, TCE and internalisation theories may recommend under certain conditions that the start-up internalises a transaction in order to minimise the risk of market failures typically associated with high-tech environments. On the other hand, the start-up may lack the resources required for this theoretical prescription.

Nonetheless, it is compatible with transaction cost logic to think of an operating mode that avoids extensive commitment of resources, i.e. the use more hybrid structures such as long term contracting or joint ventures. This requires an element of control over the arrangement in order to exploit and appropriate benefits of international operations. While the assumed governance costs of such an arrangement make it a sub-optimal choice compared with either direct exporting or the setting up of a wholly owned distribution subsidiary, it may be the only way for a start-up to provide services such as installation and technical maintenance in distant foreign markets.

A final point related to high technology environments was made by Williamson himself (1991). Issues such as timing of innovation and product launch are of crucial importance for firms which experience a short window of opportunity. If the emphasis is put on responsiveness in real-time rather than equilibrium contracting, then the prescriptions of TCE should not be the dominant decision rule. Additional modifications not yet developed are needed to maintain the predictive ability of the theory (Williamson 1991). Arguably, the defining element of international new ventures is the rapidity of their cross-border expansion which suggests that real-time responsiveness is of vital importance. Williamson's "exception" thus appears to be the norm when looking at new, technology-based

---

[13] This implies that the decision to internationalise is given.

firms. This suggests that additional approaches should be considered when explaining this phenomenon.

2.3.4. Firm-Specific Advantages

So far, the distinct prescriptions of the two approaches reviewed have somewhat conflicting implications when applied to high-tech start-ups. In this section, we would like to discuss different theories that have the potential to bridge the prescriptive gap between the process logic and transaction cost-based theories. To this end, we will briefly review Hymer's monopolistic advantage theory, the resource-based view of the firm (RBV) and the emerging knowledge-based and organisational capability (OC) perspectives. Strictly speaking, only the first is a "genuine" theory of international business. The resource-based view has its origins within the field of strategic management and is a more general theory concerned with the sources of competitive advantage, rather than a theory of international business. Still, it claims to represent a more general theory of the firm. Given its widespread application to strategy analysis of large mature firms and given that these firms increasingly compete at an international level, its implications should have some validity when applied to internationally operating start-ups. The organisational capability perspective, which is closely related to the RBV, has recently been extended to discuss international operating modes of firms. We would argue that these three theories are closely related in several points. Above all, they are all concerned with explaining organisational outcomes with firm-specific factors that are difficult to replicate by competitors. In addition, the theoretical core of all three explicitly draws on Penrose's theory of the growth of the firm and the notion of firms being bundles of resources (Penrose 1959). Surprisingly, in the discussion of the phenomenon of international entrepreneurship, this connection has largely been ignored by other researchers.[14]

---

[14] See for example Oviatt and McDougall's (1994) criticism that traditional theories of international business fail to explain the emergence of international new ventures. While they include monopolistic advantage theory in their list of "ill-suited" theories, they propose that a resource-based explanation promises to lead to better insights (Oviatt and McDougall 1994). Bloodgood, Almeida and Sapienza (1996) are a notable exception as they discuss both monopolistic advantage and resource-based approaches jointly.

2.3.4.1. Monopolistic Advantage Theory

Theoretical Core

Monopolistic advantage theory is frequently associated with the seminal contribution of Stephen Hymer (Hymer 1976)[15]. Hymer was puzzled by the inability of the prevailing neo-classical theories of international trade and international finance (portfolio capital investment) to explain the foreign activities of firms. According to neo-classical trade theory, highly developed countries where capital is abundant relative to labour are expected to export capital intensive goods and import labour intensive goods. Given tariff or non-tariff barriers, these countries may export capital as a partial substitute to goods thus reaping the benefits from relatively higher interest rates in developing countries where capital is scarce and labour abundant. Since 1945, however, empirical evidence had not been in line with the neo-classical theory. International trade and the flows of capital are now mainly occurring between industrialised countries with rather similar factor endowment. Hymer's response was to put forward a microeconomic approach that stressed the role of the individual firm as main determinant of international flows of goods and capital. His explanation of foreign direct investment extended the portfolio investment approach by emphasising that an element of control over the acquired assets can lead to higher returns than could be expected according to financial theory.

In international business, however, this approach remains best known for its attempt to explain why firms can compete in foreign settings against indigenous competitors. The latter are likely to be in a more favourable position than foreign firms, as they have better information about their environment and acquiring this knowledge may be costly. However, some firms acquired advantages in particular areas that they may find desirable to exploit in other countries. These superior abilities can stem from technological innovation, manufacturing processes, brand names, organisational talents, marketing skills (Hymer 1976). By subsequently invoking Bain's (1956) classical analysis of barriers to competition in domestic markets, Hymer identifies superior advantages as imperfections in international markets. These advantages or abilities can be leveraged in foreign host markets without substantially higher costs (Caves 1982) and create market imperfections - "quasi-monopolies." These imperfections subsequently enable multinational enterprises to reap monopoly rents that outweigh the disadvantages and costs of competing abroad.

---

[15] Hymer's original thesis was completed in 1960, but it was only after his death, in 1976, that it was published by the MIT. By that time, his ideas had already found widespread acceptance.

Critical Comments

The market power approach was later extended by industrial economists (Caves 1982; Pitelis and Sugden 1987) who perceived advantages arising from superior abilities principally as anti-competitive devices which act as barriers to entry to other firms. In contrast, it should be noted that the international firm is originally seen by Hymer as an active agent, not a passive agent in the classical industrial economics tradition, which follows the structure-conduct-performance paradigm.[16] (Cantwell 1991). Authors have also expressed concern about the term "monopoly rents". This notion may be misleading as these advantages can, for example, result from a more efficient resource allocation by multinationals (Dunning 1993) and thus rather take the character of "Ricardian rents"[17] which stem from superior co-ordination abilities. However, a common denominator is that the international growth of the firm is essentially a result of superior abilities which cannot be matched by competitors, at least in the short run, thereby creating a market imperfection. Like internalisation and transaction cost theory, monopolistic advantage theory is largely static in nature. Its main weakness is that it does not explain how superior, rent-generating abilities are created in the first place.

2.3.4.2. Resources, Organisational Capabilities and Knowledge

Theoretical Core

Monopolistic advantage theory is very close to the resource-based view (RBV) of the firm and the organisational capability (OC) perspective that see competitive advantage as stemming from superior resources and capabilities which cannot be replicated by competitors. The discussion of these more recent theories will be brief as they are not international business theories per se. However, the RBV has in the past been applied to study competition of internationally competing firms (for example Collis 1991; Tallman 1991).

The main difference between monopolistic advantage theory on the one hand, and RBV and OC on the other, is the latter's elaborate emphasis on the mechanisms how resources, skills and capabilities are generated, kept and deployed. Based on Penrose's notion of the firm as bundle of assets, the resource-based view of the

---

[16] It thus somewhat pre-empted Porter's (1980) analysis of the sources of competitive advantage.

[17] Monopoly rents are defined as returns that stem from the ability of a monopolist to maintain prices above marginal costs. Social costs arise from the contraction of output below its level under perfect competition. In contrast, there are no social costs associated with Ricardian rents which are defined as returns of scarce resources in excess of their opportunity costs (Mahoney and Pandian 1992).

firm (Wernerfelt 1984; Barney 1991; Mahoney and Pandian 1992; Peteraf 1993) argues that organisational performance is a function of the internal assets of a firm. If these resources are matched appropriately to the external environment, then the firm may command a competitive advantage over its rivals. According to the RBV, firms are inherently different as today's resource endowment is a function of previous decisions and accumulation processes (Dierickx and Cool 1989). Resources include both physical resources and intangible resources. While the former can be more easily obtained and imitated, it is especially the latter that differentiate a firm from its rivals. They include management skills, brand names, processes, organisational culture and tacit knowledge of employees. It is this idiosyncratic bundle of intangible resources that will determine how the physical resources will be deployed thus leading to firm-specific returns.

Scholars also tried to define the characteristics of those resources that lead to sustainable competitive advantage. Barney argues that, in order to yield sustainable competitive advantage, resources have to be valuable, rare, imperfectly imitable and un-substitutable (Barney 1991). Peteraf's contribution suggested that competitive advantage can be gained when resources are heterogeneous, imperfectly mobile and when there are ex-post and ex-ante limits to competition. The concept of "isolating mechanisms" (Lippman and Rumelt 1982) has been put forward to explain why rents from resources are not competed away under competition. In their exhaustive review of the RBV, Mahoney and Pandian (1992) argue that isolating mechanisms stem from bounded rationality (causal ambiguity) and asset specificity (uncertainty of imitability due to uniqueness of resource accumulation pattern).

Over the last decade, the resource-based view has developed into several closely interrelated branches. In addition to the core argument outlined above, there are different flavours that have emphasised capabilities, organisational routines, knowledge and learning processes. The organisational capability perspective (e.g. Madhok 1996; 1997; Teece, Pisano and Shuen 1997) is rooted in an elaborate framework linking "more common" assets and resources with "more sophisticated" competencies and capabilities. Teece, Pisano and Shuen (1997)[18] distinguish between factors of production, resources (or firm-specific assets), organisational routines/competencies, core competencies and "dynamic capabilities." They argue that new forms of competitive advantage are created through the latter - the "firm's ability to integrate, build, and reconfigure internal and external competencies to address rapidly changing environments" (Teece, Pisano and Shuen 1997, p.516). These dynamic capabilities can thus be seen as meta-competencies that are responsible for the development of organisational core competencies to match environmental opportunities. A discussion of these

---

[18] Teece, Pisano and Shuen's article was published in 1997. However, their ideas have been widely known to a larger audience, as the working paper version of the article has been in circulation since 1990.

dynamic capabilities lead to the insight that, ultimately, the knowledge base of a firm should become the core of a new theory of the firm (for example Kogut and Zander 1992; 1996; Conner and Prahalad 1996; Grant 1996; Spender 1996).The knowledge base here comprises both the skills, tacit and explicit knowledge of employees and organisational knowledge, routines and processes. A common denominator of these approaches is that the generation of value, rather than the economising on transaction costs, should become the focus of managerial and academic attention.

Madhok (1997), extended the OC / knowledge-based approach to the discussion of foreign entry modes. Here, Madhok draws on his earlier distinction between creation of new capabilities and exploitation of existing ones and the notion of a generic/embedded knowledge (Madhok 1996). He argues that the OC perspective manages to explain situations in which the theoretical implications of TCE are at odds with empirical observations, especially if the actions of firms are motivated by the development of new capabilities as opposed to the exploitation of existing ones (Madhok 1997; Teece et al 1997). If the focus is on the exploitation of existing capabilities, OC prescriptions are in line with those of TCE, although they are arguably less restrictive. Like TCE, OC incorporates the notion of bounded rationality, but reaches its conclusions without requiring the notion of opportunism. When the firm's entry decision is motivated by the creation of new capabilities, the OC perspective claims to be a powerful model for explaining the more recent surge in alliances and other hybrid entry modes which is somewhat at odds with the prescriptions of TCE. In addition, while the transaction cost approach makes the implicit assumption that firms can freely chose the optimal entry mode or switch between entry modes at no costs, the notion of path dependence indicates that the firm's margin of manoeuvre is constrained by its past decisions and organisational routines (Kogut & Zander 1996). Note that there are some similarities with internationalisation process theory due to the emphasis on learning and path dependencies. Thus, organisational capabilities can then be simultaneously sources of competitive advantage and constraints. This highlights the need to chose an entry mode which combines the existing capabilities of the firm with those demanded by a particular foreign market (Madhok 1997). Because of OC's dual focus on both the development and exploitation of capabilities, it has the potential to become a useful theoretical perspective to examine the entry modes of internationally operating firms.

Critical Comments

The resource-based, knowledge-based and organisational capability-based approaches have been subject to criticism from various sources. One problem, which is also evident from the present review, is that resource-based view is "far from being a coherent perspective" (Foss 1998). On the one hand, the common denominator of the theoretical contributions outlined above is that competitive advantage stems from internal assets that cannot easily be replicated due to isolating mechanisms and path dependency. On the other, there are arguably as many flavours of the resource-based view with distinct terminologies as there are theoretical contributions. This makes the theory more difficult to grasp and to apply. Besides this absence of terminological agreement in the field, Foss (1998) identified a further incoherence which is more difficult to address. He argues that there is an inherent tension between a more dynamic, evolutionary perspective that emphasises dynamic competencies and capabilities (e.g. Teece, Pisano and Shuen 1997) and approaches that examine the conditions for resources to generate rents in static equilibrium (e.g. Barney 1986; Peteraf 1993). This leads to a dilemma that the future development of these theories will have to address. The latter group of scholars has so far not addressed the mechanisms of endogenous competence creation. They thus run the danger of producing a tautological approach. Or, to use Porter's words (Porter, 1994, p.):

> "At its worst, the resource-based view is circular. Successful firms are successful because they have unique resources. They should nurture those resources to be successful. But what is a unique resource? What makes it valuable? Why was the firm able to create or acquire it?"

On the other hand, those scholars that were more concerned with a dynamic perspective became engaged in an exercise of increasingly elaborate theorising. After unravelling the chain of causality, they generally identified meta-competencies and knowledge as focal points for a theory of competitive advantage (e.g. Kogut and Zander 1992; 1996; Conner and Prahalad 1996; Grant 1996; Teece, Pisano and Shuen 1997). While these contributions are insightful, it becomes increasingly difficult to translate their propositions into testable hypotheses because they attempt "generalise about the unique" (Foss 1998).

As it stands, the resource-based view struggles with some inherent tensions between analytical clarity and operationalisability. Still, one can see these criticisms as a healthy development in the effort to create a sustainable theoretical core for what is regarded as one of the most fruitful areas of future strategy research (e.g. Madhok 1996). Furthermore, the resource-based / knowledge-based perspective has helped to put the emphasis back on managerial issues and internal, firm specific assets. Arguably, this is an important contribution to the field of strategy as it represents a counter-balance to the more deterministic view advocated by some theories rooted in industrial organisation and organisational economics.

Implications for High-Technology Start-ups

The monopolistic advantage theory has been derived from the observation of mature multinationals with a large resource base. However, it is consistent with this approach to think of a young, highly specialised company that offers an innovative solution that no competitor can match. This solution might stem from a product or process innovation, it might be an innovative product or a service or even an organisational ability (such as a particular competitive behaviour, i.e. selling goods over the internet thus saving distribution time and cost). At a given moment in time, when no competitor can provide a solution that is of equal use for the customer, it is thus possible to envisage a small start-up company leveraging this solution into foreign markets despite its higher costs relative to domestic operations. These costs can be offset by above-average returns that the start-up could collect due to the inability of rivals to provide an equal solution. This is essentially a static view that sees customers as choosing from of a given, known range of alternative solutions the one that maximises their objectives thus leading to higher returns for more innovative firms. In a more dynamic world, an innovative firm has to face the threat of eroding above-average returns due to the imitation of the solution by rivals or the emergence of more innovative solutions. But if one includes the potential presence of first-mover advantages, lock-in effects due to switching costs, inability of competitors to imitate due to causal ambiguity, perfect appropriability of returns and successful continuous innovation into the discussion, it becomes conceivable that a small high-tech start-up can manage to establish a global presence at a given time and to sustain it over a longer period.

While the initial monopolistic advantage theory explains why certain firms can compete internationally - and thus gives an indication of which firms will venture abroad - the resource-based / organisational capability perspective promises to be useful when trying to explain the operating modes. Applied to start-ups, the resource-based perspective seems to put the emphasis on gaining access to complementary resources and assets in order to achieve growth. This suggests that inter-firm collaborations are of particular importance for technology-based start-ups. Furthermore, the OC perspective, with its dual focus on capability creation and exploitation, promises valuable insights when looking at the structural forms of international activities. To the author's knowledge, the organisational capability perspective have not been applied to analyse the entry decisions of entrepreneurial start-ups.

2.3.5. Conclusions from the Review of International Business Theories

The theoretical approaches reviewed above have a number of common elements. First, they have all been derived from the empirical observation of large mature organisations and do not explicitly address factors specific to small firms. One example of this is the implicit assumption of the economics-based theories that firms can freely choose the appropriate entry mode. In addition, they all incorporate the notion that there are costs associated with doing business abroad that put foreign firms at disadvantage over their competitors. Besides these common elements, one can identify a number of distinct prescriptions that are not in line when the unit of analysis is at the same time a *young start-up* firm and operating in *high-technology* industries.

According to the transaction cost-based theories, one might expect a high-tech firm - once the decision to expand internationally has been taken - to either export directly or to use resource intensive entry-modes to minimise the risk of market failures associated with high-technology environments. However, many start-up companies do not possess the required resource-base to build up a subsidiary. Yet, exporting may not always be a feasible option if a product requires local support for installation, maintenance and repair. On the other hand, the process perspective holds that small and young firms - if they internationalise at all, which would be rather unexpected according to this view - establish cross-border operations in a careful and sequential way leading from low resource commitments to higher resource commitments. One can clearly see the conflicting prescriptions of these different theories. This can partly be explained by the fact that these approaches stem from different research methods and address different aspects of the internationalisation of firms. A direct comparison should therefore only be undertaken with caution. However, it is possible to identify cases where the conflict becomes explicit. The case of a high-tech start-up, whose first move abroad involves some form of direct investment, is clearly at odds with behavioural theory. On the other hand, a start-up at the forefront of a technological evolution that uses distributors to expand into foreign markets is arguably at odds with transaction cost theory. Furthermore, when taken to an extreme, it is possible to argue at the same time, depending on the theoretical perspective that one chooses, that a high-tech start-up can compete globally from inception or why it cannot internationalise at all. Thus it is possible to explain every single case of early internationalisation and every case of non-internationalisation - **but only ex-post**.

A potential bridging concept between the behavioural process perspective and the transaction cost logic is the resource-based / organisational capability view. It is related to the previous approaches in that it incorporates both behavioural elements (learning, path dependency, tacit knowledge) and concepts emerging from economic analysis (rent-generating mechanisms, asset specificity). By emphasising that a firm's competitive position is a result of both its tangible and intangible asset base and the evolutionary path it has followed, it allows room for a less deterministic analysis of the international activities of start-ups. According to this perspective, even a young start-up can compete globally if its product offering generates sufficient rents to offset the additional costs of competing across borders. Furthermore, it emphasises the use of collaborative entry modes as a means to access complementary resources.

In summary, our literature review shows that international activities of start-ups are not incompatible with theories of international business per se. However, the extent to which start-ups compete internationally has to be the starting point of any evaluation of these theories. Therefore, it would be interesting to investigate the characteristics of high-tech start-ups that stay domestic and those that show cross-border operations with different patterns and resource-intensities. That might enable us to uncover more factors that facilitate or prevent internationalisation and to assess how they fit into these theoretical frameworks. For this task, we can, to a certain extent, rely on previous work since, with the exception of the OC perspective, these different international business theories have been subject to empirical testing. Their joint inclusion in a multivariate approach should therefore lead to a number of insights.

3. Research Objective and Development of Hypotheses

3.1. Research Objective

The literature review has identified a number of gaps in the existing research on international entrepreneurship. Above all, it is striking how little overlap there is between the case study research and the quantitative surveys published to date. The majority of propositions generated by the case studies have, at present, not been subject to empirical testing. Furthermore, only a minority of the quantitative studies tried to examine questions at the heart of the field of international business such as the determinants of the decision to internationalise, the choice of entry mode or the market selection pattern. An empirical test of the propositions of the case studies should also include a control group in order to investigate whether they have the power to discriminate between international start-ups and domestic start-ups.

Second, the importance of the phenomenon of internationally operating high-tech start-ups remains unknown. In the light of the largely case study-based evidence on the internationalisation among international new ventures, two influential contributors argued that in order to "have a tangible effect on theory rather than being viewed as anomaly, the existence of a significant number of INVs [international new ventures], rapid growth in their numbers, or both must be shown an empirical fact" (Oviatt and McDougall 1997, p. 90-91; explanation within brackets added).

Third, the majority of empirical studies published to date did not systematically review international business theories in their attempts to explain the phenomenon of internationally operating start-ups. Nor have there been serious attempts at testing these different theories empirically. This is even more striking since various international business theories have been subject to criticism by international entrepreneurship scholars (e.g. McDougall, Shane and Oviatt 1994;

Knight and Cavusgil 1996). We argued in the theory review that the existence of international new ventures per se is not inconsistent with these theories. Yet, the review highlighted an interesting dilemma. The prescriptions of transaction cost-based approaches and behavioural approaches differ markedly when the unit of analysis is a firm that is *at the same time a young start-up **and** operating in high-technology* sectors. Theoretical approaches that attribute organisational outcomes to idiosyncratic firm-specific factors could build a bridge between transaction cost and behavioural approaches. Thus, a systematic survey of the behaviour of these firms is needed to achieve this and to shed light into the question to what extent different theories apply.

The current research aims to address these gaps. It will attempt to integrate theories of international business with existing, empirically derived knowledge on internationally operating start-ups. To this end, a cross-sectional research design was chosen. The author acknowledges that this cross-sectional approach is not suitable to track the internationalisation *process* of firms and their underlying motivations over time. Furthermore, in order to avoid the criticism with regard to the validity of the findings and the methodological foundations of previous research into internationalisation processes, longitudinal in-depth studies that analyse every market entry decision for every country and product would be required (see Andersen 1993; Leonidou and Katsikeas 1996). Yet, only a limited number of case studies can be handled using such an approach. Given the already existing rich insights from the case studies reviewed above, it is argued that knowledge in the field of international entrepreneurship is best advanced using a quantitative approach. Above all, this approach is best suited to simultaneously address the three gaps identified above.

- It can establish the prevalence of the phenomenon.

- It can accommodate a sample of international start-ups and a control group of domestic start-ups.

- Furthermore, it allows for a simultaneous consideration of different international business theories and empirical findings from previous case research in a multivariate framework.

Internationalisation has been defined as "the process of increasing involvement in international operations" both inward and outward (Welch and Luostarinen 1988, p.36). Generally, a firm's decision to extend its activities beyond domestic borders are motivated by the access to factor input or output markets. While cross-border sourcing represents a phenomenon of increasing importance, for small firms as well as for larger ones, it is the growth of the firm through the generation of revenues from foreign markets that will be central to the present study. Therefore, we will focus on activities aimed at gaining access to output markets. Furthermore, this means that the focus of the enquiry lies on commercialising existing products abroad, and not on extending production to foreign countries. This choice probably reflects the reality of cross-border operations of very young firms which usually lack the resources to set up production facilities abroad in a more accurate way. To this end, we will mainly look at entry modes that represent substitutes for commercialising a product across borders. For the purpose of this research, we will examine those dimensions of outward internationalisation, which have received the most widespread attention among researchers in the past. Like other researchers before, we will look at the decision to internationalise, the degree of internationalisation, the choice of entry mode and the pattern of foreign market selection (Welch and Luostarinen 1988; Nordström 1991; Sullivan 1994; Calof and Beamish 1995). we will also focus on an additional dimension, the timing of foreign market entry, which has received considerably less attention from researchers in the past (Tan and Vertinsky, 1996, is a notable exception).

The first part of the analysis will focus on a comparison of start-ups with international activities and start-ups without international activities. In this part, we will first determine the prevalence of the phenomenon within the UK. We will then test the applicability and discriminatory power of various propositions derived from international business theory and empirical research in international entrepreneurship. Given the ambiguous theoretical prescriptions with regard to timing and extent of internationalisation, it is, in the first instance, important to identify those factors which facilitate or hinder the outward movement of high-tech start-ups. This part will therefore consist of comparing high-technology start-ups that have international activities with those that compete domestically. Thus, we will attempt to explain why some start-ups engage in cross-border activities from an early stage of their existence whereas others only serve their home markets.

The second part of the analysis will look at the international start-ups in order to estimate the determinants of their degree of internationalisation. The applicability of different measures of the degree of internationalisation will be discussed. Since internationalisation could be interpreted as non-linear phenomenon, as "overcoming a barrier" (Buckley 1993a) or "jumping a threshold", it will also be tested whether internationalisation can be seen as a continuum or whether it represents a moment of discontinuous change in the life of a firm.

The third part of the analysis will investigate issues related to the timing of internationalisation. The unexpected, early or accelerated foreign market entry and subsequent evolution of international activities is arguably one of the defining features of internationally operating start-ups. Two different methods will be used in order to determine the key influence factors on the timing of internationalisation.

The fourth main part of the analysis will look at the entry decisions of these firms. It will describe the structural aspects of market entry of the sampled firms. It will also investigate the determinants of the chosen entry modes. As explained above, the conflicting prescriptions of different theoretical frameworks become most apparent when looking at the entry modes of these firms. A set of testable research hypotheses based on the theoretical and empirical knowledge will be developed below.

3.2. Research Hypotheses

3.2.1. Differences Between International Start-ups and Domestic Start-ups, the Degree of Internationalisation and Timing of Internationalisation

In this section, the hypotheses guiding this research will be presented. We will combine the hypotheses for the decision to internationalise, the determinants of the degree of internationalisation and the timing of internationalisation, because the theoretical arguments underlying their development are closely related. A second section will be devoted to the development of hypotheses on the choice of entry mode.

3.2.1.1. Operationalisation of Dependent Variables

We will attempt to analyse differences between internationalising and non-internationalising firms. Several operationalisations of "internationalisation" using different definitions will be used in order to test the robustness of the findings. The first measurement of internationalisation classifies firms as "international" as soon as they have entered one foreign market or generated one percent of their total revenue through international sales during their last financial year. A possible criticism is that this operationalisation could include a high share of firms that do not proactively internationalise and only had a few unsolicited orders from abroad. We therefore chose two additional cut-offs to operationalise the somewhat fuzzy notion of "substantial" international activities. Unfortunately, there is no literature available on what constitutes a reasonable threshold for "substantial" internationalisation. In comparable study in the US, McDougall (1989) used a cut-off criterion of 5% in order to classify the firms in her sample as international start-ups. In a European context, however, a threshold of 5% might be too low. We therefore choose a more conservative threshold of 10% non-domestic revenue. The second cut-off criterion includes only firms that have entered at least three foreign markets at the time of the survey.

There is considerable debate about the appropriate definition of the degree of internationalisation of a firm (Sullivan 1994; 1996; Ramaswamy, Kroeck and Renforth 1996; Reuber and Fischer 1997). This controversy was triggered by Sullivan (1994) who, in an attempt to measure the degree of internationalisation of a firm, suggested an index composed of several variables. His work, based on a search of empirical evidence in the literature of internationalisation, was partly motivated by the inability of previous research to state whether international diversification improves financial performance of a firm. He argued that the most widely used measure of the degree of internationalisation, the ratio of foreign sales to total sales, is problematic in the case of large diversified multinationals which comprise different business units with quite different strategic orientations. Sullivan's index is constructed of two structural variables (ratio of foreign assets to total assets and number of overseas subsidiaries to total subsidiaries), one performance variable (ratio of foreign sales to total sales) and two attitudinal variables (top managers' international experience and psychic dispersion of international operations). This index was subsequently contested by other researchers who questioned the validity of the employed concepts and its methodological foundations (Ramaswamy et al 1996). Critics have argued that an index neutralises any extreme scores of the measures and that the two attitudinal attributes are difficult to measure. More importantly, the index focuses exclusively on the later stages of internationalisation by emphasising entry modes that require foreign direct investment. For these reasons, Reuber and Fischer (1997) argue that Sullivan's index is of limited use when analysing the internationalisation of very young and small firms. They propose a revised measure that includes number of foreign regions entered, share of non-domestic revenues and share of employees devoting at least 50% of their time on export management. Yet, we argue that the latter measure is often both cause and effect of internationalisation. It should therefore not be used as independent variable in a cross-sectional dataset. To summarise, we agree that internationalisation is a multidimensional construct that is probably not captured using a single measure such as share of non-domestic revenue. However, we also agree with those authors that are concerned with the loss of information through the construction of an index that combines several measures (Ramaswamy, Kroeck and Renforth 1996). Furthermore, Sullivan's criticism of using the share of non-domestic revenue were largely directed to diversified multinational firms. In the absence of a preferable measure, we will therefore in the next sections consider the share of non-domestic revenues as key measure of the degree of internationalisation. This measure has in the past received the most widespread attention from international business scholars (Sullivan 1994).

The timing of foreign market entry has received relatively minor attention from researchers. The only study known to the author analysed the timing of Japanese multinational firms entering the US market using entry modes that require foreign direct investment (Tan and Vertinsky 1996). This dearth of empirical research could be explained by the fact that initial entries are more difficult to observe for firms that are older and more established. This presents an opportunity since early initiation of international activities is arguably *the* defining feature of international entrepreneurship. Start-ups should therefore represent an ideal test case for exploring issues related to the timing of the initiation of foreign entry modes. The dependent variable for this analysis will be the time lag between the first sales of the firm and the first international sales.

The reader will notice that these three dimensions, decision to internationalise, degree of internationalisation and timing of internationalisation are closely related. The first dimension treats internationalisation as a binary choice of the firm. The second explores whether internationalisation is a continuous phenomenon, i.e. whether the same factors that discriminate between international start-ups and domestic start-ups also explain the variation of different levels or degrees of international activities. The third can be seen as an extension of the first dimension in a more dynamic context. In essence, it is related to a binary choice, i.e. it assesses the impact of independent variables of internationalisation, but allows for observation periods of different duration and censoring of the data. In the present case, the censoring occurs due to the cross-sectional nature of the dataset. The observed time period between start-up and the survey may simply be too short for some of the youngest firms to get a realistic chance to initiate cross-border activities. The standard models used to examine the time lag between first sales and international sales can accommodate this potential bias. The relation between these three dimensions will be examined in more detail in the sections that discuss the methodological aspects of the modelling of internationalisation.

3.2.1.2. Hypotheses

The effects of size and age on internationalisation have received much attention from international business researchers. In accordance with the logic of internationalisation process models, one would expect older and larger firms to be more likely to internationalise because they possess the cumulative resources to overcome the cost and operational barriers of competing abroad (Johanson and Vahlne 1977; 1990). Empirical export development studies and "stage models" have reported a positive relationship between firm size on the one hand and the probability to internationalise and allocate resource commitments to foreign markets on the other (Bilkey and Tesar 1977; Bilkey 1978; Czinkota 1982). Yet, these studies are frequently criticised for their weak methodological foundations (see Andersen 1993, for an overview). More recent analyses which looked at large populations of firms merely seem to agree that there is no *negative* relation between internationalisation and size (Bonaccorsi 1992; Calof 1994). In addition, one author has argued that the variance explained by size is so small that it can be neglected for predictive purposes (Calof 1994). However, while we do not want to deny the presence of micro-firms spanning across national borders, we believe that, in general, the larger high-technology start-ups will be more likely to have initiated international activities by the time of the survey. We believe that a critical mass will be required in order to operate in several markets simultaneously. Accordingly, we hypothesise:

H1a: Larger start-ups at the time of formation will be more likely to have international activities at the time of the survey.

H1b: Larger start-ups at the time of formation will be characterised by a higher degree of internationalisation at the time of the survey.

H1c: Larger start-ups at the time of formation will initiate international activities more rapidly.

Upper echelon theory states that the characteristics of the top management of a firm have considerable influence on organisational outcomes (e.g. Hambrick and Mason 1984). In the context of international business, the international experience of its founders or managers has subsequently been shown to influence the degree of internationalisation of a firm (Aharoni 1966; Aaby and Slater 1989; Sullivan 1994). Yet, while being intuitively convincing, empirical findings have remained inconclusive. In the case of multinational firms, Kogut (1989) argues that competitive advantage stems from the management of the transfer of knowledge and resource between the dispersed international operations. Following this argument, Roth (1995) reported that living experience abroad had a significant effect on performance in firms with a high degree of international interdependence. However, another finding of the same study was that experience in managing international activities did not have a significant influence on firm performance. Studies that have looked at international entrepreneurship more specifically reported similar findings. McDougall, Shane and Oviatt (1994) report that the founders of the firms in their sample of international new ventures were characterised by first-hand knowledge and experience of foreign factor and product markets. Accordingly, they concluded that 'alertness' to business opportunities abroad was a vital precondition for the formation of international new ventures. Reuber and Fischer (1997) found that the degree of internationalisation of a firm was positively influenced by the international experience of its managers. In contrast, Roberts and Senturia (1996) report that none of the top managers of the firms in their sample had direct international experience from having lived abroad. Still, a majority in their sample had previous work experience in US companies with international activities. Bloodgood, Sapienza and Almeida (1996) found that international work experience was positively related to internationalisation activity whereas international schooling was not. In the light of these several findings, the following hypotheses were constructed:

H2a: Start-ups are more likely to have international activities, if their founders have international work or education experience.

H2b: Start-ups will be characterised by higher degrees of internationalisation if their founders have international work or education experience.

H2c: Start-ups will initiate international activities more rapidly if their founders have international work or education experience.

Increasing attention has been given to the role of external finance during the growth period of start-up companies. Those companies that obtained venture capital can benefit from higher levels of external finance than are available through traditional banks (Moore 1994; Murray and Lott 1995). In addition, venture capitalists add value to through providing access to their network and expertise (Sapienza 1992), which can extend to foreign countries. The presence of external equity finance from venture capitalists and business angels also can be interpreted as an indicator for the expectations concerning the business plan, the product and the management team of the venture. It thus represents a valuable proxy variable to capture technological and managerial quality. In order to fulfil the ambitious growth targets of venture capitalists, investee companies may frequently be strongly encouraged to include the commercialisation of foreign markets in their business plans (Murray 1996). Therefore the hypothesis was formulated as follows:

H3a: Start-ups with external finance from venture capitalists or business angels will have a higher propensity to engage in international sales.

H3b: Start-ups with external finance from venture capitalists or business angels will be characterised by a higher degree of international sales.

H3c: Start-ups with external finance from venture capitalists or business angels will initiate international sales more rapidly.

It has become popular to argue that because of spiralling research and development costs and shortening life cycles for high-technology products, firms operating in high-technology sectors cannot exclusively rely on domestic markets (Oakey, Rothwell and Cooper 1988; Ohmae 1990). Empirical investigations seem to confirm this trend. Kobrin (1991) found that technological intensity (expressed as a ratio of costs to sales revenue) was the most important structural determinant of cross-border integration in the industries which he examined. At the firm level, it has been shown that higher R&D intensity leads to a higher propensity to export among SMEs. (Cooper and Kleinschmidt 1985; Aaby and Slater 1989). Contradicting those findings, Lindqvist reported that, in her study of Swedish new technology-based firms, higher R&D intensity was not related to higher degrees of internationalisation in terms of speed of first market entry, resource-intensity of entry modes, geographical sequence and degree of international sales (Lindqvist 1991). Furthermore, Fujita (1995a; 1995b) provides evidence that many small high-tech firms did not internationalise due to competitive pressures in their domestic market. In essence, there is mixed evidence which leads us to propose that, in the case of start-ups, the relationship may be more complex than previously thought.

High research and development intensities can indicate that the start-up is still in its product development phase. During that phase, its management will have a preference to devote scarce resources to the transfer of its core technology into commercially viable products. In the absence of contract development for a foreign partner, the firm will also be expected to concentrate its initial commercialisation efforts on domestic sales which are likely to be less costly than international sales. Thus, high R&D intensities are likely prevent firms from launching their products in international markets. On the other hand, we agree with authors who argued that high-technology start-ups frequently operate in specialised niches. Sales to a domestic market may not generate the cash-flow required to recover the initial expenditures and to finance the development of next generation products or upgrades (see for example Roberts 1991; McDougall and Oviatt 1996). Firms with very low R&D intensities or no research and development activities will thus be expected to have a lower propensity to engage in international activities. In summary, we expect a curvilinear or inverted U-shaped effect of R&D intensity on the various dimensions of internationalisation. Accordingly, we thus formulate our fourth hypothesis as follows:

H4a: Research and development intensity will have a curvilinear effect on the propensity to internationalise. This means that, up to a turning point, the propensity to internationalise will increase with growing levels of R&D intensity before decreasing with further increases of R&D intensity.

H4b: Research and development intensity will have a curvilinear effect on the degree of internationalisation. This means that, up to a turning point, the degree of internationalisation will increase with growing levels of R&D intensity before decreasing with further increases of R&D intensity.

H4c: Research and development intensity will have a curvilinear effect on the speed of international market entry. This means that, up to a turning point, the speed of market entry will increase with growing levels of R&D intensity before decreasing with further increases of R&D intensity.

Besides firm-specific factors, we argue that characteristics of their products influence whether or not firms will engage in international sales. Yet, there appears to be little empirical evidence in the field of international business regarding the impact of product characteristics on internationalisation performance (Douglas and Craig 1992; Cavusgil and Kirpalani 1993). We will first look at the innovativeness of the products in question and then at characteristics that affect the transaction costs associated with the internationalisation of these products.

The innovativeness or newness of a technology incorporated in a start-up's product has been shown to be a key factor influencing its market acceptance (Roberts 1991). In the context of international entrepreneurship, it has been reported that firms which introduced technological innovations internationalised later but were subsequently quicker at entering overseas markets (Lindqvist 1991). Jolly, Alahuhta and Jeannet (1992) reported that the global start-ups in their sample all commercialised innovative products in new or emerging industries. A distinguishing feature between the "conventional" and "innovative" firms in Boter and Holmquist's sample was that the products of the latter incorporated advanced technology. These firms were the more proactive internationalisers. Similarly, Murray (1996) reported that the firms in his sample were all developing products incorporating leading edge technology. He argued that that access to sophisticated customers abroad was one of the key motivations of these firms. Yet, these findings contradict research on more established SMEs operating in high-technology industries. Two studies reported that only a minority of internationalisers developed radically new technologies. The majority of firms which internationalised had based their strategies on the incremental improvement of existing technologies (Fujita 1995a; Lindell and Karagozoglu 1997). Still, we expect international sales to be more likely among firms whose products incorporate highly specialised niche technology since buyers can arguably buy established technology from indigenous firms in their home countries. When demand for an innovative solution cannot be met locally, buyers may turn to a foreign firm, even if the firm in question is an unknown start-up. Accordingly, we hypothesise the following:

H5a: Start-ups whose products incorporate more innovative technology will have a higher propensity to initiate international activities.

H5b: Start-ups whose products incorporate more innovative technology will be characterised by a higher degree of internationalisation.

H5c: Start-ups whose products incorporate more innovative technology will be quicker at initiating international activities.

One variable that has been identified in the case studies in international entrepreneurship was the degree of standardisation of a product. Several authors report that the firms in their sample all commercialised standardised products that required little client-specific customisation (Jolly, Alahuhta and Jeannet 1992; Boter and Holmquist 1996; Murray 1996). However, the degree of product standardisation did not have a significant impact on the internationalisation behaviour among the firms sampled by Lindqvist (1991). Still, we expect that extensive client-specific customisation does represent a barrier to foreign sales. If a product or a software solution has to be adapted to suit a particular buyer's specifications, close collaboration between end-customer and manufacturer may be required. The process of customisation is thus frequently expected to be resource-intensive. In addition, the closer these customisation requirements are located to the technological core of the product, the less likely it will be that third party such as a local distributor can handle these activities (Root 1987). Arguably, these resources can be more easily deployed in a domestic setting than in foreign markets. Accordingly, we hypothesise the following:

H6a: Start-ups that sell standardised products that require little client-specific customisation and adaptation will have a higher propensity to engage international sales.

H6b: Start-ups that sell standardised products that require little client-specific customisation and adaptation will be characterised by higher degrees of international sales.

H6c: Start-ups that sell standardised products that require little client-specific customisation and adaptation will enter foreign markets more rapidly.

An important impediment to internationalisation can lie in the scale of transaction costs associated with cross-border commercialisation (Klein, Frazier and Roth 1990). Transaction costs which impact on the commercialisation of high-technology products can arise for many reasons including consultations prior to sale, installation costs, maintenance and after sales activity, and training of sales and front-end personnel (Root 1987; Moriarty and Kosnik 1989; Bell 1995; Meldrum 1995; Beard and Easingwood 1996). They represent an immediate obstacle when the firm exports directly to foreign end-customers. When a distributor is involved, the commercialisation requirements give rise to asset specificity which increase the cost of contractual safeguarding. For a small firm, these additional costs can represent important barriers to internationalisation (Morgan and Katsikeas 1997).

H7a: High costs of commercialisation will be negatively related to the propensity to engage in international sales.

H7b: High costs of commercialisation will be negatively related to the degree of internationalisation.

H7c: High costs of commercialisation will be negatively related to the timing of first international sales.

In addition to these independent variables, we include firm age as control variable. Formulating a hypothesis here would be somewhat tautological. Unless all firms in the sample have initiated cross-border activities at inception, any hypothesis stating that firms with international sales are older would probably be supported.

Still, as age is likely to account for some of the variation in the data, we include it as control variable. Age should also be positively related to the degree of internationalisation. While we accept that certain firms may de-internationalise over time, we believe that in the majority of cases, internationalisation will be a process increasing outward involvement where the countries entered or share of non-domestic revenue increase over time. We also include industry dummy variables in order to control for any industry-specific effects. With regard to internationalisation, these can for example capture the level of domestic and international competition and the presence of lead markets with the most advanced customers.

Finally, we would like to formulate a summary hypothesis related to the degree of internationalisation. In the specific context of technology-based start-ups, only two studies are known to the authors which tried to assess the effects of different variables on the degree of internationalisation (Lindqvist 1991; Bloodgood, Almeida and Sapienza 1997). The fact that in Lindqvist's study, neither size nor age of the firm appeared significantly related to the degree of internationalisation suggests that internationalisation may be best understood as 'jumping a threshold'. Once the threshold is overcome, the marginal effects of these variables on internationalisation may well decrease. On the other hand, Bloodgood, Almeida and Sapienza (1996) found a positive relationship between firm size and degree of internationalisation. Note, however, that they used a different operationalisation of the degree of internationalisation of their firms and that their sample included firms without international activities. The notion of internationalisation as continuous phenomenon is in contrast with the position of those researchers that see the initiation of international activities as a discontinuous change or organisational innovation (see Andersen 1993 for a review). However, the discussion of the hypotheses above does not suggest that the independent variables chosen for this research have a different impact on the propensity to internationalise than on the degree of internationalisation.[19] We will therefore hypothesise that the same factors that determine the decision to internationalise also determine the firm's degree of internationalisation.

H8: The same factors that will account for the differences between international and domestic start-ups will explain the variation in the degree of internationalisation.

---

[19] Note however, that other influence factors not discussed here will certainly have an impact on these two dimensions of internationalisation. It is also likely that there will be number of factors that will have a different impact on the dimensions. Yet, as it is one of the main purposes of this research to integrate previous empirical findings from the field of international entrepreneurship with the main body of literature from the field of international business, we can only account for a limited number of independent variables.

In summary, we can provide a broad categorisation of the hypotheses presented here. While most of them have been derived from empirical research in the field of international entrepreneurship, it is possible to make the link to the theoretical frameworks in the field of international business. Size has been used previously in empirical studies to operationalise the propositions of internationalisation process and stage theories (Andersen 1993; Leonidou and Katsikeas 1996). A resource-based perspective can be associated with variables describing top management team's international experiences (McDougall, Shane and Oviatt 1994; Roth 1995), external finance and expertise from venture capitalists and business angels and R&D intensity (Dierickx and Cool 1989; Mahoney 1992). Note however, that R&D intensity has been used both in resource-based approaches (Mauri and Michaels 1998) and in transaction cost-based approaches as proxy for product-market environments where costs of technology transfer are high (Teece 1986; Davidson and McFetridge 1988). The use of R&D intensity in resource-based approaches is somewhat problematic since most operationalisations are based on *input* variables such as expenditures or number employees. Sustained investment in research and development can result in the building up of heterogeneous resources and capabilities (Dierickx and Cool 1989). When these are embodied in a firm's end-products, their ability to generate above-average rents may offset the additional costs arising from cross-border operations. However, a high score along possible technology indicators does not *automatically* translate into superior capabilities. Conversely, a firm may invest relatively little in research and development but can come up with a highly innovative solution that enables it to generate above-average rents. For this reason, we argue that product innovativeness is a more appropriate resource-based measure to capture possible firm- or product-specific advantages that have a positive impact on internationalisation. Finally, product characteristics that impact on commercialisation can be linked with transaction cost arguments. However, we would like to make clear that a test concerned with the ability of these cost variables to discriminate between internationalisers and non-internationalisers is not a test of transaction cost theory per se. Since the latter is explicitly aims at comparing the efficiency of particular governance modes, or market entry modes in an international setting, it treats the decision to internationalise as a given. A significant impact of the cost variables on the above dimensions of internationalisation is therefore not suitable to test for the predictive ability of transaction cost and internalisation theory.

3.2.2. The Choice of Market Entry Mode

3.2.2.1. Operationalisation of the Dependent Variable

For the purpose of this study, our dependent variable is defined as the dichotomous choice between selling abroad by either direct exporting or through the use of distributors. Three related arguments support this approach. First, we receive empirical support from previous studies which report that exporting and the use of intermediaries are in practice the two main alternatives employed by entrepreneurial high-technology firms (Lindqvist 1991; Bell 1995).

Second, the choice between direct exporting and the use of distributors is of utmost managerial relevance for technology entrepreneurs. With the singular exception of the US economy, the finite market opportunities in many countries may not justify the development expenditures for certain highly-specialised niche technologies unless international expansion is considered from inception. Technology-based start-ups therefore face a dangerous dilemma. On the one hand, they may be forced to venture abroad to help amortise their initial development expenditures and to generate sufficient revenues to finance ongoing development activities. On the other hand, as many technology-based start-ups experience negative cash-flows during their early years, they may lack the necessary human and financial resources required for the effective commercialisation of their products on their own. Given these resource constraints, identifying end-customers and providing pre- and after-sales support services may be better handled by a local partner. The downside of this arrangement is that revenues have to be shared between the start-up and the distributor. Additional costs can be incurred by the start-up because of the need to provide technical training and the creation of monitoring mechanisms. Early on, technology entrepreneurs therefore have to make complex and highly strategic trade-offs given that the choice of the foreign sales mode may have profound implications both in terms of costs and revenue generation.

Third, the main theoretical frameworks in the field of international business which analyse entry modes come to somewhat different conclusions when applied to firms that are at the same time young (or inexperienced) and operate in high-technology sectors. Process models (Johanson and Vahlne 1977; 1990) see commitment to internationalisation as a function of experiential knowledge of foreign markets. Accordingly, a start-up company would be expected to gain initial experience through reactive exporting before proactively venturing into foreign markets. The choice between direct exporting and the use of more complex and proactive entry modes is thus dependent on firm experience and foreign market knowledge. Despite having received empirical support, process models and the subsequently developed "stage models of internationalisation" (e.g. Cavusgil 1980; Reid 1981) are frequently criticised for being too deterministic and for failing to take firm-specific factors other than experience into account (Andersen 1993). A rival approach, the transaction cost economics (TCE) approach, has been very influential because it provides a decision rule with regard to individual entry decisions. Firms are expected to choose the governance or entry mode that minimises the costs of carrying out particular transactions. In its application, TCE is essentially concerned with comparing different institutional arrangements for carrying out economic activity (Williamson 1985). As the choice between direct exporting and involving a foreign distributors is essentially a choice between an internal arrangement and an arrangement involving an external third party, the tools of TCE are applicable to model the decision. Yet, the TCE approach implicitly assumes a capacity for discretionary resource deployment. For example, the commercialisation of a product incorporating very advanced technology may require a high degree of asset specificity. If this asset specificity leads to a substantial increase of the costs of involving a distributor, a firm is expected to switch from direct exporting to a sales subsidiary once its foreign sales to a particular country exceed a certain level. However, this may not reflect the reality of resource constraint start-ups. They may rather be inclined to establish collaborative relationships with intermediaries in order to get access to assets, resources and capabilities which they do not own. The widespread use of collaborative strategies in technology-intensive industries has triggered the development of the organisational capability (OC) perspective. Compared to TCE, its proponents argue that it represents a superior approach for the analysis of collaborative governance arrangements (Madhok 1997). To date, we do not know of any study that has applied the organisational capability perspective to the internationalisation of smaller, entrepreneurial firms.

Given that these three approaches put their emphasis on different variables, we therefore incorporate some of their elements in our set of hypotheses. This integrated multivariate approach should provide further evidence of whether or not they explain the choice of entry modes made by high-tech start-ups. Following established research practice, we have chosen the *entry decision* and not the firm as the unit of analysis. Like other researchers, we argue that entry decisions are a function of firm-specific factors, product-specific factors and target country specific factors (Cavusgil, Zou and Naidu 1993; Erramilli and Rao 1993). The international business theories reviewed above have primarily been applied to comparisons of exporting, contractual / hybrid entry modes (joint ventures, alliances, licensing), and direct investment. Yet, the choice between direct exporting and sales via distributors is a choice between an internalised transaction or an externalised transaction involving intermediaries. We find ourselves within the established tradition of researchers that have conceptualised entry modes choices as a binary choice (see for example Davidson and McFetridge 1984; Kogut and Singh 1988; Erramilli and Rao 1993; Barkema and Vermeulen 1998). Based on the theoretical frameworks described above, we will develop a set of hypotheses to test which variables account for the choice between direct exporting and exporting via distributors as the two predominant modes of foreign market entry for technology-based start-ups.

3.2.2.2. Hypotheses

Firm size is widely seen as proxy for the availability of resources which can be committed to foreign markets. According to the well known internationalisation process perspective, larger firms are expected to make bolder commitments to foreign markets (Johanson and Vahlne 1990). However, the resource implications of choosing intermediaries over direct exporting to end customers are not clear-cut. Exporting may involve relatively high cost in identifying and selling to end-customers (Zacharakis 1997). Yet, once the customers are identified, the operating costs may be relatively low and - in the best case - represent only the costs of shipping a product abroad. Selling via a distributor may reduce the cost of identifying foreign customers considerably. Distributors are also likely to have invested in long-term relationships with their customers. However, using intermediaries will normally require certain preparatory costs prior to the first sales. These can arise for the following reasons. Suitable partners have to be identified before engaging in a commercial relationship (Root 1994). Formalising a distribution agreement frequently involves legal and other administrative costs. The distributor's staff need to be trained in selling the product, installing it and providing subsequent maintenance or upgrades. Furthermore, there may an imbalance of bargaining power between both parties, especially if the supplier is , as yet, an unestablished, young firm (Zacharakis 1997). In this situation it may well be the distributor who chooses the supplier rather than vice versa. A distributor will normally have a portfolio of related products and will promote those products which maximise his net income. Aligning the objectives of the two parties through appropriate governance mechanisms has been widely studied in a domestic context (e.g. Anderson and Narus 1990; Heide and John 1994). In a foreign country, the task of monitoring a distributor is likely to be even more difficult for a small entrepreneurial firm. Therefore, selling via an established distributor relationship is likely to require higher up-front investment than exporting. In the particular case of technology-based start-ups, the availability of resources is probably an even more crucial predictor of subsequent firm actions (Oakey, Rothwell and Cooper 1988). Accordingly, we argue that this route to foreign markets will be employed by start-ups commanding greater resources.

H9: Firms that sell into foreign markets via intermediaries are larger than firms that export directly.

A related hypothesis concerns the experience of the firm. The internationalisation process perspective argues that firms increase their commitment to international sales over time as their experiential knowledge of foreign markets increases (Johanson and Vahlne 1977; 1990). According to this logic, firms that are more experienced in international sales are expected to engage in more complex entry modes. In addition, some firms may change their entry mode over time, and move along the establishment chain from direct exporting to more complex or resource intensive entry modes such as the use of distributors or the setting up of a sales subsidiary. Following the argument developed for hypothesis 1, we believe that, from a start-up manager's point of view, using a distributor represents in most cases a more complex and committed foreign entry mode than direct exporting.

H10: Firms that sell into foreign markets via intermediaries are more experienced in international operations than firms that export directly.

It is, however, not necessary that experience in international operations has to be gained by the firm as organisational entity. A *young* firm initiating its *first* market entries cannot be expected to have direct experiential knowledge of international operations embodied in its processes and routines. As Oviatt and McDougall (1994) point out, this may not be a disadvantage. For international new ventures, organisational routines that make no difference whether sales are domestic or international can be a source of future competitive advantage. In the case of start-ups, the founders' international experience can be a substitute for organisational experience. If key staff of the firm who are involved in international operations have been previously exposed to foreign environments, a firm may initiate cross-border activities by using more complex entry modes. The international experience of senior managers has in the past been used to predict the scale and scope of international activities of start-up firms (Bloodgood, Sapienza and Almeida 1996; Reuber and Fischer 1997).

H11: Managers of firms which sell into foreign markets via intermediaries will be more likely to have international experience than managers of firms which export directly.

The experience of the firm is also a key variable in contributions that applied the organisational capability (OC) perspective to the choice of entry modes (Aulakh and Kotabe 1997; Madhok 1997). OC theorists argue that present outcomes are influenced by past experiences and routines which have become embedded in the organisation (Madhok 1997). If a firm uses a particular sales channel in its domestic market, it may be expected to further exploit this experience (i.e. negotiation of contracts, incentivising and motivating intermediaries) in foreign markets. Thus, the higher costs or risks of arranging more complex foreign sales modes can arguably be reduced through leveraging experiences gained earlier in a domestic market. Incidentally, Roberts and Senturia (1996) observed that, over time, the internationally operating high-tech firms in their sample had a tendency to replicate their domestic sales model in foreign markets. We believe that this is partly caused by experience or learning effects and hypothesise the following:

H12: Firms will sell into foreign markets via intermediaries rather than export directly if they already use distributors for their domestic sales.

The OC perspective argues that a firm's value-creating activities are a function of its resource and capability base. (Madhok 1997; Teece, Pisano and Shuen 1997). Madhok distinguishes between activities where the focus is on capability development and activities where the focus is on the exploitation of an existing advantage. In the case of start-ups - given our focus on sales modes - we argue that the objective of their international sales is to exploit to the full the commercial value of their technological competency in order to ensure their survival. Madhok also introduces the notions of 'ownership effect' and 'locational effect'. The former is represented by the ratio of embedded-to-generic firm-specific know-how, whereas the latter is defined as the ratio of embedded-to-generic market-specific knowledge (Madhok 1997). According to Madhok, a firm will carry out a transaction itself (internalisation) if there is a high potential for the erosion in the value of a firm's know-how stemming from the ownership effect. On the other hand, a firm will have a preference for collaboration, if there is a high potential for the erosion in the value of a firm's know-how from the locational effect. In summary, collaborative arrangements will be preferred in countries where the idiosyncratic ways of doing business erode the value of firm-specific know-how. Conversely, a firm is less likely to involve third parties if firm-specific know-how is inimitable or immobile thereby making the sharing of routines with intermediaries difficult (Hill, Hwang and Kim 1990; Madhok 1997). This suggests that a firm will have a higher propensity to avoid the use of intermediaries if its technology is very advanced or unfamiliar with potential users in its target market. Given the importance of tacit knowledge for such products, market-based support infrastructures may not be effective or available (Meldrum 1995). Effective commercialisation may therefore only be possible by internalising the sales process. Thus, idiosyncratic, country-specific ways of doing business abroad may represent a lesser barrier than in the case of more established technologies, especially if the product is sold to industrialised countries. Collaborations are expected to occur more frequently when the technology is more mature and established, a proposition that has received some validity in earlier research on international technology transfers (Davidson and McFetridge 1985).

H13: The products of firms that sell into foreign markets through direct exports incorporate newer technology than those of firms that sell via intermediaries.

Previous research on internationalisation has found that product characteristics affect the way that firms manage their international activities (Cavusgil, Zou and

Naidu 1993; Cavusgil and Zou 1994). They have also been found to influence the chosen entry modes in the case of young technology-based firms (Lindqvist 1991). The importance of client-specific customisation as a barrier to internationalisation has been reported in studies that examined product characteristics of international start-ups (Murray 1996; Roberts and Senturia 1996; Lindell and Karagozoglu 1997). The transformation from offering bespoke technology solutions to standardised or "shrink-wrapped" products in which the technology is embedded is associated with an increasing market orientation of the firm (Roberts 1991). Companies whose products are tailor-made for particular customers have been found to be more likely to sell directly without involving intermediaries (Bell 1995). Furthermore, it is more probable that the technological skills required to tailor a particular product to the needs of a customer reside within the company that developed the product rather than with the distributor in a target country.

H14: Products sold into foreign markets via intermediaries require less client-specific customisation than those of firms that export directly.

The tools of transaction cost economics (TCE) have also been widely used to analyse the determinants of entry mode choices. In essence, TCE is concerned with finding the most efficient institutional or contractual arrangement for economic transactions (Hennart 1989). As opposed to following the methods used by researchers who measured transaction costs indirectly by defining situations in which asset specificity and uncertainty are supposedly high (see for example Anderson and Gatignon 1986; Hennart 1990), we follow the approach of Klein, Frazier and Roth (1990) and attempt to measure the costs involved in the selling process of high-technology goods directly. During the sales process of high-technology goods, the vendor may be required to spend considerable time advising and educating the potential customer on the key features and relative merits of the product. After the sale, more complex products may require installation by trained staff, regular after sales service and periodic upgrades (Hutt and Speh 1992; Cavusgil and Zou 1993). To carry out these tasks, the sales and technical staff of the vendor will require particular skills. In the case of exporting, these skills are normally resident within the manufacturer. Selling a product via an intermediary, however, requires those skills also to be already present within, or transferable to, the distributor. The producer may therefore have to provide regular training to the staff of the intermediary in order to transfer the necessary skills and routines in order to effectively support the product. High up-front investments into these specific assets reduces the subsequent bargaining power and margins of the party incurring these costs. Zacharakis (1997) argues a small entrepreneurial firm is more likely to be obliged to reduce the distributor's set-up costs through the provision of training or other transfers than a large established multinational. Furthermore, a distributor may not be motivated to push a complex product which requires substantial pre-sale consulting and installation efforts. Therefore, products and services which incur substantial costs during the sales process should make it more difficult to align the interests of the start-up and a potential distributor. However, selling a technologically advanced product is likely to require an effective support infrastructure (Meldrum 1995). Using distributors which can exploit economies of scale and scope not available to the young firm may be the only way to provide the necessary infrastructure to service foreign customers. Furthermore, the costs of learning how to perform the relatively standardised tasks of installation, end-user training and maintenance are likely to be relatively low when the distributor already has a portfolio of related products in place. Therefore, we hypothesise that, in international markets, distributors represent the preferred vehicle for start-ups to ensure effective customer support for products whose commercialisation is resource-intensive.

H15: The pre- and after-sales transaction costs of products sold into foreign markets via intermediaries are higher than those of firms which export directly.

We include R&D intensity as a control variable. It has in the past been used as a proxy variable in studies that applied the framework of transaction costs to international market entry choices (Davidson and McFetridge 1985) in order to operationalise asset specificity and information asymmetries in exchange relations. We argue that there are two problems with this measure. First, it constitutes an *input* variable and may not necessarily have an impact on the asset specificity required to commercialise the *output* of the firm. High R&D expenditures may not give rise to asset specificity or information asymmetries per se. Indeed, higher R&D investment may even allow a reduction in transaction costs by designing out complexity for the customer. Second, it is usually measured at firm level not at product level because it is difficult to obtain R&D intensity (R&D expenditure divided by sales) on a product group basis. While high R&D expenditures and the need to amortise them quickly probably affect the decision to internationalise, we do not think that this variable has an impact on the entry mode chosen. Furthermore, instead of being responsible for high levels of asset specificity, R&D expenditures can actually be an indicator that the firm invests into features that minimise transaction costs (see Roberts 1991, for a convincing statement on the R&D expenditures involved to switch from customised solutions to "shrink-wrap" products). Therefore, we argue that these dimensions are better represented by measuring transaction costs directly and by measuring the maturity of the technology (see above). Due to its widespread use in empirical studies, however, we include R&D intensity as a control variable to detect any firm-level effects it might have on the choice of entry mode. We do not present any hypotheses regarding the target country, but also include it as a control variable.

We follow the approaches of Erramilli and Rao (1993) and Barkema and Vermeulen (1998) and include country risk, absolute size of the target country and GDP per capita as additional variables. We also include further dummy variables to control for any industry-specific effects that may impact on the chosen sales mode (see also section 3.2.1.2.).

To summarise, like other researchers before us (e.g. Cavusgil, Zou and Naidu 1993), we attempt to explain the international entry modes using firm-specific variables, product-specific variables and variables specific to the environment in which the firms operate. Firm size and experience in international activities can be seen as operationalisations of the internationalisation process model. Experience with the domestic sales mode and the innovativeness of the technology can be seen as operationalisations of the OC perspectives, whereas product characteristics are proxies for the transaction cost perspective. We will now discuss the methodological approach used for gathering the data and testing the above research hypotheses.

4. Methodology

As already mentioned in the introduction, the current research is part of a larger Anglo-German project on the international activities of British and German start-ups in high-technology industries. The expertise of the German research team was of particular benefit to the identification of data sources and the sampling process. A number of methodological issues arose from the comparative nature of the larger research project. We will, when appropriate, elaborate on them in the following sections.

4.1. The Survey Instrument

As argued in chapter 3.1., we decided to use a cross-sectional research design in order to address the research questions identified after a review of the relevant literature. It was argued that this method could establish the prevalence of the phenomenon. Not only can it accommodate a sample of international start-ups and a control group of domestic start-ups, but also allows for the simultaneous inclusion of different international business theories and empirical findings from previous case research in a multivariate framework.

Nevertheless, a cross-sectional survey design has a number of limitations. Foremost among them is the problem of operationalising the theories outlined in the literature section. Whereas the gathering of information through interviews allows for a richer operationalisation of the relevant concepts, this approach has the disadvantage of being very costly and time-consuming. Therefore, unless extensive resources are committed, this approach is unsuited to generating a dataset with a large number of cases. A larger number of responses can be achieved with a mail survey but at the expense of richness of information. The most appropriate solution to this problem is a careful screening of the literature in order to identify questions that have been successfully applied by other researchers in similar contexts.

Furthermore, there may be problems of understanding the questions. The respondents may not understand a question in the way that it was intended by the researchers. We therefore tried to incorporate questions that have successfully been applied in previous research. In addition, pre-testing of the questionnaire helps to identify ambiguous questions.

Another problem is the response behaviour of the target sample. If the survey receives a low response rate, the chances increase that the findings are not representative of the whole sample. Repeated mailings, pre-paid return envelopes, phone reminders and the promise to share results are frequently used in order to increase the response rate. In addition, there can be a sample selection problem, since only those entrepreneurs that have a particular interest may decide to participate in the survey. In this type of research, it is problematic if only relatively successful entrepreneurs respond. In both cases, the results are biased as the respondents do not reflect the characteristics of the population as a whole. In order to test for this bias, various non-response bias tests have been developed. While they cannot correct for a potential bias, they do at least increase the researcher's awareness to this problem and indicate whether the findings can be generalised.

Arguably, the above limitations are the price paid for the ability of this approach to consolidate existing knowledge in the field and subject it to rigorous testing. We will now discuss the process of obtaining data from the firms. First, we will discuss how the target group of firms, high-technology start-ups, has been operationalised to obtain a contactable population of firms. Then we will describe the data source used in the survey. After that, we will describe the sampling process and the handling of the survey. Finally, we will assess the possibility of non-response bias.

4.2. Definition of High-Technology Start-ups

As already stated above, there are a wide number of definitions for the terms high-technology start-up and new technology-based firm (Autio 1997; Storey and Tether 1998). In the first study on high-tech start-ups in Europe, sponsored by the Anglo-German Foundation in 1977, the consultancy Arthur D. Little coined the term "new technology-based firm." To fulfil this definition of a new technology-based firm, a company has to meet the following criteria (Little, 1977):

- It must not have been established for more than 25 years.
- It must be established by one or more individuals and not be the subsidiary of an established firm.
- It must have as main business purpose the exploitation of an invention or a technological innovation.

This definition excludes subsidiaries of other firms, buy-outs / buy-ins and de-mergers from existing firms. Note that this definition includes firms which are up to 25 years old. This is in contrast to internationally accepted definitions of researchers who have opted for different age thresholds to define start-up companies or new ventures. In the American literature on entrepreneurship, the majority of researchers have defined a new venture as younger than eight years or six years (Oviatt and McDougall, 1997). While the validity of the US definition is acknowledged, we decided to deviate from this practice by focussing on firms that were up to ten years old. Due to the lack of data from other studies in the area of international entrepreneurship, we had no a priori expectations about the share of firms with international activities among the total population of high-tech start-ups. However, we expected international activities to be more prevalent among slightly older and larger firms. As it was vital to obtain data from a critical number of internationalisers, we opted for a slightly different definition of the term "start-up" to include older firms.

The criterion of "high-technology" is more difficult to operationalise. Researchers have in the past repeatedly highlighted the weaknesses of available definitions (see Koberg, Rosse and Bergh 1994 for a review). Nonetheless, most researchers agree on a list of common attributes or dimensions of "high-technology." The most import of these are the uncertain returns of research and development investments, the uncertain market reaction, partly due to the difficulty of ex-ante performance evaluation in the absence of comparable solutions, the short windows of opportunity due to faster rates of obsolescence and the presence of high levels of human capital in high technology firms (e.g. Moriarty and Kosnik 1989; Koberg, Rosse and Bergh 1994; OECD 1997; Storey and Tether 1998). Definitions also distinguish between market and technology uncertainty (Moriarty and Kosnik 1989; Meldrum 1995) and product and process innovation (OECD 1997). The problem with these attributes is that they are notoriously difficult to operationalise. Even if there were objective indicators, considerable measurement problems exist. Many indicators measure R&D input variables as opposed to technology or innovation output. Since firms with low R&D expenditures may develop and manufacture technologically advanced products, the relation between input and output variables is not straightforward. On the other hand, methods that use output indicators such as patents ignore those firms that decide not to disclose their output, i.e. those that don't file patents and trademarks. There is a further problem of measurement as small and young firms frequently do not record research and development expenditures separately.

Despite these problems, R&D expenditures as a percentage of total sales and R&D employees as a percentage of total employees have become the most frequently used proxy variables to operationalise high-technology (Butchart 1987; Koberg, Rosse and Bergh 1994; OECD 1997). The majority of experts that developed the Oslo and Frascati Manuals of the OECD for measuring innovation and R&D indicators (OECD 1997) agree that these indicators represent reasonable approximations in order to identify technology intensive or knowledge intensive organisations. These measures have also found widespread use as indicators in the field of innovation economics. Furthermore, the weakness of measuring R&D input can be addressed by including objective (e.g. patents) or subjective output measures in a survey.

An operationalised definition of high-technology industries in the UK based on the above indicators has been proposed by Butchart (1987). He provides a definition of high-tech industries based on the ratios of R&D expenses per sales turnover and employees working in R&D per total employees. He thus established a list of 19 SIC codes of industries that are characterised by "substantially above average" scores on at least one of the criteria and "above average" scores on the other (Butchart 1987). A list of these industries can be found in table 3. Like Butchart himself, we acknowledge that this definition is not an accurate operationalisation of "high-technology" as there will be a sizeable proportion of firms in those industries which do not carry out any research and development activities. However, we argue that, as opposed to targeting low-technology sectors in the search of high-technology start-ups, including only firms from the above industries results in an increased likelihood of obtaining responses from firms that fulfil the specified criteria for inclusion in this study.

To conclude, we are aware of the weaknesses of the established definitions of technology, but, in the absence of a more appropriate method, stick to conventional practice and use an industry definition based on average R&D expenditures. Furthermore, since this definition has in the past been used for a large European research project on new, technology-based firms (Storey and Tether 1998), it should therefore improve the comparability of our findings with previous research.

4.3. Identification of Data Sources: The Use of Credit Rating Data

The next step consisted of identifying suitable sources of primary data in order to construct a data base of firms from these industries. Start-up firms pose particular challenges to researchers since the coverage of both official sources and commercial data providers of young firms is quite incomplete. However, as mentioned above, we were particularly interested in identifying the extent to which British high-technology firms were engaged in international activities. It was therefore important to identify a data source with a wide coverage of start-ups firms.

It would, in principle have been possible to compile a contact database using different industry directories. However, it has not been possible to identify directories for all high-technology industries using the above definition of

Butchart (1987). Furthermore, industry directories may be biased towards large and older firms and not contain data on the youngest start-ups in an industry. Using data from industry directories was therefore ruled out.

Instead, we decided to use data from credit rating agencies. Using credit rating data is getting increasingly popular in research on start-ups (McDougall 1989; Small Business Research Centre 1993; Licht and Stahl 1995). The main advantage of credit rating data is that they offer a degree of coverage similar to official government data sources, such as the Company House database, while containing additional information unavailable through public sources. Using this additional information, researchers can construct more suitable sampling frames and carry out more accurate non-response analyses. However, it should be noted that considerable problems exist with credit rating data as well. The data quality can suffer from recording errors, recording lags or inaccurate information provided deliberately by the researched firms. The latter is a particular problem with smaller firms where it is not uncommon to observe that the owner / managers do not want to reveal information about their company. Yet, while the problems of credit rating data are well known, experts still believe that they represent the best starting point for constructing enterprise panels and carrying out large surveys of entire populations (Licht and Stahl 1995).

The coverage of any credit rating agency is generally quite exhaustive as far as larger firms are concerned. When the firms in question are very small, the issues related to data quality become more important and have to be addressed. First, as with available public data sources, the reliability of credit rating data and the proportion of excluded firms within a population increases with decreasing firm size. Statements about the larger population become more inaccurate when the survey includes small firms, as the total size of the population is unknown. On the other hand, with increasing firm size, visibility and the chance of being included in a credit rating database increase significantly. Accurate information on the rate of omission is, unfortunately not available. Second, industrial economists interested in populations of firms are well aware that the large majority of firms in any industry are micro-firms. Among these micro firms, there is a substantial proportion with little or no business activity. They may have been set up by their founders for reasons not related to any business activity. Adopting a cut-off criteria is likely to exclude the majority of these firms. Furthermore, it substantially reduces the likelihood of omission from the credit rating database. In addition, given the objective of the study, one can argue that internationalisation is not an issue for these firms. Their inclusion in the sampling would therefore neither produce a target sample suitable for the purpose of this research project nor be an economically reasonable strategy. Therefore, we decided to chose an additional cut-off criterion. Target firms needed to employ at least three people at the time of the latest credit rating to be included in the sample. The exclusion of firms with fewer than three employees reduces the possibility of a bias due to non-inclusion in the credit rating agency's database and increases the likelihood of obtaining responses from target firms for this research.

To summarise, independent new firms with at least three employees, founded between 1987 and 1996 inclusive, and operating in the 19 UK SIC codes defined by Butchart (1987) were chosen as target population for the study.

4.4. The Primary Data Base

Several information providers were contacted in order to obtain information on the number of eligible firms. We decided to use a database from Dun & Bradstreet, the leading British credit rating agency in terms of company coverage. After initial discussions, Dun & Bradstreet generously decided to make the database available. Dun & Bradstreet offers a number of services to their clients, the most important being assessment of credit risks and provision of data bases for direct marketing purposes. Typically, firms are included in Dun & Bradstreet's data base for two reasons:

- First, D&B proactively gathers information from public sources such as Company House and telephone directory publishers such as the Thompson Directory. They do so themselves in to order achieve the broadest possible coverage for their customers. All companies that have registered with Company House are included in the database. Registration with Company House is compulsory for all limited companies.

- Second, customers or suppliers who would like to obtain information on a firm concerning the financial situation, payment score, etc., can solicit information from the agency. If a firm is not contained in the data base, it is contacted by a Dun & Bradstreet researcher to gather the required information.

In both cases, newly included firms are contacted on a regular basis by Dun & Bradstreet researchers in order to update the available information. The Butchart definition of high-technology industries relies on 1987 UK SIC codes (Butchart 1987). Dun & Bradstreet, however, uses 1982 US SIC codes on a global basis in order to classify firms in its database. In order to make the data comparable with the German classification, the Anglo-German research team chose to translate all industry classification codes in NACE codes, the recent European standard classification developed by Eurostat. Based on the description of the Butchart definition, all different classifications were translated into the NACE system. The conversion of the various codes into NACE, Revision 1, is listed in table 3.

4.4.1. The Clean-up of Primary Data

Our inclusion criteria resulted in a primary dataset of 7788 firms. A closer look revealed that nearly two thirds of the records obtained originate from companies in the service sector whose business activity is related to computer and software (NACE codes 7220 and 7260). This distribution is due to classification problems in the relatively new computer-related industries. Both NACE and SIC codes do not allow for a more detailed classification of these firms. As a result, these industry classifications also include companies that sell (wholesale, distribution, retail) and repair (including various maintenance activities) computers. In addition, service firms such as systems integrators fall under these "high technology" industry definitions.

Despite this obvious classification problem, these two sectors were included in the definition of high-technology sectors by Butchart. Yet, given the core element of the definition of a high-technology firm, the performance of research and development activities, the majority – though not all - retailers, system integrators and maintenance firms can be expected to fall outside the scope of this research project. In order to increase the probability of obtaining survey data from firms that meet the inclusion criteria of this study, we decided to exclude these firms. Using the "line of business description" and an additional classification code (the Thompson directory classifications) contained in the Dun & Bradstreet source file, companies unlikely to perform research and development activities were identified. This was accomplished using various "negative" criteria for a text field search. For example, companies whose line of business activity or company name included keywords such as "retail", "distribution", "wholesale", "maintenance" and "repair" were earmarked. Among telecommunications firms, radio stations were excluded from the sample as their business activity normally does not entail regular research and development activities comparable with those of the other firms in the sample. Research and development laboratories were also excluded because the survey instrument would have required substantial modification to address the peculiar characteristics of these organisations. We examined each of these earmarked company records in order to ascertain whether an exclusion is warranted on the basis of the negative criteria. The same procedure was carried out for firms in the manufacturing sector (negative criteria: retail, distribution, repair, maintenance, wholesale). However, due to the more precise classification nomenclature in the manufacturing sector, only a relatively small number of firms had to be excluded from the original datafile.

Altogether, this procedure lead to an exclusion of 3904 service companies and 322 manufacturing companies. An industry break-down of the original sample, the Dun & Bradstreet source file, and the adjusted sample of 3562 firms is shown in table 3. The services group consists of the telecommunications service codes (NACE 64.20) and computer related service codes (72.20 - 72.60). As one can see from table 3, these firms, which represent about 40% of the total cleaned sample, essentially belong to one industry, namely software. According to the NACE classification system, the remaining manufacturing firms - about 60% of the sample - operate in 16 different industries.

Table 3: Dun & Bradstreet Source Data and Cleaned Primary Database

Description (NACE Rev.1)	NACE Rev. 1	Description ('82 US SIC)	'82 US SIC	# of firms	after clean-up	%
Plastics in Primary Form	24.16	Plastic Material and Synthetic Resin	2821	43	42	1.18%
Synthetic Rubber in Primary Form	24.17	Synthetic Rubber Manufacturers	2822	7	3	0.08%
Pharmaceutical Products and Preparations	24.41	Pharmaceutical Products and Preparations	2834	60	43	1.21%
	24.42	(included above)				
Office Equipment	30.01	Calculator Manufacturers	3574	22	12	0.34%
		Misc. Office Machinery	3579	6	3	0.08%
Computers and other Information Processing Equipment	30.02	Computer Manufacturers	3573	311	276	7.75%
Electric Motors, Generators and Transformers	31.10	Power, Distribution and Transformers	3612	45	44	1.24%
		Switchgear & Switchboard Manufacturers	3613	120	112	3.14%
		Motor & Generator Manufacturers	3621	28	26	0.73%
Electricity Distribution and Control Apparatus	31.20	Power, Distribution and Transformers	3622	88	84	2.36%
Electronic Valves, Tubes and other Components	32.10	Radio & TV Tubes	3671	3	2	0.06%
		Cathode Ray Tubes	3672	14	12	0.34%
		Special Purpose Electronic Tubes	3673	4	3	0.08%
		Semiconductors	3674	101	89	2.50%
		Electronic Capacitors	3675	1	1	0.03%
		Resistors, Electronic Application	3676	1	0	0.00%
		Electronic Coil and Transformers	3677	23	21	0.59%
		Connectors, Electronic Applications	3678	3	3	0.08%
		Misc. Electronic Components	3679	309	278	7.80%
Television and Radio Transmitters and Apparatus for Line Telephony and Line Telegraphy	32.20	Telephone & Telegraph equipment manufacturers	3661	52	49	1.38%
		Radio & TV Broadcasting Equipment	3662	249	206	5.78%
Television and Radio Receivers, Sound or Video Recording and Reproducing Apparatus	32.30	Radio & TV Equipment manufacturers (excluding Communication)	3651	77	68	1.91%

Medical and Surgical Equipment and Orthopaedic Appliances	33.10	X-Ray Apparatus and Manufacturers	3693	22	21	0.59%
		Surgical/Medical Instruments	3841	88	85	2.39%
		Orthopedical/Surgical Appliances and Supplies	3842	164	86	2.41%
Electronic Instruments and Appliances for Measuring, Checking (except Industrial Process Control)	33.20	Engineering and Scientific Equipment Manufacturers	3811	90	87	2.44%
		Environmental Control Devices	3822	22	19	0.53%
		Fluid meter and Counting Devices	3824	12	11	0.31%
		Electric Meter Manufacturers	3825	60	53	1.49%
		Misc. Meter and Control Devices	3829	61	54	1.52%
Electronic Industrial Process Control Equipment	33.30	Industrial Instruments Manufacturers	3823	105	95	2.67%
Optical Instruments	33.40	Ophthalmic Goods	3851	11	9	0.25%
		Optical Instruments and Lenses	3832	19	17	0.48%
Photographic Equipment		Photographic Equipment	3861	42	30	0.84%
Aircraft and Speedcraft Manufacturing	35.30	Aircraft Manufacturers	3721	9	9	0.25%
		Aircraft Engine Manufacturers	3724	8	6	0.25%
		Misc. Aircraft Part Manufacturers	3728	22	20	0.17%
		Guided Missile and Space Vehicle	3761	1	1	0.56%
		Guided Missile and Space Vehicle Engines	3764	0	0	0.03%
		Misc. Guided Missile and Space Vehicle	3769	1	1	0.00%
Telecommunications	64.20	Telecommunications	4811	87	24	0.03%
		Telecommunications	4821	5	2	0.67%
		Telecommunications	4832	55	0	0.06%
		Telecommunications	4833	25	0	0.00%
		Telecommunications	4899	213	145	0.00%
Software Consultancy and Supply	72.20	Computer Programming and Software Services	7372	2403	1305	36.64%
Data Processing	72.30	Data Processing	7374	55	0	0.00%
Database Activities	72.40					
Other Computer Related Activities	72.60	Misc. Computer Services	7379	2457	105	2.95%
Research and Development in Natural Sciences and Engineering	73.10	Research and Development Laboratories	7391	184	0	0.00%
Total			Total	7788	3562	

4.4.2. Sampling Procedure

A so-called stratified random sampling approach was adopted in order to select target firms for the mailing. We will describe the process and elaborate on the reasoning behind choosing this approach over a standard random sampling. In a first step, the remaining 3562 companies were stratified into two industry groups (manufacturing and services) and four size classes (by employees). In order to obtain the target sample of 2000 firms for the mail survey, we calculated a target number of firms per cell. Our target was to include 1500 manufacturing firms and 500 service firms. Furthermore, in order to obtain a roughly equal distribution of firms among different size classes, we also calculated an approximate target number per size class.

Table 4: Sample Composition After Stratification
(Number of firms per cell and percentage of total)

Employees	Cleaned Sample			Target Sample		
	Manufacturing	Services	Total	Manufacturing	Services	Total
3-5	673	742	1415	344	112	456
	19%	21%	40%	17%	6%	23%
6-9	474	370	844	384	112	496
	13%	10%	24%	19%	6%	25%
10-19	472	292	764	427	132	559
	13%	8%	21%	21%	7%	28%
20 +	362	177	539	345	144	489
	10%	5%	15%	17%	7%	24%
Total	1981	1581	3562	1500	500	2000
	56%	44%	100%	75%	25%	100%

In the next step, using the above targets as thresholds, a random sample of 2000 companies was drawn to establish the *target sample* for the mail survey. Furthermore, we also drew a *reserve sample* of 671 firms, roughly a third of the target sample. The latter was intended to replace firms that ceased to exist or moved address and whose envelopes were expected to be returned unopened within a few days of the mailing. The remaining 891 firms were discarded. Table 4 shows the sample composition using the above stratification criteria for the cleaned Dun & Bradstreet sample and the *target sample* for the mailing. Table 5 shows the drawing probability per strata.

After having described the procedure, it is of course necessary to highlight the reasoning for adopting this approach. As one can see from both tables, the stratified sampling resulted in an artificial over-representation of manufacturing firms as opposed to service firms and larger firms as opposed smaller firms. For example, the group of the smallest service firms represents 21% of the cleaned up Dun & Bradstreet sample, but only 6% of the target sample (Table 4). This translates into a drawing probability of 15% (Table 5).

Table 5: Drawing Probability per Strata *

Employees	Manufacturing	Services
3-5	50%	15%
6-9	80%	30%
10-19	89%	46%
20 +	98%	81%

* The table shows the final drawing probability after inclusion of 62 firms from the reserve sample (see section on the mailing below).

Several issues are addressed by this procedure. First, as already mentioned above, due to the dearth of empirical research in international entrepreneurship, the extent of cross-border activities among British high-technology start-ups was completely unknown. Theory, however, suggests that larger start-ups are more likely to have international activities. As the main research question consists of comparing internationalisers with non-internationalisers in a multivariate framework, it is vital to obtain data on a sufficient number of firms with international activities. Oversampling larger firms therefore increases the likelihood of realising that objective. Second, given the size distribution of firms in any given industry, the majority of responses would be expected from these smallest of firms. If there are systematic differences firm behaviour related to size, a more balanced sampling frame that produces a more even distribution of firms across different size classes is more suitable to pick that effect up. Third, since we are interested in discovering industry effects at a more disaggregated level than "manufacturing vs. service", it is not desirable to devise a sampling frame where 36.6% of firms originate from one industry (NACE 72.20) and the remaining 63.4 % from all other 18 industries. The stratified random sampling allows for an incorporation of these objectives through deliberate over- or under-representation of particular strata.

There is, however, an important downside to this approach. The stratified sampling process deliberately introduces a bias into the data that prevents researchers from drawing conclusions on the *population* as a whole without making further adjustments to the results. In order to correct for that bias, the standard procedure consists of calculating weights which reflect the different drawing and response probability per strata. Based on the assumption of absence of non-response bias *within* each strata, the descriptive results can easily be corrected for that bias by incorporating these weights into the calculation. Given that descriptive results refer to a univariate data pattern, it is not unreasonable to make that assumption when a sufficient number of firm responded.

In a multivariate approach, however, the impact of stratification and the appropriability of weighting is more difficult to assess given the multitude of different multivariate pattern. On the one hand, the stratification deliberately introduces a bias through over- or under-sampling. On the other hand, as firms are quite diverse entities, both management and distribution theory suggest that the individual multivariate pattern are not completely determined by the stratification criteria. In other words, one does a priori not expect the multivariate vectors of service firms to be consistently different from those of manufacturing firms unless there is an extremely high correlation between the stratification criteria (service vs. manufacturing) and all other variables in the questionnaire. Consequently, it is common not to attach weights to the regression models after stratification. To conclude, the stratification is likely to result in some sort of bias, though it is virtually impossible to assess its impact on the results. Still, if the number of data points is sufficiently high, the results of the estimations should not impaired in a consistent way. The stratified sampling has thus been chosen because the benefits outlined above outweigh its the potential downside.

4.5. The Questionnaire

In parallel to drawing a target sample for our survey, we developed a four page questionnaire based on the existing literature in the field, including both international business in general and exploratory studies in international entrepreneurship. We first asked respondents about general characteristics of the firm, characteristics of the founders and their skill sets and product characteristics. As the questionnaire was designed to operationalise the dominant theories in the field of international business, variables to measure transaction costs during the sales process were included. Furthermore, we operationalised variables that have been used in previous research to operationalise the resource-based view to test the propositions of internationalisation process models. We also asked respondents to provide information about the three most important foreign markets for their best selling product. The latter was done in order to analyse the market entry as unit of analysis as a function of product characteristics and country characteristics. Finally, we asked the respondents to rank different motivations for international activities and the costs and constraints experienced during this process.

The design of the questionnaire and the individual questions were then discussed with the German research team. These discussions lead to a number of changes reflecting the experiences of the German researchers with German start-up firms. A copy of the questionnaire can be found in appendix 1. Key questions of the survey instrument are described in more detail in section 6.1., which deals with the operationalisation of the independent variables.

4.6. The Pilot Case Studies

In order to test the survey instrument, four pilot case studies were carried out in the UK. Different methods were chosen to test whether the survey instrument was comprehensive. The first method (2 cases) involved visiting the pilot respondent and observing him while filling out the questionnaire, asking him to "think loudly" during the process (Hall and Hofer, 1993). Questions were discussed when the pilot respondent felt that they were worded ambiguously. During this process, we took notes which served as basis for further improvements. The second method (2 cases) did not require our presence. It involved sending the questionnaire directly to two pilot respondents. After the questionnaire was filled out, we discussed the answers with the respondents over the phone in order to determine the comprehensiveness of the questions and whether they effectively measured the constructs that the we were interested in. The pilot testing resulted in a number of suggestions for modifications. After discussions with the German researchers who also carried out pilot-tests, a number of changes to both the layout and wording of the questions were incorporated.

4.7. Mailing and Response Pattern

The questionnaire and a cover letter explaining the purpose of the project were sent to the target firms during the last week of September 1997. The cover letter explicitly stressed that the we were equally interested in responses from internationalisers and non-internationalisers. Three waves of reminders within three to four weeks distance from each other were subsequently mailed. The cover letters of the reminders were worded differently for each mailing (see appendix 2 to 5). After the first reminder, we started contacting a random sample of 75 firms by phone in order to solicit participation in the survey. As this method did not yield a substantially higher response rate among the contacted firms, we decided to send out additional reminders rather than pursuing a telephone follow-up. The last questionnaires were received in February 1998. Subsequently, we contacted respondents in all cases where the answers given to important questions required clarification or were not provided at all. This resulted in the following response pattern (see also table 6).

Table 6: Response Pattern

Description	Return Code	Number of cases Abs.	rel. (%)
Usable Questionnaires	1	362	17.6
Answering only the first questions and then breaking-off	2	7	0.3
Refusal, questionnaire sent back	3	27	1.3
Refusal by mail or telephone	4	34	1.6
Firm responded but does not belong to the target population	5	94	4.6
Firm not known at the address or firm moved and new address unknown (envelope was sent back unopened)	6	134	6.5
Firm no longer existed or is in receivership	7	9	0.4
No response at all	8	1395	67.7
Total		2,062	100

Out of the 2000 questionnaires that were mailed out, 62 were returned unopened within four days. The return information provided by the Royal Mail indicated that the firms in question had ceased to exist or were not known at the given address. We therefore selected an additional 62 firms from the reserve sample so that the total number of contacted firms increased to 2062. Out of these, 1919 firms were still in business and received the survey instrument (1919=2062-(134+9)). 456 firms sent back completed questionnaires (return codes 1 + 5). This translates into a response rate of 24 % which is in line with other studies on small firms based on credit rating data (McDougall 1989; Small Business Research Centre 1992; Licht and Stahl 1995).[20]

Two figures in the table merit further comment. First, there was an unexpectedly high percentage (4.6 %) of firms that filled out the questionnaire correctly but that had to be excluded from the study because they fell outside the definition adopted for the purpose of this study (return code 5). This category is made up of three different groups. Firms of the first group stated that they were more than 10 years old. The second group stated that they were not founded as independent new firms, but as subsidiaries, buy-outs or buy-ins. The remaining firms indicated that they were acquired by larger firms after their formation. A filter question in the questionnaire was used in order to shed further light on the formation of these firms. In those cases where the best-selling product was developed *after* the current legal incorporation, we recontacted the respondents. Questions concerning the process of their formation were asked to determine the reasons for the

---

[20] The Cambridge surveys yielded a response rate of 32% (Centre for Small Business Research 1993). Licht and Stahl (1995) reported response rates of 25% for their enterprise panel. In contrast, McDougall's (1989) study based on Dun & Bradstreet data resulted in a 10% response rate.

separation from their previous incubator organisation. Two criteria were used in order to establish whether these firms could be retained in the database. First, the de-merger, buy-out or buy-in had to be staged in order to pursue the development of a new product idea. Second, the customer base of the firm had to be different than the one of its parent organisation. In 36 cases, both criteria were fulfilled and the firms were classified as eligible respondents (return code 1) as they actually constitute new businesses despite "inheriting" some assets from incubator organisations (see also Katz and Gartner 1988, for a discussion of emerging organisations). Return code 5 represents all remaining de-mergers, MBOs, MBIs and subsidiaries that were removed from the analysis.

Second, the group of firms with unknown addresses (6.5 %) contains an unknown number of firms that have entered receivership. The return code 7 ("Firm does no longer exist") therefore understates the number of firms the have ceased to exist as it only represents those firms that wrote back to the researchers indicating that they were in the process of receivership.

4.8. Non-Response Analysis

In order to assess whether the firms that participated in the study systematically differ from non-respondents, we perform a non-response analysis following the methods recommended by Armstrong and Overton (1977). Following that approach, we compare the 456 firms that sent back questionnaires with the remaining 1606 firms using several variables of the original Dun & Bradstreet data base. Note that the 94 firms that had to be excluded because they did not meet the inclusion criteria of the study (return code 5) were included among the respondents. As mentioned above, these firms were mainly subsidiaries of larger firms, set up as buy-outs or buy-ins or simply too old to be included. Due to the different processes of their formation and subsequent management, it is reasonable to assume that this may lead to different growth trajectories. Yet, given the unexpected high share of these firms among the respondents, we expect that the Dun & Bradstreet database also contains a substantial percentage of firms that fall under that category. As we cannot identify that type of firm ex ante in the source data, we include them as respondents in the non-response analysis. We then tested for differences of employees, information quality and credit score. The latter is of particular interest as it represents a summary proxy variable that credit rating agencies assign to assess the financial viability of a business. This variable is therefore likely to be a good indicator of the overall performance of a start-up. The information rating is a variable assigned by the Dun & Bradstreet researchers in order to judge the quality and amount of disclosed information. Table 7 shows the means, standard deviations and t-values of the respondents and non-respondents of the different variables selected for comparison.

Table 7: Comparison of Respondents and Non-Respondents

	Respondents	Non-Respondents	Standard Error	Z	P>|t|
Employees	18.38	17.84	1.65	-0.33	0.74
Credit Score	9.25	9.23	0.177	-0.099	0.92
Info Rating	2.94	2.97	0.043	0.816	0.41

When we compare the means of respondents and non-respondents of each of these indicators, we realised that none of the differences is significant in a statistically sense. Particularly the financial indicator used to compare the two groups suggest that there are no performance differences between respondents and non-respondents. The absence of significant differences in the information rating variable suggests that the initial Dun & Bradstreet information on those firms that did participate in the survey was of the same quality as the information provided by non-respondents. Stated differently, significantly lower score among non-respondents would have indicated a systematic bias in favour of firms that are more willing to disclose firm-specific information to outsiders.

A t-test is, however, only a crude way of assessing a potential bias. In order to improve the analysis of non-respondents, the information on the 75 firms contacted over the phone during the mailing phase was used. These firms were asked to provide information on their size by employees and whether they had international sales. Not all firms wanted to disclose information. For 58 of the firms, information was available. The average of 16 employees and 38 firms with international sales are in line with the parameters for the total sample (see section 5.3.1.). We therefore conclude that non-response bias could not be detected using these tests.

5. Descriptive Data Analysis

5.1. Methodological Considerations

In this chapter, we will give an overview of the sample of eligible firms by providing some basic descriptive statistics and discussion of the results. As mentioned in the previous chapter, 362 usable questionnaires could be retained for analysis. Given that our mail sample was generated using a stratified random sampling procedure (see chapter 4), we deliberately introduced a bias into our data. For example, there was a deliberate over-sampling of larger firms and a deliberate under-sampling of service firms. In order to infer from our sample on the estimated larger population of high-tech start-ups, this bias had to be neutralised. To this end, the values of the firms in each of the eight strata have been adjusted using a weighting procedure. The next section briefly discusses how these weights were calculated.

5.1.1. Calculation of Weights

In order to calculate the weights for each strata, two different factors, the drawing probability and the response probability, were taken into account. The drawing probability accounts for the bias introduced through the deliberate over- or under-sampling due to the stratified random sampling. It is calculated by dividing the number of firms in the *mail* sample by the number of firms in the adjusted (cleaned) Dun & Bradstreet *source* sample per strata. As we are interested in inferring from our sample on the total population of firms, we also adjusted these drawing probabilities with the response probability per strata. The latter is calculated for each strata according to the same method used to calculated the overall response probability (see section 4.7.). The weight for each strata is then given by the inverse of the product of drawing probability and response probability. Table 8 gives an overview of the drawing probability, the response probability and the resulting weight for each of the strata.

These weights were used when basic descriptive statistics were calculated, such as the mean, the median and the standard deviation. First, the mean of any variable was calculated for every strata. A weighted average was then calculated using the different weights in order to estimate the population mean. In practice, this is a relatively straightforward task as the majority of statistical software packages allow the incorporation of weights in their calculation routines.

Table 8: Calculation of Weights per Strata*

Strata	Drawing Probability	Response Probability	Weight
Manu 3-5 employees	0.50	0.17	11.84
Manu 6-9 employees	0.80	0.24	5.29
Manu 10-19 employees	0.89	0.25	4.55
Manu 20 + employees	0.98	0.25	4.15
Service 3-5 employees	0.15	0.25	26.25
Service 6-9 employees	0.30	0.27	12.23
Service 10-19 employees	0.46	0.28	7.75
Service 20 + employees	0.81	0.29	4.24

* Weight=1/(drawing probability x response probability)

The following example using the number of employees at the time of the survey highlights the implications of this procedure. The *sample mean* is 20 employees. Given that we deliberately over-sampled large firms, we expected the population mean to be somewhat lower. Accordingly, we obtain a *weighted mean* of 15 employees which is an *estimation of the mean of the total population* of high-tech start-ups. In the next section, the majority of the descriptive results will be shown both weighted and unweighted. The discussion is mainly based on the weighted results but we provide further explanations when substantial differences are evident.

5.1.2. Industry Groups

In order to analyse the characteristics of the firms in more detail, they are grouped in five industry categories. These are services, IT/communications hardware, electronics, life sciences and "other". Table 9 indicates the classification logic and the number of firms per industry group. The percentages are shown both weighted and unweighted and represent the share of the estimated total population and share of sample respectively.

The classification was motivated by the desire to obtain homogeneous industry groups. Note that the services / software industry group is mainly composed of software firms. Furthermore, the line of business description of three of the five telecommunications firms (such as "internet access provider" or "phone system management software") reveals that their activity is based around software solutions. In the following, this group is referred to as "software". The IT and telecommunications hardware firms mainly consist of two NACE codes. The product descriptions of firms in these industries suggest that they predominantly manufacture products in relatively large volumes from commodity components. The group "engineering / precision engineering" represents those firms which specialise in the development and manufacture of electronic instruments, control and measurement devices. The group "life sciences" consists of medical engineering firms and biotechnology firms. These two NACE codes have been grouped together because they face somewhat similar challenges during the development and commercialisation phases of their products. For example, the products of these firms are in many cases subject to regulatory approval by health authorities in their target markets. Furthermore, the commercialisation of these products is usually carried out through medical equipment distributors. As the project is largely concerned with the internationalisation of these firms, which is arguably a sales driven process for start-ups, we believe that they represent a rather homogeneous subgroup.

All remaining firms were classified as "Other". We do admit that it appears somewhat arbitrary when merely looking at the different NACE descriptions ranging from synthetic rubber to aircraft manufacturing. However, there is a logic behind this classification. First, the inclusion of some of these NACE codes in the other four groups would arguably lead to lower degree of homogeneity among these. Second, and more important, the product description of these firms revealed that the majority, 67%, produce components for other products. This compares to 19% for the other industry subgroups. We therefore believe that there is some homogeneity even in this more eclectic subgroup.[21]

We will now turn to a description of the firms, both at start-up and at the time of the survey, and discuss the characteristics of their products. Certain indicators will be shown at an industry level using the five industry groups described above. Furthermore, for certain indicators, a break-down by the different size classes will be provided. Size is here defined in terms of employment. The groups are identical to the size groups used for the stratification procedure (1-5 employees, 6-9 employees, 10-19 employees and 20 and more employees).

---

[21] During our descriptive analysis, we received further evidence that this firm is quite distinct from the other firms along a number of dimensions.

Table 9: Sample Composition by Industry

Industry Groups	# of firms	% *)	% **)	Description (NACE Rev.1)	NACE Rev. 1	# of firms
Services / Software	104	44.03	28.73	Telecommunications	64.20	5
				Software Consultancy and Supply	72.20	92
				Other Computer Related Activities	72.60	7
IT / Communication Hardware	79	17.42	21.82	Office Equipment	30.01	0
				Computers and other Information Processing Equipment	30.02	30
				Television and Radio Transmitters and Apparatus for Line Telephony and Line Telegraphy	32.20	44
				Television and Radio Receivers, Sound or Video Recording and Reproducing Apparatus	32.30	5
Engineering / Precision Engineering	56	12.57	15.47	Electronic Instruments and Appliances for Measuring, Checking (except Industrial Process Control)	33.20	38
				Electronic Industrial Process Control Equipment	33.30	13
				Optical Instruments / Photographic Equipment	33.40	5
Life Sciences	34	6.86	9.39	Pharmaceutical Products and Preparations	24.41	3
				Medical and Surgical Equipment and Orthopaedic Appliances	33.10	31
Other	89	19.12	24.59	Plastics in Primary Form	24.16	8
				Synthetic Rubber in Primary Form	24.17	2
				Electric Motors, Generators and Transformers	31.10	20
				Electricity Distribution and Control Apparatus	31.20	12
				Electronic Valves, Tubes and other Components	32.10	42
				Aircraft and Speedcraft Manufacturing	35.30	5
Total	362	100.00	100.00			362

*) Weighted share of estimated **population**   **) Unweighted share of the actual **sample**

During the descriptive analysis, we will use the method of kernel density estimation in order to explore the distribution of several continuous variables. This method is a non-parametric estimation very similar to a histogram. The main difference between the two is that a histogram divides the data in several non-overlapping intervals, so-called bins. The observed pattern therefore depends to a large extent on the chosen number of bins. On the other hand, a kernel density estimator allows intervals to overlap and estimates the centre point of these intervals. It thus approximates the density of the value for a particular dependent variables, i.e. the frequency at which it occurs. As a result, the distribution of the dependent variable is approximated as a continuous line. It can be overlaid with a normal distribution around the mean in order to explore the distribution of the dependent variable (for a detailed explications of this method see, for example, Tapia and Thompson 1978).

5.2. Descriptive Data Analysis: General Firm Characteristics

5.2.1. Firm Characteristics at Start-up

Table 10 shows descriptive statistics of the firms at the time of start-up. A breakdown of the number of founders reveals that 70% of firms have been set up by at least two founders. This distribution applies across all different industry groups and size classes. Including the founders, the mean number of employees at start-up was four employees with a median of two. As one would expect from a population of start-ups, the distribution of this variable is highly skewed to the right with values ranging from 1 to 50. 88% of the firms had five employees or less at the time of start-up. At industry level, there are certain differences with regard to start-up employment. Average start-up employment varied between 3.0 (IT/Com hardware and engineering) and 4.60 ("other"). Software firms started with an average of 3.9 employees and life sciences firms with 4.1 employees.

Table 10: Firm Characteristics at Start-up *

	Weighted			Unweighted		
	Mean	Median	SD	Mean	Median	SD
Founders	2.13	2	1.21	2.16	2	1.27
Employees at start-up	3.78	2	5.42	4.36	3	6.45
Sales in first year (in 000)	216	100	405	274	124	507

* Employment in full-time equivalents; sales data in thousands of pounds

In their first financial year, these firms generated a mean turnover of £216,000. The average firm, however, had a much lower level of sales (median £100,000). This distribution becomes less skewed when excluding the "de-merged start-ups." The remaining population had mean sales of £179,000 with values ranging from 0 to £2,175,000. Note that there is sometimes a gap of several years between the year of formation and the first financial year. This is largely due to the long development cycle of certain products and the fact that some new organisations take a number of years to "emerge" (Katz and Gartner 1988). While 87% of firms generate their first sales within their first or second year of operation, the remaining 13% of the start-ups experienced a lag ranging from two to six years.

5.2.2. Firm Characteristics at the Time of the Survey

The target firms for the sample were founded between 1987 and 1996 inclusive. At the time of the survey, the responding firms were on average 5.4 years old (base year: 1997). Figure 1 reveals that the age distribution is somewhat uneven with the highest percentage of responding firms centred around the mean age.

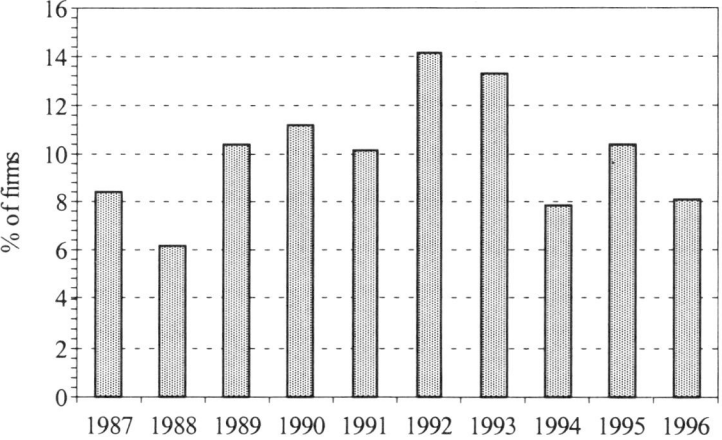

Figure 1: Firms by Year of Formation

The slightly lower share of older firms among the respondents (left tail of the distribution) is probably due to the likelihood of survivor bias inherent in any dataset on entrepreneurial start-up firms. This "drop" is already present in the Dun & Bradstreet source dataset. When looking at the right end of the tail, one can observe a slightly lower than expected percentage of responding firms starting from the formation year 1994. A likely explanation for this decline could be the lack of interest in the survey topic among the youngest firms or greater demand on management during the start-up period.

Table 11 provides information on firm size at the time of the survey. During the period between start-up and the time of the survey, the firms created on average 12 additional jobs with values ranging from -17 to 167 (median 6). Accordingly, a start-up employed on average 15 people including the founders (full-time equivalents). These figures are in line with previous studies on the employment of new, technology-based firms (for reviews of existing empirical data see Autio 1997; Storey and Tether 1998). As one can see from the table, the firms generated average sales of £1,380,000 (median £650,000) with values ranging from £16,000 to £16,100,000. The average annual sales per employee were £59,300 with values ranging from £2,600 to £ 250,000. We also asked the respondents to state their sales forecast for the current financial year, which usually coincided with the financial year at the time of the survey. The firms in our sample had a very optimistic outlook on the future with 93% of firms expecting an increase of their sales during the following financial year.

Table 11: Firm Size at the Time of the Survey *

	Weighted			Unweighted		
	Mean	Median	SD	Mean	Median	SD
Age	5.41	5	2.67	5.74	6	2.64
Employees today	15.36	8	20.84	20.01	12	24.18
Sales in last year	923	480	1508	1246	654	1799
Sales per Employee	59.3	49	45.21	62.6	52	44.26
Expected sales next year	1264	600	2054	1608	860	2225

* Sales data in thousands of pounds; Employee data in full-time equivalents

Table 12: Firm Size by Industry*

	Total Sample	Software	IT/Com Hardware	Engineer.	Life Sciences	Other
Employees today	15.36	15.32	16.37	11.44	17.44	16.35
Sales in last year	923	890	1222	731	771	923
Sales per Employee	59.3	58.1	77.6	63.9	44.2	56.5
Expected sales next year	1264	1308	1693	971	889	1109

* Weighted results; employment in full-time equivalents; sales in thousands of pounds

When looking at firm size by industry (table 12), a number of differences became apparent. In terms of both employment and sales, the firms in the engineering industry group were smaller than the other firms. Note also that the life sciences firms indicated relatively low sales figures compared to the sample average despite having the highest average number of employees. Their low ratio of sales per employee suggest the presence of a number of firms that are still in the development process or that have launched their products without yet reaching their full sales potential. Software firms reported the highest projected sales increase from their last financial year to the year-end forecast of the financial year at the time of the survey. The growth rates of the firms will be discussed in more detail in section 5.2.7.

5.2.3. External Finance: Venture Capital, Business Angels and Public Grants

We asked respondents to indicate whether they received any form of external finance to start their firm. We asked them whether they benefited from investments from venture capitalists and business angels or successfully applied for government grants. Table 13 reports the results to this question.

Table 13: External Finance

	% of firms at start-up			% of firms today		
	# of obs.	Weighted	Unweighted	# of obs.	Weighted	Unweighted
Venture Capital	35	7.44	9.67	39	8.78	10.77
Business Angels	29	7.10	8.01	40	8.92	11.05
Public Grants	50	12.27	13.81	62	12.93	17.12

The figures show that 7.4% of the firms received venture capital at start-up. This percentage increased slightly when considered at the time of the survey. A roughly equal percentage of firms benefited from investments though business angels (7% at start-up; 9% at the time of the survey). These figures are in line with those provided by Moore (1994), who reported that 10% of the high-tech firms in his sample benefited from venture capital. Given that Mason and Harrison (1994) estimate the that business angel sector in the UK is of at least equal size than the official venture capital sector, the percentage of firms with business angel investment is also within the expected range. Note that the percentage of firms receiving funds from a business angel increased to a greater extent over time than the percentage of VC investee firms.

The figures for government support requires some comments. The previous two questions on venture capital and business angels enabled respondents to clearly state their involvement at start-up and the time of the survey. One does expect an increasing involvement over time as a disinvestment is unlikely at such an early stage of the companies' life. The section on public grants, however, is less straightforward as many grants and awards represent one-off payments instead of ongoing equity participation's. The answer to "support today" therefore underestimates the amount of firms that have *ever* benefited from such schemes. Accordingly, when just looking at the results as indicated by the respondents, the share of firms that received some sort of government grant over time is constant. We therefore also calculated the share of firms that did receive a grant at the time of start-up but indicated "no support" at the time of the survey. Accordingly, the weighted share of firms that have received some government support or participated in some government financed scheme since inception increases to 20.7%. Note, however, that this figure is likely to include refundable loans. According to the comments provided on the questionnaire by many entrepreneurs, this percentage does not only cover non-refundable grants and innovation, technology or design awards, but also the participation in the Small Business Loan Guarantee Scheme which underwrites refundable loans administered by retail banks. 27 of the firms (7.5% of the sample, 5.9% of the estimated population) benefited from an export assistance grant or participated in a government programme designed to assist them in their international expansion. 23 of these firms indicated that they have international sales at the time of the survey. Three of the firms that received export assistance did not sell into foreign markets during their last financial year but had international sales at some stage in the past. In only one case, there were no international sales recorded despite the provision of export assistance.

We also asked respondents to indicate the amount of funds provided through these external financiers, expressed as percentage of total equity. Note that this does not mean that the venture capitalists or the business angels hold the same amount of the shares or voting rights. Note also that this is of course less applicable to government grants which are in the majority of cases accounted for as extraordinary revenues and therefore appear in the profit and loss report, but not the balance sheet. Still, it gives a rough indication of the amount of finance made available to the entrepreneurs through these sources of finance and a comparison is quite informative. On average, venture capitalists provided an investment which represented a share of 39% of the firms' equity. When looking at the firms today, the average share amounted to 36%. It was somewhat surprising to find out that the mean share of business angels' investment was higher than the venture capitalists'. Among those firms that benefited from investments from business angels, we found a start-up investment of 52% and 41% today respectively. Note also a certain decrease in the relative importance of the amount of these investments over time. A possible explanation for this relative decrease is that both venture capitalists' and business angels' investments are likely to represent a larger share of the total equity at company start-up compared to later stage investments. Finally, public grants were less important as sources of finance than these two sources of equity finance. We found that the value of the grants amounted to 37% at start-up and 32% at the time of the survey respectively.

Further analysis revealed some industry-specific differences. Life sciences firms had a higher share of venture capital investments both at start-up and today whereas engineering were more likely to benefit from business angel investments than the remaining firms. On should, however, bear in mind that such a breakdown conveys the danger of making inferences about a larger population based on very small numbers. The breakdown of the presence of business angels by industry resulted in sub-groups consisting of 5 to 11 cases. Any interpretation therefore has to be made with extreme care.

5.2.4. Founders

When looking at the characteristics of the founders (table 14), we observed that the majority of firms, 70% of the population, were set up by teams of at least two founders. This figure applies across all different industries and size classes. 79% of the founders had joint working experience prior to starting their firm. We then looked at the international experience of the founders. We asked respondents to state whether they had previous work experience abroad, work experience in the UK for an internationally operating company or whether they have been educated abroad. The results show that 51% had work experience in a foreign country and 46% worked in the UK for an internationally operating firm respectively.

Table 14: Founder Characteristics

	Weighted			Unweighted		
	Mean	Median	SD	Mean	Median	SD
Number of Founders	2.13	2.00	1.21	2.16	2.00	1.27
Joint work experience* (in %)	78.53		41.14	81.60		38.82
Work experience abroad (in %)	51.43		50.05	52.21		50.02
Work experience in UK for international firm (in %)	46.08		49.92	48.90		50.06
Education abroad (in %)	13.06		33.75	12.71		33.35

* for firms with at least 2 founders

Combining these two indicators, 67% of founders that had some sort of international business exposure. International education was less common with only 13% of the founders stating that they spent time abroad as part of their education. Only one founder stated that he was educated abroad but had no foreign exposure in a professional setting. No important differences were found when looking at the different size classes with the exception of smallest firms having a lower percentage of international exposure. On the scores indicating international business experience, firms operating in life sciences and engineering had the highest percentages of founders with international exposure.

Management Skills

We asked respondents to indicate whether they experienced shortages of particular skills when they started their firm and at the time of the survey. In table 15, we show the percentage of those firms that said they faced a substantial shortage of skills at start-up and at the time of the survey respectively. We operationalised "substantial" as those firms that ticked a score of 4 or 5 on the five point Likert scale. As one can see from the table, the largest learning effects over time were in managerial areas such as marketing, sales and financial management. The situation in technical areas such as production and research and development stayed relatively stable over time. There were neither industry-specific differences nor differences with regard to the size classes.

Table 15: Shortage of Management Skills*

	At start-up	Today
	% of firms with "substantial" shortages of skills	% of firms with "substantial" shortages of skills
Marketing	31.68	18.14
Sales / Distribution	30.41	23.15
Financial Management	22.72	9.73
General Management.	12.49	10.76
Production, Manufacturing	17.63	12.63
Research & Development	20.23	19.17

* Weighted Results

5.2.5. Research and Development Activities

Given that our survey targeted technology-based start-ups, we included a number of questions in order to determine to what extent the responding firms were involved in research and development (R&D) activities. In accordance with widespread practice (see also section 4.2.), we chose several indicators. We first asked firms about the *regularity* of their R&D activities. As additional indicators, we used *R&D intensity* (measured as R&D expenditures as percentage of total sales), the share of *R&D employees* (measured as employees devoting at least 50% of their time to the development of future or existing products as percentage of total employees) and the number of *employees with technical training* in the company. The results are as follows.

We asked respondents to state how regularly they engaged in research and development activities. 36 (11%) firms stated that they did not perform any research or development. 106 (33%) firms indicated that they were involved in R&D activities on an occasional basis. The remaining 220 (56%) firms stated that they regularly undertook research and development activities. Looking at the industry breakdown of this indicator revealed that the firms grouped under "other" had a substantially lower share of firms with regular research and development activities (36%). This indicator was highest for the IT/Communication hardware and life sciences firms, with 72% and 69% respectively. An analysis by size class revealed that larger firms had a higher tendency to engage in research and development on a regular basis. The percentages for permanent R&D activities are 45% (3-5 employees), 60% (6-9 employees), 60% (10-19 employees) and 75% (more than 20 employees) respectively. Table 16 shows the R&D intensity of the firms in our sample.

Table 16: R&D Indicators - R&D Intensity

	Weighted			Unweighted		
	% of firms	Mean R&D Intensity	Median	% of firms	Mean R&D Intensity	Median
No R&D Activities	10.51	0	0	9.94	0	0
Occasional R&D	33.20	7.64	2.00	29.28	8.25	2.00
Regular R&D	56.29	22.61	15.00	60.77	20.26	12.00
Total	100.00	15.26	7.00	100.00	14.72	8.00

Firms that regularly engaged in research and development activities reported an average R&D intensity of nearly 23% (median 15%) with values ranging from 0% to 200%. The distribution is skewed to the right with 80% of firms showing an R&D intensity of 30% or less. 13 firms with regular R&D activities reported R&D intensity of 0%. However, they did provide an estimation of R&D employees (see below). These firms do probably not a have a separate R&D budget and their managing directors felt unable to provide a detailed account of the expenses for the questionnaire. As one would expect, the firms that performed development activities only on an occasional basis reported lower R&D intensities (mean 7.6%, median 2%). A breakdown by firm size (in terms of employees) revealed small differences. The mean values per size class ranged from 14.9% for smallest firms (1-5 employees) to 16.9% for the largest firms (more than 20 employees).

We then looked at a different indicator for the technology intensity of the firms. In accordance with common practice in studies that are concerned with measuring the technology intensity or knowledge content of firms (see for example OECD 1997), we asked respondents to state how many employees devoted more than

50% of their time to research and development of current or future products. We asked respondents to provide the information in full-time equivalents. The results are displayed in table 17.

Table 17: R&D Indicators - R&D Employees*

	Weighted			Unweighted		
	% of firms	Mean R&D Employees	Median	% of firms	Mean R&D Employees	Median
No R&D Activities	10.51	0	0	9.94	0	0
Occasional R&D	33.20	35.04	28.57	29.28	30.33	21.98
Regular R&D	56.29	36.82	33.33	60.77	30.85	25.00
Total Firms	100.00	31.77	25.00	100.00	27.67	22.22

* in full-time equivalents

According to the respondents, roughly a third of the workforce of the start-ups is involved in research or product development. However, as opposed to the highly skewed distribution of the R&D intensity, the values of the share of R&D employees approximately follow a normal distribution. It is also quite noticeable that the "occasional" R&D performers reported equal levels of R&D employees. A separate analysis looking at the size classes revealed that smaller firms had a higher share of employees working on product development. The smallest size group (1-5 employees) had a mean of 34% as opposed to 25% for the group of the largest firms. This could reflect the phenomenon that task sharing is very common in small structures and development staff are likely to be involved in other activities. As a result, R&D employees may be overcounted in a survey addressed to small firms.

Table 18: R&D Indicators - Employees with Technical Education

	Weighted			Unweighted		
	% of firms	Mean Tec. Employees	Median	% of firms	Mean Tec. Employees	Median
No R&D Activities	10.51	9.08	0	9.94	8.44	0
Occasional R&D	33.20	27.19	16.67	29.28	24.93	16.67
Regular R&D	56.29	46.52	42.85	60.77	40.59	36.60
Total Firms	100.00	36.17	28.57	100.00	32.80	25.00

As a final indicator, we looked at one human capital indicator that is frequently associated with the knowledge intensity of a firm. We asked the respondents to indicate how many employees had technical or scientific education at degree level. The results (table 18) show that the firms in the sample (both weighted and unweighted) have a highly educated workforce. As expected, firms that regularly perform R&D activities top the list with 46.5% of employees having technical or scientific education at degree level.

We then looked at the industry breakdown of these figures (see figure 2). Some industry-specific differences are remarkably consistent. Software firms achieve the highest scores on the three indicators nearly doubling the values of the industry group "other". On average, the software firms had an R&D intensity of 19.4% (median 10%), an R&D employee share of 41.7% (median 34.5%), and nearly half of their workforce (mean 48.4; median 50%) was educated at degree level.

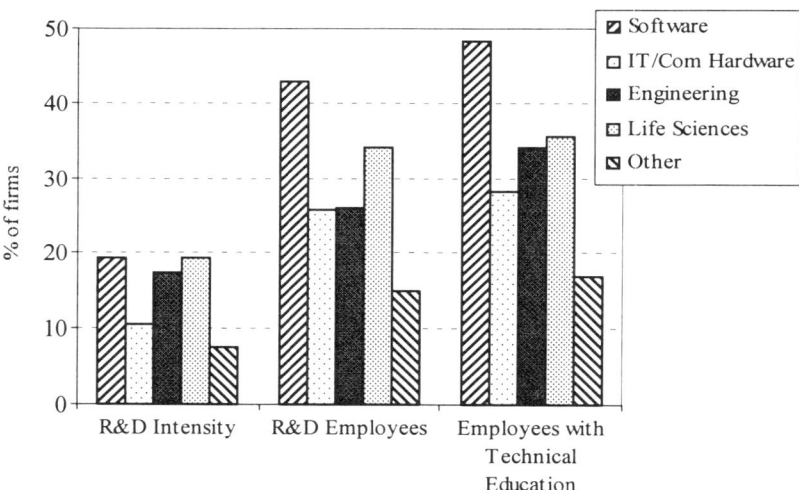

Figure 2: R&D Indicators by Industry

The differences between the software firms and the other firms become quite substantial when looking at the two employee indicators. Yet, the high scores of software firms relative to firms from the remaining four industry groups are not surprising given that software, a service industry, is characterised by a relatively low capital intensity and the fact that its main expenses are usually labour costs.It is also quite noticeable that the industry group "other", mainly electronic components firms, is consistently found at the lower end of the spectrum. The differences between the remaining three industries are less marked with life sciences scoring slightly higher than IT/Communications hardware and engineering when looking at the share of R&D employees.

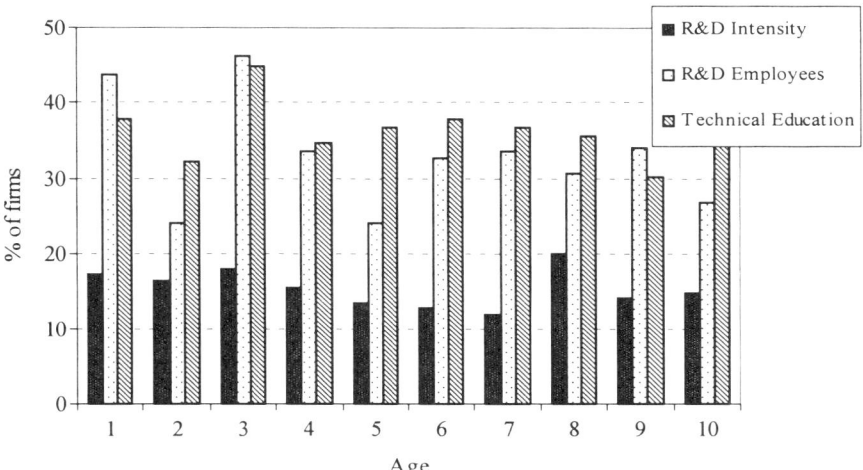

Figure 3: R&D Indicators by Firm Age

In a further step, kernel density estimations were performed in order to explore the distribution of R&D intensity in the different industries. Figure 4 and 5 show the results. The estimations reveal that the research and development expenditures as share of total turnover are distributed quite evenly across the five industries. In all industries, the distribution is skewed to the right with the highest density being lower than the mean. In all industries, one can observe a number of extreme firms that spend sums in excess of 50% of their total turnover on research and development. Note, however, that the firms with the highest R&D intensities were not necessarily the youngest firms. An analysis of the R&D indicators by different age groups did not reveal age specific differences (Figure 3).

Descriptive Data Analysis

Figure 4: Kernel Density Estimation of R&D Intensity by Industry

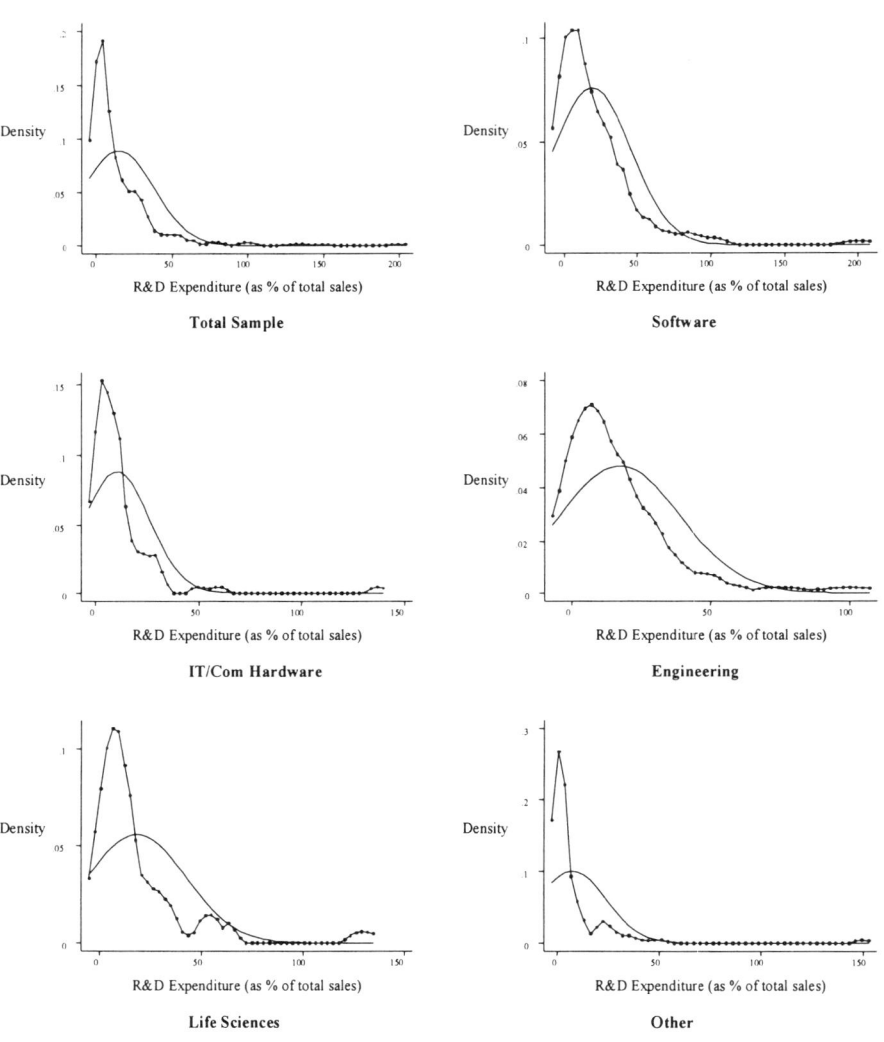

Descriptive Data Analysis: General Firm Characteristics   111

Figure 5: Kernel Density Estimation of R&D Employees by Industry

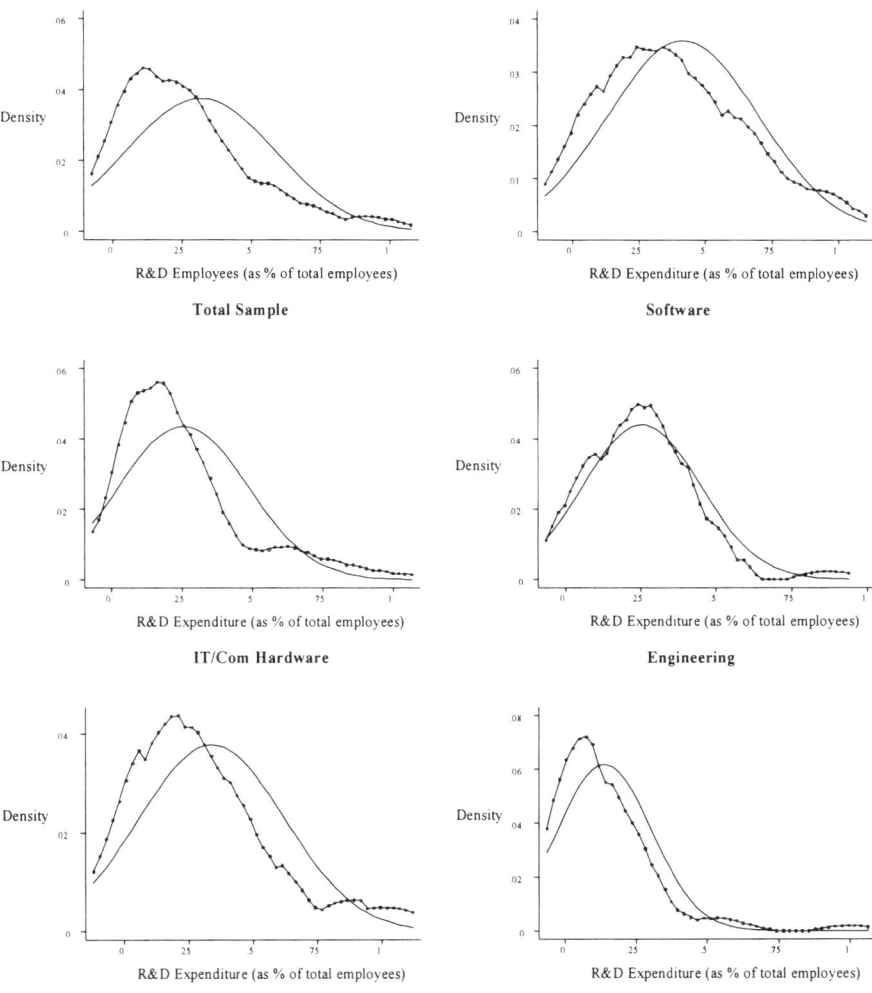

The kernel density estimations for the share of R&D employees by industry (figure 5) reveal that this indicator is approximately normally distributed for the software, engineering and life sciences firms. The distributions of the indicator for IT/Communications hardware firms and "other" firms is characterised by higher degrees of skewness.

To summarise, from looking at both the weighted and unweighted means, one can conclude that the majority of firms that replied to the survey do actually fall within the category of one could call "technology-based" or "knowledge-intensive" according to those criteria commonly used in the relevant literature. Compared to the figures given by Butchart (1987) for the different high-technology industries, they are characterised by higher levels of research and development expenditures, higher levels of research and development employees and a workforce with a high degree of technical/scientific skills. It is worth pointing our that the weighted results for all research and development indicators show slightly higher values than the unweighted results. The results by industry suggest, that the differences can be largely attributed to the fact that the weighting corrects for the undersampling of software firms, the firms with the highest scores on the majority of indicators. However, to a lesser extent, it also reflects the phenomenon that smaller firms indicated slightly higher values for various indicators.

5.2.6. Product Characteristics

Due to the main focus of the present research project, the analysis of the scope and determinants of international activities of start-up firms, we also asked respondents to provide us with information on the products they commercialise. As we expected a sizeable proportion of firms to sell a range of different products, we asked respondents to provide us with information on their *best selling* products or product groups. We first asked them to indicate the share of turnover that their best-selling product was contributing to their total turnover. On average, their best-selling product contributed 61% to total turnover. For 58% of firms, their best-selling product contributed more than 50% to total turnover. We will now report the characteristics of the best-selling products. Table 19 gives a breakdown of how the firms characterised their best-selling product.

Product Category

We asked respondents to state whether their products are consumer goods, capital goods, components or products ready for use by the end-user. Note that these categories are not always mutually exclusive as products such as software solutions can be at the same time be sold as an end product to a customer or be incorporated as a component into other, more complex solutions. Note also that there is a quite high percentage of products that are neither capital goods nor consumer goods. These are frequently products sold to industrial buyers but do not represent major investments. Not surprisingly, components were most prevalent among firms of the industry group "other". 67% of firms in this group classified their best-selling product as a component. This compares to a sample average of 20%. There were no differences across different firm size classes.

Table 19: Classification of Best-Selling Product

Product Category	Weighted % of firms	Unweighted % of firms
Product ready to use for end-user	48.90	44.44
Component of other products	20.00	21.67
Both component and end-product	8.07	9.72
Neither component nor end-product	23.03	24.17
Total	100.00	100.00
Capital good	33.63	33.89
Consumer good	13.86	11.94
Both capital and consumer good	0.51	0.83
Neither capital nor consumer good	52.00	53.33
Total	100.00	100.00

Innovativeness or Newness of the Product

We then asked respondents to indicate how they would characterise their best-selling product in terms of the newness or innovativeness. As mentioned above this *output* indicator was meant to add further information on the innovativeness of their technology in addition to the R&D *input* indicators. Table 20 gives a breakdown of this indicator.

Table 20: Innovativeness of Technology

Degree of Innovativeness / Newness	Weighted % of firms	Unweighted % of firms	R&D Intensity (in %) *	Share R&D Employees (in %) *
Product incorporates tried and tested combinations of existing technology	24.94	23.31	7.30	20.83
Product incorporates new combinations of existing technology	26.40	27.81	14.53	31.65
Product incorporates novel technology developed elsewhere	15.88	12.92	13.55	31.75
Product incorporates novel technology developed specifically in-house	32.78	35.96	22.88	38.95
Total	100.00	100.00	15.26	27.67

* weighted results

One third of the respondents classified their products as "incorporating novel technology developed specifically in-house." The results indicate that there is a certain correlation between the R&D intensity of the firms and the innovativeness of the technology. Accordingly, firms with more innovative products were characterised by higher levels of R&D expenditures. Note, however, that firms whose products incorporate "new combinations of existing technology" and "novel technology developed elsewhere" are characterised by roughly equal levels of R&D intensity. Figure 6 gives a breakdown of this indicator by industry group.

Figure 6 reveals that the highest share of firms whose products incorporate novel technology developed in-house can be found in the life sciences field (50%). This is followed by engineering (45%) and IT/Communications hardware firms (40%). The degree of technology differentiation among the software firms was evenly balanced. Firms from the industry group "Other" had the highest share of firms that classified their technology as "tried and tested" (41%). This is in line with expectations as this category largely consisted of manufacturers of electronic components.

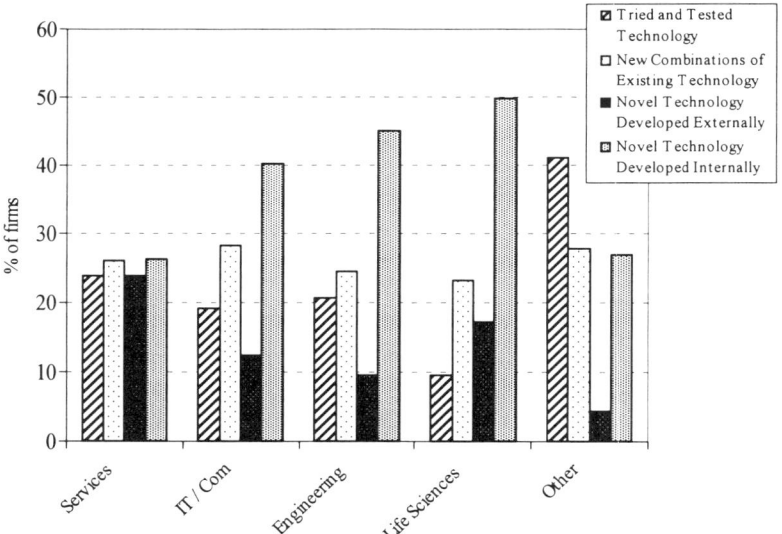

Figure 6: Degree of Technology Differentiation by Industry

Commercialisation

To determine the extent to which their products require tasks to be performed during their commercialisation, we asked the firms to rate the level of pre-sales consultation, installation, maintenance/upgrade, training and system requirements on a five point Likert scale. We are reporting here those firms that indicated that their products require substantial commercialisation efforts. We operationalised "substantial" as scoring of 4 or 5 on the 5 point Likert scale.

As one can see from figure 7, there are a number of industry-specific differences. The products of software firms for instance require far more maintenance than the products of the firms in other industries. More than half of the software firms (51%) stated that their products require substantial maintenance. This is probably due to the fact that a substantial share of these firms are actually small software programmers whose main activity consists of contract programming of tailor-made solutions. Products of firms in the engineering and life sciences sectors require more pre-sales consultation than other products (81% and 82% respectively). This, however, does not appear to be caused by customisation requirements as these products require on average fewer customisation efforts than products of firms from other industries.

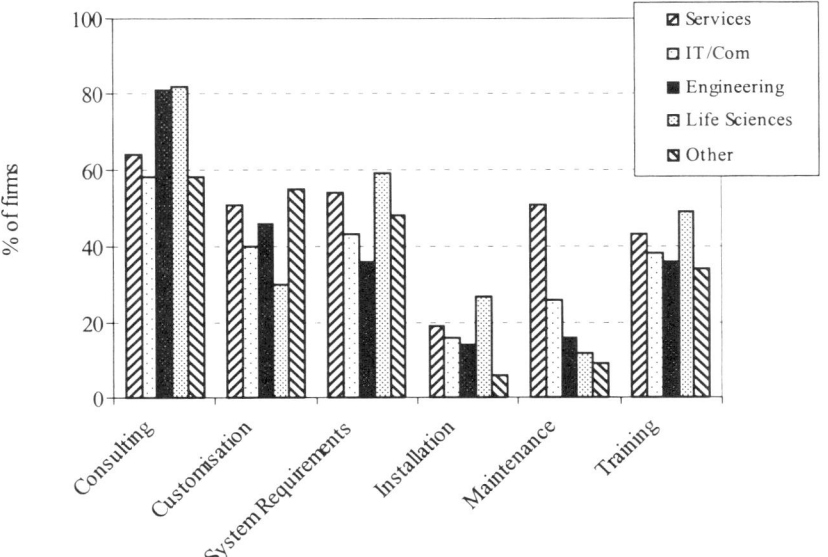

Figure 7: Commercialisation Requirements by Industry

Life sciences had the lowest share of firms whose products are characterised by substantial client-specific customisation (30%). In this industry, however, we could observe the highest share of firms that stated that their products require substantial training (49%) and installation efforts (27%). We also asked respondents to indicate their chosen sales in the UK. 12% of the firms indicated that they exclusive sold through third parties such as distributors. 57% of the start-ups stated that they exclusively sell directly to the final customers. A further 26% of the firms used both sales channels. The remaining 5% used other sales channels, such as licensing.

5.2.7. Growth Rates

The final section of the chapter on general firm characteristics is concerned with the growth rates of the firms in our sample. We calculated annual average growth rates for employment and sales growth based on figures provided by the entrepreneurs.[22] It is not unproblematic to calculate growth rates for start-up firms. The observation of the growth figures alone can lead to the conclusion that the firms in the sample are exceptionally successful. Yet, an inflated growth rate can have two reasons. First, it is caused by the fact that the majority of start-ups were quite small when they were founded (median 2 employees). Starting with a small base will inevitably result in a high growth rate as soon as the firm starts recruiting additional employees.

Second, the firms in the sample are quite young. The younger the firms, the more spectacular the growth rate (see figure 8). The difference between employment growth and sales growth for firms that one year old can, in many cases, probably be explained by the time lag to accomplish the development phase (during which product and market developers have to be hired) and the generations of the first sales. The following example will illustrate the point further. A firm that was set up by one founder in 1993 which had 5 employees at the time of the survey will have an average annual employment growth rate of 49% over a four year period. Yet, one can hardly speak of it a "fast growing" company in the terms used by policy makers and academics interested in the topic (see, for example, Storey 1996). In order to get a complete impression, we will therefore discuss the median growth of these firms where appropriate.

---

[22] The formula to calculate the employment growth rate is as follows:

$$Average\ Annual\ Employment\ Growth = \left(\frac{Employment\ Today}{Employment\ at\ Start-up}\right)^{1/Age} - 1$$

The sales growth rate is calculated in a similar way, except that "age" is replaced by the time difference between the first financial and the last or current financial year respectively.

Figure 8: Average Annual Growth Rates by Firm Age

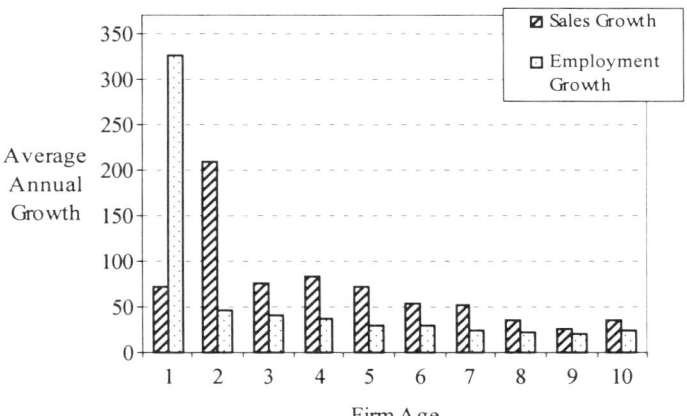

The results are displayed in table 21 to table 23. The employment growth rate and three different sales growth rates are shown. In addition to the sales during the first financial year and the last completed financial year, we also asked the entrepreneurs to indicate the year-end forecast for their current financial year.[23] We therefore show the sales growth between start-up and the last financial year, growth between the first year and the year-end forecast for the current year and the last year compared to the year-end forecast for the current year.

When looking at the employment growth, both weighted and unweighted calculations show an average annual rate of 51%. The median growth is reported at 26%. As expected, the sales growth rate is very high with a calculated annual average rate of 112%. The differences between the weighted and the unweighted figures indicate that smaller firms have higher average growth rates. Note also that the expected growth rate between the last financial year and the year-end forecast for the current year is quite high at 53%. The average firm reported an expected sales growth of 28% which shows that the majority of start-ups in our sample are quite optimistic about their future.

---

[23] During the subsequent interview phase of the Anglo-German project, carried out between six and nine months after the survey, 20 managing directors were interviewed. In all but one case, the estimated turnover target was met by the firms. This suggests that the information given by the respondents is actually quite accurate and reinforces the importance of this measure.

Table 21: Average Annual Growth Rates

Growth Rates (in %)	Weighted			Unweighted		
	Mean	Median	SD	Mean	Median	SD
Annual Average Employment Growth	51.50	25.99	119.97	51.25	29.13	109.72
Average Sales Growth (start-up - last financial year)	112.31	46.14	250.16	87.44	42.81	204.63
Average Sales Growth (start-up - current year end forecast)	70.60	44.37	101.15	61.91	40.68	83.48
Average Sales Growth (last year - current year end forecast)	53.04	28.57	127.78	45.62	25.00	108.09

Table 22: Average Annual Growth Rates by Industry*

Mean Growth Rates (in %)	Sample Mean	Software	IT/Com Hardw.	Engin.	Life Science	Other
Average Employment Growth	51.50	63.33	39.84	34.27	62.05	40.69
Average Sales Growth (start-up – last financial year)	112.31	154.87	76.98	92.86	87.11	78.05
Average Sales Growth (start-up - current year end forecast)	70.60	82.20	66.92	67.19	70.39	52.67
Average Sales Growth (last financial year - current year end forecast)	53.04	68.02	48.33	45.83	42.23	31.98

* weighted results

Table 23: Median Annual Growth Rates*

Median Growth Rates (in %)	Sample Median	Software	IT/Com Hardw.	Engin.	Life Science	Other
Annual Employment Growth	25.99	25.74	31.95	28.47	23.86	25.89
Annual Sales Growth (start-up – last financial year)	44.37	47.87	51.17	44.22	33.51	38.95
Annual Sales Growth (start-up – current year end forecast)	46.14	47.56	52.42	46.14	39.50	37.97
Annual Sales Growth (last financial year - current year end forecast)	28.57	34.62	22.30	25.00	27.90	18.42

* weighted results

Tables 22 and 23 give average and median growth rates for the different industries. The differences at the industry level are not straightforward. Compared to the total sample, the software and life science firms reported the highest employment growth but only relatively low median rates. This suggests that there are a number of extreme firms that cause the distribution to be highly skewed to the right.

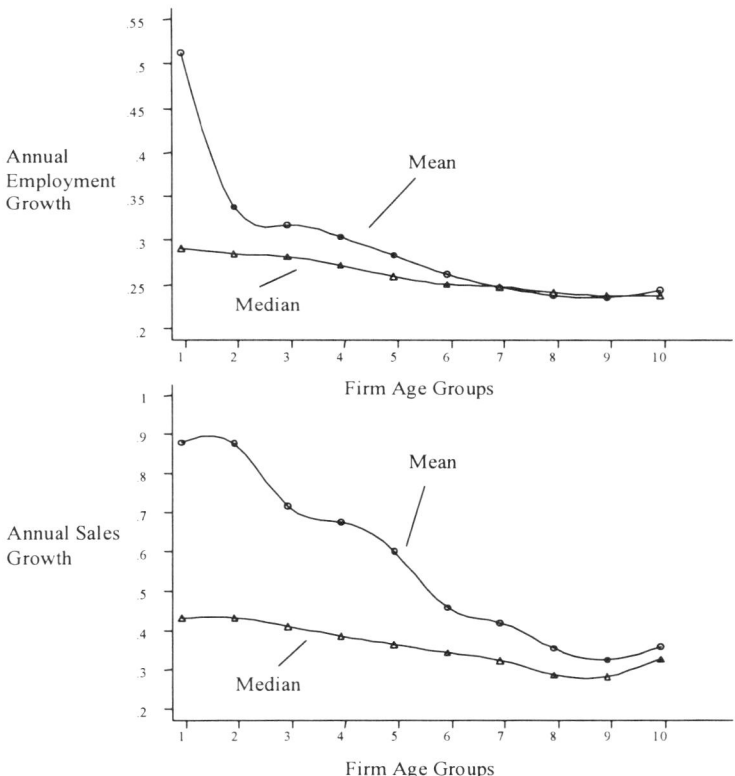

Figure 9: Convergence of Growth Mean and Median by Age Group

In order to obtain a more realistic picture of the growth pattern of the firms in our sample, we decided to plot the median and mean growth rates for the different age groups. Figure 9 shows the results. The x-axis on the chart has be to interpreted as follows. Firm age group "1" contains all firms. In age group "2" only firms that were at least two years old at the time of the survey were included, an so on. Group "10" contains only the oldest firms in the sample. Along the x-axis, the number of observations thus gradually decreases from 362 firms to 39 firms.

Given the cross-sectional rather than longitudinal nature of the sample, this can only be an imperfect approximation of the growth pattern over time. Nonetheless, it does convey an important message: The older the firms in our sample, the more the values between mean and median converge. Separate kernel density estimations of the growth rates for the different age groups show that, for older firms, the growth rate distribution increasingly converges to a normal distribution (results not shown). Taking this convergence as an indicator, the results suggest that the growth rates decrease as the firm grows older to a level of about 25% annual growth for employment and about 30% for sales growth. These figures are probably a more realistic estimate of the growth potential of these firms than the calculated average growth rates for the whole sample.

It was not possible to identify studies that reported similar growth rates. The majority of empirical studies on the growth of entrepreneurial firms surveyed by the author were not comparable as they focus on firms from different industries or provide growth rates at a certain given year rather than average annual growth rates. As these figures are highly sensitive to the chosen age range, comparisons with studies that use different age cut-offs cannot be made. A study looking at average annual growth rates since inception for a sample of firms covering ten years of their life could no be identified in the literature.[24] Note, however, that these figures are roughly in line with recent data provided by Keeble et al (1998). They reported that their sample of new, technology-based firms in the Oxford and Cambridge region experienced an employment growth of 99% and a sales growth of 233% over a three year period. This corresponds to an annual average of 26% and 49%. As these figures are based on older firms, they approximate the converged longer term mean and median values that one can observe among the older firms in our sample (see figure 9).

5.2.8. Summary of the Descriptive Analysis of Firm Characteristics

To summarise, we have a sample of firms that are on average five and a half years old and that employ 15 people. The majority of these firms are actively involved in research and development activities. Furthermore, all R&D indicators used in this study indicate that they devote substantial resources to the development of current and future products.

When looking at the impact of the weighting, it becomes evident that for the majority of variables, the stratification did not result in substantial differences between the (unweighted) sample mean and the estimated (weighted) population mean. In a univariate context, the main differences are found when looking at those indicators that measure or incorporate some notion of size. As mentioned earlier, this is a direct consequence of the sampling strategy and the differences

---

[24] Note that the average annual growth rates among the start-up firms in the German sample is roughly equal. This lends some support to the accuracy of the growth rates reported here.

between the weighted and unweighted results can be attributed to the undersampling of service firms and smaller firms. It lends further support to the argument that a weighting should not necessarily be introduced into the multivariate analysis (see also section 4.4.2.), as this would lead to an over-emphasis of certain *multivariate pattern*, despite the evidence in the descriptive statistics that there are hardly any differences when looking at the *univariate* distribution of the variables discussed above.

5.3. Descriptive Data Analysis: International Activities

5.3.1. Prevalence of the Phenomenon

One of the key objectives of the present research is an estimation of the extent to which British start-up firms in high-technology industries have engaged in international activities. In section 3.2.1., we discussed the use of different definitions or threshold in order to separate internationalisers and non-internationalisers. Accordingly, we will use a first operationalisation that classifies firms as "international" as soon as they have entered one foreign market or generated one percent of their total revenue through international sales during their last financial year. In addition, we will use two additional cut-off criteria and consider only those firms as internationalisers that have entered at least three markets or generate at least 10% of their total revenues from international sales. The sample also contains 30 firms that had international activities at some stage but did not generate any revenues from international sales during their last financial year. All but six of these firms were classified as domestic start-ups.[25] The group of domestic start-ups therefore also contains 24 "de-internationalisers." The following tables will report the results for the three indicators and report the time lag between formation and international sales.

Table 24 gives an overview of the international activities of the start-ups in our sample. 246 out of 362 of the firms in the sample (68%) did engage in international operations. Due to the weighting, the estimated share of internationalisers among the population of British start-ups decreases slightly to

---

[25] In three of those cases, the firms were set up in 1996. They have entered foreign markets in 1997. As their financial year 1997/98 was not completed at the time of the survey, they correctly answered in the questionnaire that - despite competing internationally - they did not generate revenues through international sales in their **last** financial year. In the remaining three cases, the founders stated in the questionnaire that their firm was actively competing in several foreign markets. However, they did - exceptionally -not generate any revenues through foreign sales during their last financial year. These three cases are there kept within the sample of internationalisers.

60%. If one counts the 24 "de-internationalisers" among the international start-ups, the percentages change further. It thus follows that 66% of the estimated population of British start-ups have at some stage of their lives been involved in international activities (75% of the sample). When adopting a stricter definition of "international activities" using the additional indicators introduced above, the percentages decrease. 45% of firms had activities in at least three foreign countries and 47% of the firms generated more than 10% of their annual turnover through non-domestic revenues. When we adopt Oviatt and McDougall's (1997) most recent definition of an international new venture, which includes only firms younger than six years, we can still find that 51% of the firms (unweighted: 62%) have initiated international sales. These results provide clear evidence that international activities are much more prevalent among British high-tech start-ups than previously assumed. The finding actually suggests that the majority of British high-tech start-ups compete internationally rather than limiting themselves to their domestic home market.

Table 24: International Activities of Sample Firms

	# of obs	Weighted Mean	Unweighted Mean
% of firms with international sales	246	59.30	67.96
Time lag between start-up and international sales	244	2.22	2.16
Time lag between first domestic sales and international sales	244	1.54	1.41
% of firms with international sales into least three countries	184	44.86	50.83
% of firms that generating at least 10% of revenues through international sales	193	47.30	53.31
% of firms that generating at least 50% of revenues through international sales	97	23.55	26.80

The table also shows that, on average, international start-ups initiated their cross-border sales during the third year of their life. Only 2.2 years (median 2) elapsed between start-up an the first international sales. Given that a sizeable proportion of start-ups have no sales in their early years because they are still engaged in development activities, we also calculated the time lag between the first sales and the first international sales. The resulting lag of 1.5 years (median 1) shows that the average firm with international sales decided to venture abroad shortly after product launch. These results strongly suggest that, at least in the UK, international activities among start-ups are much more prevalent than expected. Tables 25 and 26 compares these indicators at the industry level and by different size classes respectively.

Table 25: International Activities of Sample Firms by Industry *

Mean	Total Sample	Software	IT/Com Hardware	Engin.	Life Sciences	Other
% of firms with international sales	59.30	47.72	68.73	79.21	84.91	55.10
% of firms with international sales into least three countries	44.86	35.31	55.21	67.32	69.42	33.82
% of firms generating at least 10% of revenues through international sales	47.30	37.57	51.30	69.00	76.86	41.29

* weighted results

Table 26: International Activities of Sample Firms by Size Class*

Mean	Total Sample	3-5 employees	6-9 employees	10-19 employees	20 + employees
% of firms with international sales	59.30	51.19	50.44	64.26	75.47
% of firms with international sales into least three countries	43.46	34.27	39.56	44.88	57.94
% of firms that generating at least 10% of revenues through international sales	46.57	38.40	40.97	49.46	60.50

* weighted results

The industry breakdown reveals that software firms and firms grouped under "other" had the lowest propensity to engage in international sales. This could be explained by the presence of a large number of contract programmers and developers among the software firms. Similarly, the industry group "other" is to a large extent made up of manufacturers of electronic components. Arguably, both groups are more likely to subcontract for domestic clients than for international ones. The life sciences firms had the highest scores on all indicators for internationalisation. When looking at the time lag between start-up (or first sales) and first international sales, the life sciences firms were also the quickest to enter foreign markets (after 0.9 years). No further industry level differences were observable for the timing of internationalisation. The analysis by size class (table 26) shows that smaller firms obtain lower scores on all operationalisations of international activities. This provides some evidence that internationalisation requires a certain critical mass of resources. Nonetheless, the fact that 51% of the firms of the smallest size class engaged in cross-border activities suggests that resource-related barriers to internationalisation can be overcome.

Before looking at the degree of internationalisation, a word of caution is warranted since we sampled a cross-section of firms. The reported share of internationalisers is probably a realistic approximation of the share of internationalisers 5.7 years (the average sample age) after formation. However, the share of internationalisers among the older firms is higher than among the younger firms. This reflects the fact that for the majority of the youngest firms in the sample, the observed time period of the survey instrument is therefore too short to give them a realistic chance to internationalise. Given their survival, the percentage of firms that will have a longer term propensity to internationalise will be larger.

In an attempt to establish the impact of this bias, we used additional information given by the entrepreneurs. We asked them whether they planned international activities in the future. Thus, we can divide the sample up into four groups of firms. First, we have those start-ups that had international activities during their year of formation. We then have a group of internationalisers that have initiated cross-border activities in the second year since formation or later. There is a third group of firms which are currently not engaged in international activities but plans to do so in the future. Finally, there are those start-ups that have no international activities and do not plan any future involvement. These figures are presented in table 27.

Table 27: Timing and Expected Involvement in International Activities*

	Timing [1]		Timing [2]	
	# of firms	% *	# of firms	% *
"Born international" (International activities within year of formation)	69	16.06	112	25.79
International start-ups (international activities in second year or later)	177	43.24	134	33.51
No international activities, but future involvement anticipated	63	21.08	63	21.08
No international activities and no future involvement anticipated	53	19.62	53	19.62

* weighted results
[1] Base year: year of formation
[2] Base year: first financial year

The table shows that 16% (unweighted: 19%) of the firms in our sample had international activities within their year of formation. Taking their first financial year as base year - remember that some firms will spend their first years developing their products without generating any sales - the percentage or "born international" firms increases to 26% (unweighted: 31%). More importantly, however, there are only about 20% of the firms (unweighted: 15%) that do not envisage any international activities in the future. In the absence of non-response bias, this shows that 80% of the British high-technology start-ups have already started international activities or plan to do so in the foreseeable future.[26] This figure is somewhat lower, but in line with the share of firms with international activities in the sample that are 8 years and older (74% weighted, 77% unweighted). Overall, these descriptive analyses have provided compelling evidence that international activities are of foremost concern for British start-ups firms in high-technology sectors.

5.3.2. The Degree of Internationalisation

After having established that a majority of start-ups in our sample engaged in international activities, we were of course interested in the extent to which they engaged in international activities. There is considerable debate about the appropriate definition of the degree of internationalisation of a firm (Sullivan 1994; Ramaswami, Kroeck and Renforth 1996; Reuber and Fischer 1997). We agree that internationalisation is a multidimensional construct that probably cannot be captured using a single measure such as share of non-domestic revenue. However, we also agree with those authors that are concerned with the loss of information through the construction of an index that combines several measures (Ramaswami, Kroeck and Renforth 1996). In the next sections, we will therefore consider several indicators of the degree of internationalisation. We chose the share of non-domestic sales, number of markets entered and percentage of firms that generate more than 50% of their turnover form foreign sales. A sub-sample of 246 high-tech start-ups engaged in international activities. Table 28 provides a summary of some indicators of interest for this sub-sample.

There are little differences between the weighted and the unweighted results. On average, these firms generated 38% of their total turnover form international sales (median 31%). The values observed range from 0 to 100%. On average, these firms sell into 10 foreign countries (median 6) with the maximum observed number of foreign market entries being 90. As reported in the previous section, firms with international activities on average started selling abroad two years after their formation. 27% of all internationalisers had international revenues within their first year of formation. These firms now generate on average 47% of their revenues from foreign sales. Today, 38% of the international start-ups generate more than 50% of their revenues through non-domestic sales.

---

[26] Note, however, that some firms may at that stage fall outside the internationally accepted definitions of new ventures.

Table 28: The Degree of Internationalisation - Descriptive Statistics *

	Weighted			Unweighted		
	Mean	Median	SD	Mean	Median	SD
% of non-domestic revenues	38.50	32.0	31.18	38.44	30.0	31.66
Number of foreign markets entered	9.51	6	11.07	9.99	6	11.86
% of firms generating at least 50% of revenues through international sales	38.26		48.70	38.93		48.86

* international start-ups only

These figures are slightly lower but in line with the data provided by recent studies. Keeble et al. (1998) surveyed of British technology-based firms in the Oxford and Cambridge region and reported that the average share of non-domestic revenue amounted to 44%.[27] In a study of Canadian NTBFs, Preece, Miles and Baetz (1999) reported an average of 53% of non-domestic revenues. Table 29 gives a breakdown of these figures by industry. A breakdown by industry reveals that firms from the industry group medical engineering / life sciences were the most "international" firms in the sample.

Table 29: Degree of International Activities by Industry*

	Total	Software	IT/Com Hardware	Engin.	Life Science	Other
% of non-domestic revenues	**38.47**	35.48	33.61	44.64	50.28	37.25
Number of foreign markets entered	**9.42**	9.23	10.43	6.18	13.63	7.92
% of firms generating at least 50% of revenues through international sales	**38.26**	32.54	33.39	49.35	52.26	36.19

* weighted results

On all indicators, this group obtains the highest scores. Software, the only service group in the sample, has the lowest share of firms with international activities. Once these firms have initiated international activities, however, the chosen indicators suggest that their internationalisation performance is not substantially different form the sample average.

---

[27] Note that firms in Keeble's sample were older SMEs rather than start-ups.

Figure 10: Kernel Density Estimation of the Share of Non-Domestic Revenue by Industry (Compared to Normal Distribution)

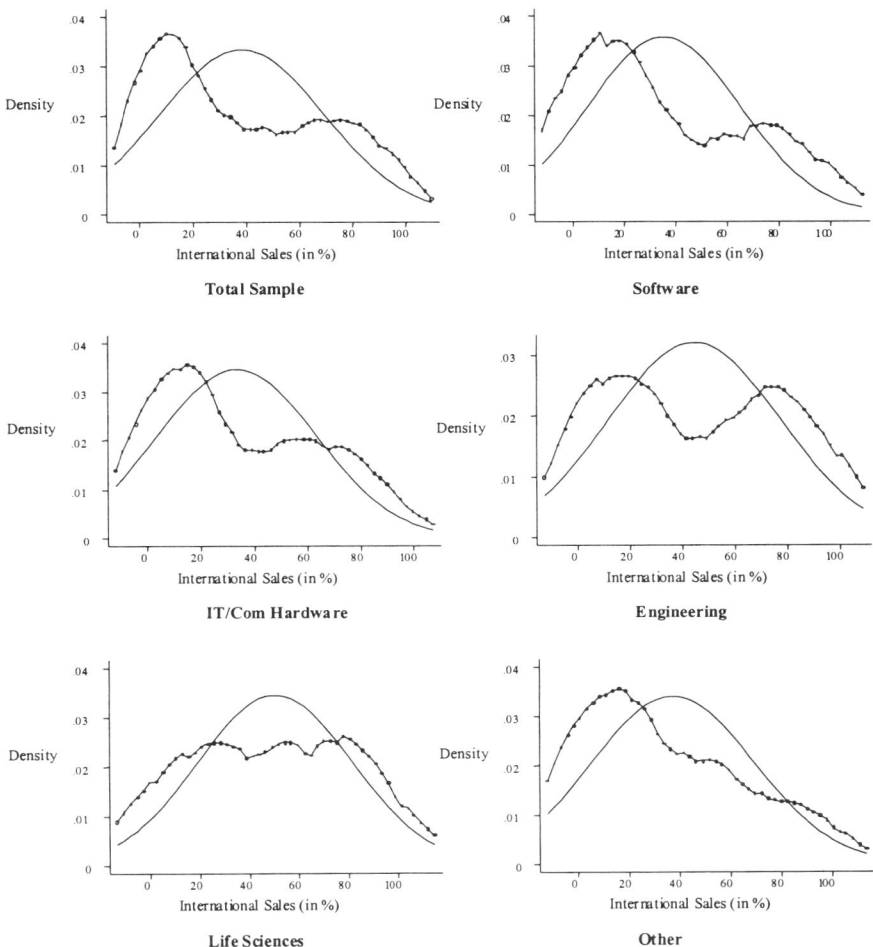

Figure 10 shows the results of a kernel density estimation for the share of non-domestic revenue. The dotted line shows the distribution of the share of non domestic revenue (or share of international sales) which is overlaid with a normal distribution around the mean. As one can see from the estimation for the total population, the distribution is skewed to the right with the high percentage of firms (41%) having a share of non-domestic revenue of less than 20%. From then on, however, the distribution is fairly flat with a stable density of firms having international sales of up to 90%.

There are also a number of industry-specific differences in the distribution of the share of non-domestic revenue. The international sales distribution of firms in the software, IT/Communications hardware and "other" industries is very similar to the total sample. The distribution of the engineering and life sciences firms, however, is markedly different. The graph suggests that there are two distinct groups of engineering firms with international activities. The share of international sales of the first group oscillates around 15% whereas the second group has a mean of 75%. The distribution of the share of non-domestic revenues for the life sciences firms is quite flat with a stable number of firms reporting international sales between the 20% and 90% level.

5.3.3. Entry Modes

As one of our chosen areas of analysis is the market entry decision, we asked respondents to provide us with information on their three most important foreign markets defined by their contribution to the sales of the firm's best-selling product. We chose the operationalisations of Root (1987) and Klein, Frazier and Roth (1991) to define different entry modes. The differences between agents and distributors were explained in the questionnaire. Accordingly, an agent sells ad hoc on a commission basis whereas a distributor sells on a regular basis.

This resulted in a dataset of 547 market entry decisions. 10 cases had to be excluded from the analysis, because respondents could either not provide country level sales or indicated that they used entry modes that were difficult to classify. Respondents did, for example, report sales modes such as the formation of export co-operatives and global distribution deals with multinationals. In the latter case, the sales transaction has been carried out between the UK subsidiary of the multinational and the start-up, whose international activities mainly consisted of setting up technical support offices abroad. Due to their heterogeneity, these entry modes were excluded from further analysis. The results are displayed in table 30.

Out of the 547 market entry decisions in our sample, the preferred current entry mode used by the firms was distributors (42%) followed by direct exporting (36%) and the use of sales agents (11%). Market entry modes that required some form of foreign direct investment were not extensively used by the firms in our sample. 27 entries (5%) were carried out through joint ventures and 15 entries (3%) via wholly owned subsidiaries. The generation of international sales revenues through licensing also had a marginal role (9; 2%). On average, an individual market entry accounted for 8.3% of the total turnover of the start-up with mean values ranging from 5.9% for joint ventures to 14% for entry modes that involved building up a subsidiary.

Table 30: First and Current Entry Modes

Entry Mode	First Entry	%	Current Entry	%
Exporting	241	44	199	36
Agents	68	12	60	11
Distributors	198	36	227	42
Sales joint venture	12	2	27	5
Wholly-owned sales subsidiary	7	1	15	3
Licensing	11	2	9	2
Missing / other	10	2	10	2
Total	**547**	**100**	**547**	**100**

Note: The table shows the first and current entry modes used in the most important foreign markets for the company's best selling product.

In comparison with the first entry modes used by these firms, it appears that *aggregate* changes of entry modes over time reflect a tendency to use arrangements that represent a higher commitment to international sales. These descriptive findings provide further evidence of the validity of our decision to compare direct exporting and exporting via distributors as the main strategic options for high-tech start-ups.

After analysing the changes of *individual* market entry decision, a similar picture emerges. Table 31 maps out first entry mode, intermediate mode and anticipated future changes. Out of the 515 entry decisions surveyed, 345 (67%) have never been subject to operating mode changes and the respondents did not anticipate any changes in the future. Arguably, these firms may be too young and their international experience too short to have experienced changes in entry modes (average age 6 years, see above). Respondents reported 187 actual and anticipated changes. The large majority represents in increase in commitment (151 cases) and only a relatively small number of market entries (21) represent a decrease of commitment.

Table 31: Evolution of Market Entry Modes

		change representing increasing commitment	change representing decreasing commitment	Missing / change in commitment not classifiable
No changes	345			
Different first entry mode	101	88	11	2
Different intermediate entry mode	10	7	2	1
Expected different future mode	76	56	8	12
	187	**151**	**21**	**15**

5.3.4. Pattern of Market Selection

Tables 32 and 33 give an overview of the geographical spread of the international firms in our sample. The most important markets for British high-tech start-ups are found in Western European countries followed by North America and East Asia. In terms of the first market entered - which may not be the firms' largest market - a similar picture emerges. While the majority of firms (138; 57%) had their first international sales in Western Europe, the most popular country of first entry was the US (52; 21%). It is noteworthy that 43% of first entries were made to countries that do not belong to the EU/EFTA. When looking at the second, third, fourth and fifth market entries, a similar pattern emerges (results not shown).

Table 32: Geographical Focus of International Activities (by Target Region)

Unit of Analysis	Entries		Firms	
Entry Mode	Current Entries	%	First Country Entered	%
EU/EFTA	307	56	138	57
US & Canada	106	19	56	22
East Asia (Japan, HK, Sing., Korea, Taiwan)	37	7	14	6
Australia & New Zealand	25	5	6	2
Emerging Markets, Europe	12	2	2	1
South America	3	1	3	1
Middle East	22	4	11	5
Emerging Markets, Asia	13	2	4	2
Other	22	4	10	4
Total	**547**	**100**	**244**	**100**

Looking at individual countries, however, (table 33) the most frequently entered export market is the US with 96 entries, followed by France (68) and Germany (64). A similar pattern is evident from the choice of the initial market entry. These results corroborate the findings of Lindqvist (1991) and Bell (1995). A breakdown of market entries at a regional level shows that a majority of firms chose geographically close countries for their first international sales. An analysis at the country level, however, reveals that the size of the target market rather than its closeness to the home market coincides with the entry frequency. Note also that an important minority of firms entered spatially distant markets in South East Asia, South America and the Middle East first.

Table 33: Geographical Focus of International Activities
(10 Most Frequently Named Target Countries)

Unit of Analysis		Entries		Unit of Analysis		Firms	
Current Entries	Rank	# of obs.	%	First Country Entered	Rank	# of obs.	%
USA	1	96	18	USA	1	52	21
France	2	68	12	France	2	29	12
Germany	3	64	12	Germany	3	24	10
Ireland	4	28	5	Ireland	4	18	7
Netherlands	5	24	4	Sweden	5	15	6
Belgium	6	20	4	Netherlands	6	14	6
Australia	7	18	3	Belgium	7	8	3
Spain	7	18	3	South Africa	8	7	3
Sweden	7	18	3	Australia	10	6	2
Japan	10	16	3	Norway	10	6	2
Other countries		177	32	Other countries		65	27
Total		547	100	Total	100	244	100

5.3.5. International Production

207 firms (85%) were not involved in any foreign production. Of the remaining 36 firms, eight (3%) said that their manufacturing is exclusively carried out abroad. Six firms were using local subcontractors, one firm engaged in a production joint venture and one firm had both a production joint venture and a manufacturing subsidiary in one country. Among the 28 firms (12%) that stated that their products are produced both in the UK and abroad, 18 firms used the services of a local sub-contractor, eight firms set up their own production facility and one firm chose to set up a manufacturing joint venture in one country and to produce via sub-contractors in another. These figures indicate that the main focus of international activities of the start-up firms in our sample is on commercialisation, not production. Only 11 out of 243 firms (3%) were involved in equity investments into foreign production operations.

5.3.6. Growth and International Sales

This section will explore some issues related to firm growth and internationalisation. Unfortunately, we do not dispose of data on firm size in the year **prior** to the first international sales. We are thus merely comparing overall firm growth of those start-ups that have initiated international sales at some stage of their lives with those that only compete domestically. As already mentioned in section 5.2.7., it is not unproblematic to calculate growth rates for start-up firms.

Given that some firms started very small, a consideration of the average growth rates could result in a misleading picture. Median and Mean growth rates are therefore presented together in tables 34 and 35.

We were surprised to find that on all growth indicators, firms without international activities scored higher than those with international activities. Firms without international activities experienced higher employment and sales growth between start-up and the time of the survey. Furthermore, they had a more optimistic outlook on their current financial year. This became apparent from comparing both mean and median values for the third item reported in the tables. The average domestic start-up expects a growth of 33% whereas the average international start-up expects a growth of 25%. As expected, the differences were more spectacular when looking at the mean values than at the median values.

Table 34: Mean Annual Growth Rates of the Sample Firms - Comparison of International Start-ups and Domestic Start-ups

Mean Growth	Weighted			Unweighted		
	Total Sample	Intern. Firms	Domestic	Total Sample	Intern. Firms	Domestic
Annual Employment Growth (start-up to present day in %)	51.50	50.84	52.46	51.24	43.48	68.23
Annual Sales Growth (start-up to current year end in %)	70.60	60.31	84.99	61.91	60.50	65.12
Annual Sales Growth (last year to current year end in %)	53.04	51.46	55.67	45.62	44.60	48.12

Table 35: Median Annual Growth Rates of the Sample Firms - Comparison of International Start-ups and Domestic Start-ups

Median Growth	Weighted			Unweighted		
	Total Sample	Intern. Firms	Domestic	Total Sample	Intern. Firms	Domestic
Annual Employment Growth (start-up to present day in %)	25.99	25.74	30.66	29.13	**28.12**	**31.95**
Annual Sales Growth (start-up to current year end in %)	44.37	42.87	50.00	40.68	**39.91**	**43.49**
Annual Sales Growth (last year to current year end in %)	28.57	25.00	33.33	25.00	25.00	27.95

Due to the lack of data on firm size in the time period prior to internationalisation, the following analytical dilemma arises. One explanation for the lower growth rates of international start-ups could be related to their domestic setting. It may well be the case that internationalisers have been "pushed" to venture abroad because structural or strategic factors inhibited them from growing in their home market. While the internationalisation efforts may be quite successful, they will report a lower overall growth rate for their consolidated operation. The second possible explanation could be that internationalisers were relatively successful firms in their domestic market. Given the conventional view that competing internationally is more resource-intensive than competing in a domestic setting, it could well be that their overall growth rate decreases as a result of initiating cross-border activities.

In order to shed further light on these issues and get a better understanding of the growth rate differentials, we used a tool similar to the one used during the discussion of growth rates in general (section 5.2.7.). Since the results from table 26 suggest that smaller and younger firms are less likely to have engaged in international sales – yet, they are the firms with the highest calculated growth rates - we plotted median growth rates for the firms for different age groups and compared internationalisers to non-internationalisers. The results are displayed in figure 11. The x-axis on the chart is to be interpreted as follows. Firm age group "1" contains all firms. In firm age group "2" only firm that were at least two years old at the time of the survey were included, an so on. Group "10" contains only the oldest firms in the sample. Along the x-axis, the number of observations thus gradually decreases from 362 firms to 39 firms. Like in the section on firm growth in general, the same disclaimer about the cross-sectional nature of the dataset applies here.

The plots show that, when looking at annual sales growth, the higher sales growth rates can be attributed to the presence of the youngest firms in the analysis sample. When only considering firms that are at least three years old, international start-ups have median growth rates that are consistently higher than those of domestic start-ups. These differences are not as clear cut when looking at the plot for the median employment growth rate. As with sales growth, one can attribute the fact that that non-internationalisers have higher aggregate employment growth rates almost exclusively to the inclusion of very young firms in the analysis. When only considering those firms that are at least three years old, the growth rates between internationalisers and domestic start-ups are quite similar.

Figure 11: Median Employment Growth Rates by Age Groups

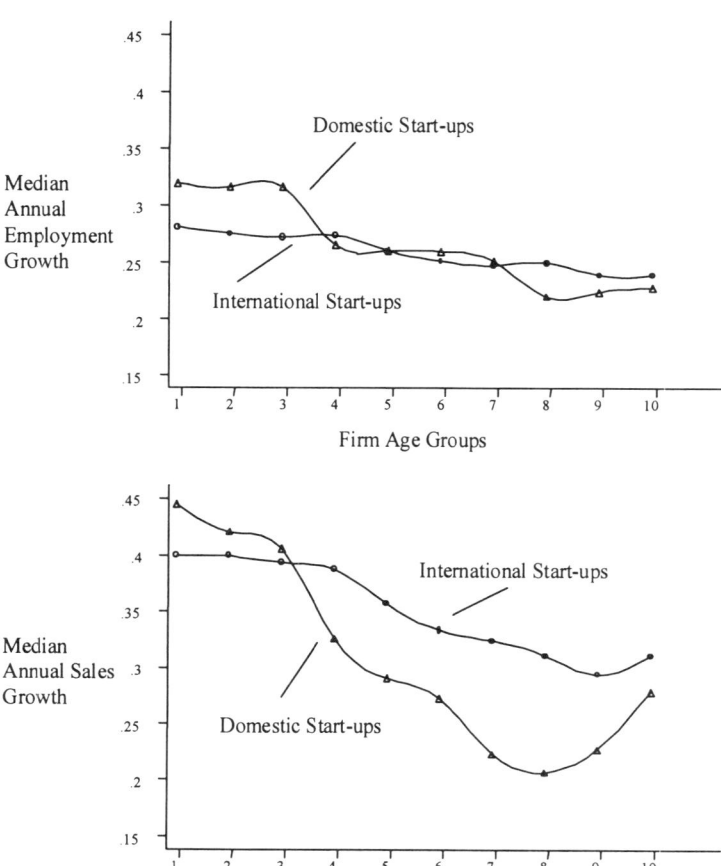

These findings therefore strongly suggest that the differences are a statistical artefact stemming from the composition of the sample rather that reflect performance problems of international firms. The higher reported growth rates among domestic firms therefore seem to stem from the fact that domestic firms are on average smaller and younger at the time of the survey. Their inclusion leads to an inflation of annual growth rates. We can therefore not support the proposition that internationalisers have lower growth rates per se.

Note, however, that we cannot make any statements concerning the degree of causation between growth and internationalisation. A statistical relationship between growth and internationalisation cannot be established with this cross-sectional sample but requires a longitudinal dataset. Nonetheless, exploratory analysis of our data allows us identify the youngest firms as being responsible for observed growth differentials. This result should be informative for further research looking at the internationalisation-performance relationship of start-up firms.

5.3.7. Motives, Triggers, Costs and Constraints

The questionnaire also included several questions where entrepreneurs were asked to assess their international activities. Respondents were asked to rank their motives for starting international sales, the constraints encountered and the cost incurred during internationalisation (questions 34, 35 and 36 of the questionnaire). Unfortunately, despite the pre-testing during four pilot case studies, the questions that required a ranking rather than checking a Likert scale (questions 34 and 36) were not always answered in the way intended by the researchers. For example, respondents did not rank all items or provided identical ranks for different items. Nonetheless, part of the information obtained can be used. Rather than use the rankings, we will count the cases where a particular item been classified as the "most important" motive or constraint. As a result, the aggregate of this variable should still indicate the relative importance of the different motives for and constraints as perceived by the firms' managers. The question on costs encountered during the internationalisation process used a Likert scale. In this case, no such problems were evident from the response behaviour. Table 36 provides an overview of the responses.

Table 36: Motives for Initiating International Sales

Motives	# of counts as most important motive
Potential of foreign markets for generating long term company growth	165
Insufficient sales potential in domestic market	49
Amortisation of research and development costs	11
Learning from internationally leading customers, suppliers and competitors	11
Reputation benefits of being viewed as internationally competitive company	20

The overwhelming majority of the entrepreneurs stated that securing long term company growth was the main motivator for international sales. Admittedly, the first and second item are difficult to untangle. However, the fact that the item "potential of foreign markets for generating long term company growth" was rated as most important motive more than three times more often than "insufficient sales potential in the domestic market" suggests that British entrepreneurs see international expansion as growth opportunity rather than as reactive move to counter limited demand in their home market. Amortisation of research and development costs and learning effects represented motives of minor importance.

The results should be interpreted in light of the following limitation. For this question, the entrepreneurs were asked to rate different items among a given set alternatives. A more open-ended approach to this question could have revealed additional reasons for selling abroad. Note also that this question makes the entrepreneurs evaluate their motives long after the decision has been taken. The real motives at the time of the first international sales may have been different. Nonetheless, the results suggest that British high-tech entrepreneurs have a quite proactive attitude to international activities. The results displayed in table 37 lend further support to this argument.

Table 37: Preparation and Existing Relationships Prior to the First International Sales

Preparation / existing relationships prior to the first international sales	% of firms (internationalisers only)	
	Weighted	Unweighted
Product developed with the intention to sell it internationally	77.54	76.33
Commitment to international sales in the business plan	70.29	69.51
Country-specific market research undertaken	23.18	25.20
R&D collaboration with foreign partners	9.13	8.94
Sales to UK subsidiary of foreign customer	24.18	23.58

Table 37 reports how the firms prepared for their internationalisation and whether they had any existing relationships with foreign partners prior to international sales. The proactive attitude identified through the questions on motives for selling internationally also became apparent when looking at the first item of table 37. 78% of the international start-ups intended already at the development stage to sell their product into foreign markets. However, the results also suggest that this international orientation was unrelated to existing R&D cooperations with foreign partners. Altogether, only 9% of the international start-ups engaged in collaborative research and development with foreign partners. Existing commercial relationships with UK subsidiaries of foreign firms, on the other hand, were more important triggers for international sales. Nearly a quarter of the firms already sold to UK subsidiaries of their foreign customers before starting to sell abroad. 70% of the international start-ups did have a commitment to international sales, but only 23% undertook specific market research prior to entering their first foreign market.

This apparent contradiction can be explained when looking at the immediate triggers for foreign sales. Firms were asked to describe what led to their first international sales. We coded the answers into ten different categories. Table 38 gives an overview of the most important triggers. The most important triggers for international sales were proactive actions such as deliberate contacting of potential foreign customers (24), international marketing actions (23) and visits to trade shows (18). Arguably, many of these can be carried out without undertaking detailed country-specific market research.

Table 38: Triggers for First International Sales

	Trigger	# of firms	% *	% **
Proactive Strategy	Deliberate strategy to contact potential foreign customers	24	9.92	10.96
	Order after PR, direct marketing or advertising action	22	9.45	10.05
	Contact during visit of trade fair	18	7.31	8.22
Personal Contacts and Relationships	Personal contact from previous employment	46	20.31	21.00
	International reputation of founder	9	3.00	4.11
Third Party Referrals	Contact via UK subsidiary of foreign customer	23	10.01	10.50
	Recommendation / contact via third party	16	7.02	7.31
Unsolicited	Unsolicited order	30	14.50	13.70
Internet	Contact through internet advertising	6	4.04	2.74
	Other	25	14.44	11.42
	Total	**219**		

* weighted   ** unweighted

The table also reveals that international sales frequently originated from the founders' personal networks of contacts and relationships. These include contacts from previous employment (46 mentions) and reputation effects (9 mentions). The latter are particularly pertinent in science-based industries where communities of researchers frequently interact across national borders. Referrals from third parties (16 mentions) and UK subsidiaries of foreign customers (24 mentions) triggered the international sales of the firms in the sample.

Unsolicited orders lead to the first international sales in 30 cases. Note however, that the distinction between unsolicited orders and third party referrals is only made on the basis of the respondents' answers. In reality, these two groups of triggers are likely to overlap. Internet advertising, despite offering a low-cost way of achieving international visibility, did not play an important role in triggering international sales. Only 6 firms reported that their first international sales resulted from a foreign customers visiting their website. The small differences between the weighted and unweighted results indicate that proactive action was a slightly less common among smaller firms and software firms. A further question asked respondents to rate the additional costs of international sales that were not client-specific.

Table 39: Costs of International Sales

Costs	Mean Score *	# of counts as most significant cost driver
Cost of accessing information on foreign markets	2.86	23
Costs identifying and forming commercial relationships	3.49	47
Costs of market entry and setting up foreign sales channels	3.52	55
Cost of product launch in foreign market (marketing costs)	3.34	52
Operating costs of the chosen sales channel	2.89	26
Costs of monitoring foreign activities	2.89	21

* weighted

The results in table 39 show that relationship building with foreign partners, market entry / set up of the sales channel and product launch in foreign markets were rated as most important cost drivers of international expansion. Accessing information, monitoring foreign distribution partners and operating cost of the chosen sales channel were named less frequently as important cost drivers. Additional costs mentioned by entrepreneurs in the questionnaire were mainly related to the recent appreciation of the British pound which reduced demand and margins in export markets. Finally, we asked respondents to rate factors that constrain them in their ability to internationalise further. The results are displayed in table 40. Here, the results indicate that scarcity of management time and additional costs of internationalisation were seen as the biggest current constraints. Only a minority of firms regarded increased exposure to risk and lack of experience with international activities as important constraints to internationalisation.

Table 40: Barriers to International Sales

		# of counts as most important constraint	
Constraints	Total	International Firms	Domestic Firms
Scarcity of management time	129	95	34
Limited managerial experience in international activities	41	26	15
Additional costs of foreign sales	61	41	20
Increased exposure to risk	44	39	5

5.3.8. Summary of the Descriptive Analysis of Internationalisation

Our results provide compelling evidence that British high-technology start-ups are involved in international activities to a much greater extent than one would expect from these young firms. Not only have the majority of firms in our sample (67%) started to sell abroad, but they entered on average 10 foreign markets (median 6) in the relatively short time period between inception and the time of the survey. Today, the internationalisers generate on average 38% of their revenues through foreign sales. A quarter of the firms in the sample generate at least 50% of their sales from international activities. The fact that we identified two recent studies that reported similar figures do support the representativeness of our findings (Keeble et al 1998; Preece, Grant and Baetz 1999). The international activities of our firms were oriented towards the commercialisation of their products rather than production. When we looked at growth rates, it appeared at first glance that firms without international activities had higher growth rates than internationalisers. Our analysis showed, however, that this effect can be attributed to the fact that the youngest firms (with the highest calculated growth rates since they start from a low base) have a higher share of non-internationalisers. When looking at the older firms, the relationship was inverse and internationalisers had higher growth rates than domestic firms. This is, of course, only a crude analysis, as our dataset does not allow us to establish the extent to which the growth is determined by international or domestic sales. *Any interpretation has to be made with extreme care and should bear this important limitation in mind.* In any case, it does highlight the need for gathering longitudinal data to look into the internationalisation – performance relationship.

The above descriptive results suggest that there is some support for the theoretical claims of process models when looking at the *aggregate sample*. The majority of firms were involved in low commitment entry modes and few firms engaged in activities that required foreign direct investment. The firms' entry mode changes over time reflect an increase of commitment to foreign markets. Finally, a majority of firms first sells into relatively close markets. However, there are important numbers of *individual firms* that that deviate from this pattern. The fact that the single most important target country, both in terms of first entry and absolute numbers of market entries, is the US suggests that entry mode choices are also driven by more compelling strategic reasons than psychic distance alone. The economic size of the target market or the recognition of significant, country-specific opportunities may be more persuasive factors. We will now present the results of our multivariate analyses and investigate the determinants of the decision to internationalise, the degree of internationalisation, the timing of foreign market entry and the choice of entry mode.

6. Multivariate Data Analysis

6.1. Operationalisation of Independent Variables

In our hypotheses, we stated that the various dimensions of internationalisation are expected to be a function of firm size, international experience of the founders, external finance, technology intensity, innovativeness, the extent to which products are customised and the costs of commercialisation. Accordingly, we have to measure these influence factors. Firm size was operationalised in several ways. In the questionnaire, we asked respondents to state employees and sales both at start-up and at the time of the survey. The descriptive analysis revealed that the distributions are highly skewed to the right. Such a distribution is to be expected in a sample of start-up firms. Consequently, the direct operationalisations of size, i.e. the inclusion of the absolute sales volume or number of employees risk producing statistically insignificant parameter coefficients. Highly skewed distributions can be normalised using logarithmic transformations. We therefore first calculated log values of our various size measures. Second, for the regression models shown here, we constructed an index of the log values for firm size measured by number of employees and firm size by sales. The levels of the alpha coefficient (0.72 at start-up; 0.88 today) are above the recommended thresholds (Nunally and Bernstein 1994), therefore indicating construct validity. Since the actual firm size at the time of the survey could at the same time represent the cause and effect of international activities, we primarily used size at start-up in our regressions. We thus avoid possible effects of endogeneity in the models. Nonetheless, in most cases we also report parameter coefficients when size today is entered into the regression equation in order to explore whether the results are consistent.

International work experience was operationalised by asking the respondents in the questionnaire whether they had previous living experience abroad, whether they had work experience for an internationally operating firm or whether they were educated abroad. These measures are consistent with those used by Roth (1995), Bloodgood, Almeida and Sapienza (1996) and Reuber and Fischer (1997). The exact wording of these questions can be found in the questionnaire in appendix 1. The respondent's answers have then been included as dummy variables in the models. Dummy variables have also been coded to indicate industry affiliation and the involvement of venture capitalists and business angels.

In accordance with standard practice (Butchart 1987; Koberg, Rosse and Bergh 1994; OECD 1997), we chose two indicators to measure technology intensity (questions 8 and 9 in the questionnaire, see appendix 1). We asked respondents to state technology intensity measuring R&D expenditure as percentage of total turnover and R&D employees as share of total employed (see also section 4.3.). In all regressions, we compare the impact of their inclusion on the model results. The innovativeness of the technology employed was measured using a four-item scale (question 17 in the questionnaire, see appendix 1). We developed this scale after a review of the relevant literature (Roberts 1991; OECD 1997) and refined it through discussions with our pilot-case study respondents. Respondents were asked whether their products are best classified as incorporating tried and tested combinations of existing technology, new combinations of existing technology, novel technology developed externally or novel technology developed specifically for this product by the company.

The extent to which a product requires client-specific customisation and the transaction costs incurred during the sales process were each measured using a 5 point Likert scale (question 18 in the questionnaire, see appendix 1). The four items measuring transaction costs (pre-sales consulting intensity, installation intensity, maintenance intensity, training intensity) were then combined into a single item (alpha 0.73). Finally, country GDP and risk data were obtained from the IMF's *World Investment Report* and the publication *Institutional Investor*.

A summary table (table 41) of the independent variables is presented below. Table 42 displays the first order correlations of the dependent and independent variables. We will now present the results of the various regression models on the differences between international and domestic firms, their degree of internationalisation and the timing of their initial market entry. Since we hypothesised an identical variable vector for these three distinct dimensions of internationalisation, I will first report the results of the model estimations. After that, I will discuss the impact of the independent variables in a joint section. A summary of the expected relationships is displayed in table 43.

Table 41: Summary of Independent Variables

Variable	Explanation	Measurement
Int. Act.	International activities	Dummy variable (1=yes)
Degree of int.	Degree of internationalisation	Share of non-domestic revenue in %
Speed	Speed of foreign market entry	year of first foreign sales – year of formation, recoded so that highest values represent highest speed
Size	Firm size	Index of log values for sales and employees at start-up
Age	Firm age	Base year 1997
Exp. abroad	Work experience abroad	Dummy variable (1=yes)
Exp. mult	Work experience for internationally operating firm in the UK	Dummy variable (1=yes)
Exp. edu.	International education	Dummy variable (1=yes)
R&D Expend.	R&D expenditure	Ratio R&D expenditure to sales
R&D Emp.	R&D employees	Ratio R&D employees to total employees
VC	Venture capital investment at start-up	Dummy variable (1=yes)
Angel	Business angel investment at start-up	Dummy variable (1=yes)
Inno_1	Technology newness: new combinations of existing technology	Dummy variable (1=yes)
Inno_2	Technology newness: tried and tested technology	Dummy variable (1=yes)
Inno_3	Technology newness: incorporates novel technology developed externally	Dummy variable (1=yes)
Inno_4	Technology newness: incorporates novel technology developed internally	Dummy variable (1=yes)
Custom	Customisation requirements	5 point Likert scale
Cost	Cost of commercialisation	Index of consultation installation, training and maintenance requirements
Software	Industry: Software	Dummy variable (1=yes)
IT/COM	Industry: IT/Com hardware	Dummy variable (1=yes)
Engin.	Industry: Engineering	Dummy variable (1=yes)
Life Sc.	Industry: Life Sciences	Dummy variable (1=yes)
Other	Industry: "Other"	Dummy variable (1=yes)

Table 42: Correlation Matrix of Dependent and Independent Variables

	Intern. activities	Degree of int.	Speed	Size	Age	Exp. Abroad	Exp. multi.	Exp. edu.	R&D Expend.	R&D employ.	VC	Angel	Inno_1	Inno_2	Inno_3	Inno_4	Custom	Cost	Softw.	IT/COM	Engin.	Life Sc.	Other
Int. Act.	1.0000																						
Degree of in	0.0779	1.0000																					
Speed	0.0561	0.2443*	1.0000																				
Size	0.0934*	0.0114	0.2370*	1.0000																			
Age	0.2095*	0.1023	-0.3782*	-0.1603*	1.0000																		
Exp. Abroad	0.2200*	0.1231*	0.0959	-0.0518	0.0270	1.0000																	
Exp. Mult	0.2454*	0.1466*	0.1070*	0.0385	0.1131	0.2831*	1.0000																
Exp. edu.	0.1198*	0.1069*	0.0481	-0.0276	-0.0128	0.2986*	0.1578*	1.0000															
R&D Exp.	0.1185*	0.2654*	0.1167*	-0.0163	-0.0371	0.0640	0.0608	0.1857*	1.0000														
R&D Emp	0.0992*	0.2776*	0.0614	-0.1162*	-0.0067	0.1267*	0.0819	0.1501*	0.4203*	1.0000													
VC	0.0844	0.0896	-0.0765	0.1446*	-0.0378	-0.1446*	0.1101*	0.1278*	0.1007*	0.0539	1.0000												
Angel	0.0718	0.0664	0.0178	0.0130	-0.0351	0.0379	0.0167	-0.0209	0.0651	0.0999*	0.0068	1.0000											
Inno_1	-0.2234*	-0.1335*	0.0549	0.0721	-0.0092	-0.1613*	-0.0975*	-0.0860	-0.1857*	-0.2604*	-0.0622	-0.0671	1.0000										
Inno_2	0.0461	0.0778	-0.0329	0.0129	-0.0022	-0.0182	0.0237	-0.0235	-0.0344	-0.0343	0.0116	-0.0473	-0.3422*	1.0000									
Inno_3	0.0108	0.0455	-0.0394	0.0273	-0.0676	-0.0152	-0.0227	-0.0429	0.0404	0.0396	-0.0112	0.0690	-0.2124*	-0.2391*	1.0000								
Inno_4	0.1446*	0.0013	0.0159	-0.0940*	0.0580	0.1673*	0.0773	0.1208*	0.1687*	0.2353*	0.0559	0.0556	-0.4131*	-0.4650*	-0.2886*	1.0000							
Custom	-0.2362*	-0.0948	-0.0741	-0.0355	-0.0594	-0.0611	-0.0433	0.0169	-0.1247*	-0.1494*	-0.0370	-0.0060	0.1180*	-0.0324	0.0407	-0.1041*	1.0000						
Cost	0.0524	0.0621	-0.0573	-0.0173	0.1131	0.0678	0.0960*	0.0672	0.0866	0.1360*	0.0141	0.0724	-0.1653*	-0.0721	0.1499*	0.1081*	0.2296*	1.0000					
Software	-0.1527*	-0.0490	-0.0663	0.0234	-0.0261	-0.0403	-0.0104	0.0694	0.1712*	0.3101*	0.0195	0.0150	-0.0702	0.0088	0.1819*	0.0087	-0.0764	0.2380*	1.0000				
IT/COM	0.0762	-0.0655	0.0104	-0.0151	-0.0816	0.0101	-0.0485	-0.0409	-0.0678	-0.0405	-0.0823	-0.0327	-0.0960*	0.0089	0.0010	0.0766	-0.0727	-0.0340	-0.3354*	1.0000			
Engin.	0.1464*	0.1045	0.0322	-0.1112*	0.0790	0.1034*	0.1011*	-0.0256	0.0284	-0.0291	0.0668	0.1270	-0.0193	-0.0099	-0.0744	0.0790	0.0010	0.0367	-0.2716*	-0.2260*	1.0000		
Life Sc.	0.0993*	0.1173*	0.0764	-0.0012	0.0505	0.0616	0.0261	0.1330*	0.0542	0.0518	0.0228	-0.0601	-0.0888*	-0.0097	-0.0112	0.0957*	-0.1049*	0.0015	-0.2044*	-0.1701*	-0.1377	1.0000	
Other	-0.1028*	-0.0719	-0.0308	0.0834	0.0052	-0.0959*	-0.0451	-0.1023*	-0.1756*	-0.2977*	-0.0131	-0.0503	0.2430*	-0.0028	-0.1216*	-0.1251*	0.1318*	-0.2980*	-0.3625*	-0.3017*	-0.2443	-0.1838*	1.0000

* significant at p < 0.10

Table 43: Summary of Expected Relationships

Hypothesis	Decision to Internationalise	Degree of Intern.	Timing of Entry	Entry Mode (Distributor)
Firm Size	H1a: +	H1b: +	H1c: +	H9: +
International Experience (Founder)	H2a: +	H2b: +	H2c: +	H10: +
International Experience (Firm)				H11: +
Domestic Sales Mode (Distributor)				H12: +
External Equity	H3a: +	H3b: +	H3c: +	
Technology Intensity	H4a: curvilinear	H4b: curvilinear	H4c: curvilinear	
Technological Differentiation	H5a: +	H5b: +	H5c: +	H13: -
Customisation	H6a: -	H6b: -	H6c: -	H14: -
Cost of Commercialisation	H7a: -	H7b: -	H7c: -	H15: +

H8 hypothesised that the variable vector that discriminated between internationalisers and non-internationalisers accounts for differences in the degree of internationalisation

6.2. Differences Between International Start-ups and Domestic Start-ups, Degree of Internationalisation and Timing of Foreign Market Entry

6.2.1. Differences Between International Start-ups and Domestic Start-ups

6.2.1.1. Model Estimation

We model the decision to internationalise using a binary choice model. In our case, we specified a series of Probit models in order to determine the key influence factors that differentiate between internationalisers and non-internationalisers.[28] The Probit models estimate international sales (1=yes, 0=no)

---

[28] The Probit and the Logit model are the most widely used binary choice models. Whereas the Logit model is based on the cumulative logistic distribution, the Probit model is based on the cumulative normal distribution. They produce similar results although the parameter coefficients are not directly comparable (Amemiya 1981; Greene 1997). The choice of one over the other is usually based on convenience or the availability of calculation routines in computer packages.

as dependent variable. In table 44 to 47, we report the results of our models. All models estimate the probability to internationalise as a function of start-up size, age, international experience of the founders, technology intensity, the presence of external finance, innovativeness of the technology, customisation requirements, commercialisation costs and industry dummy variables. In model I, we chose to operationalise technology intensity by using research and development expenditures as percentage of total turnover (R&D expenditure). Furthermore, we use firm size at start-up. In model II, technology intensity is operationalised using the percentage of employees that work for at least 50% of their time on the development of current or future products (R&D employees). Firm size at start-up is used. Model III is identical to model II with one exception. We entered size today in the regression equation. In model IV, we assess the impact of the weighting on the multivariate result for the decision to internationalise. In model V and VI, more conservative thresholds are used to operationalise the notion of an international start-up. Using a polar approach, the firms had to sell into either three foreign markets or generate at least 10% of their total revenues through foreign sales. Firms with international activities that stayed below these thresholds were removed from the analysis.

For all models, the likelihood ratio chi-square test indicates significant overall solutions compared to a constant-only model. The pseudo R^2 ranges from 0.24 in model I to 0.34 in model V. However, there are problems of interpretation associated with these test statistics. The pseudo-R^2 does not allow for an intuitive interpretation of goodness of fit other that stating that one model is "better" than another based on identical functional model specification and numbers observations. This test statistic is not comparable to the traditional R^2 of regression analysis as is does not represent the amount of variance explained. In addition, the likelihood ratio tests only examine the null-hypothesis of obtaining the stated parameter estimates from our sample while the true population parameters are in fact zero. We therefore also calculated a "hit-rate" of correctly classified cases. In the models using the basic definition of "international activities", the classification ratio ranges from 77% to 78%. Using the more conservative thresholds for internationalisation, the models resulted in classification ratios of up to 81%. In all cases, these ratios compare favourably to the maximum chance score of correct classifications that one would obtain by assuming that all firms in the sample have international activities.

Table 44: Probit Models to Test the Propensity to Internationalise

Variable	Model I Coefficients		Model II Coefficients	
Firm Size (index of log values at start-up)	0.0861	***	0.0980	***
Age	0.0375	****	0.0371	****
Work Experience in UK for Multinational	0.1504	***	0.1424	***
International Work Experience	0.1069	*	0.1035	*
International Education	0.0852		0.0916	
R&D Intensity (% of turnover)	0.7744	**		
(R&D Intensity % turnover)²	-0.4697	±		
R&D Intensity (% of employees)			1.1532	****
(R&D Intensity % employees)²			-1.1596	***
Venture Capital Investment at Start-up	0.0170		0.0276	
Business Angel Investment at Start-up	0.0738		0.0976	
New Combinations of Existing Technology	0.1454	**	0.1364	**
Novel Technology Developed Externally	0.1741	**	0.1693	**
Novel Technology Developed Internally	0.0927		0.0829	
Customisation Requirement	-0.0567	****	-0.0516	***
Commercialisation Cost	0.0217		0.0178	
Industry: IT/Com Hardware	0.2277	****	0.2265	****
Industry: Engineering	0.2482	****	0.2548	****
Industry: Life Sciences	0.1933	**	0.2036	**
Industry: Other	0.1724	**	0.1863	***
No. of Observations	354		354	
Log Likelihood	-168.15		-165.97	
Chi-square (df):	105.58 (18)	****	109.93 (18)	****
Pseudo-R²:	0.2389		0.2488	
Correct classifications (in %):	77.40		77.12	
Maximum Chance Criterion (in %):	67.96		67.96	

Note: The reference category is a software firm selling products that incorporate "tried and tested" technology. The table shows marginal parameter estimates.
**** significant at p<0.001, *** significant at p<0.01, ** significant at p<0.05,
* significant at p<0.10, ± significant at p<0.15 (two-tailed tests)

Table 45: Probit Models to Test the Propensity to Internationalise

Variable	Model II Coefficients		Model III Coefficients	
Firm Size (index of log values at start-up)	0.0980	***		
Firm Size (index of log values today)			0.0703	**
Age	0.0371	****	0.0244	**
Work Experience in UK for Multinational	0.1424	***	0.1421	***
International Work Experience	0.1035	*	0.0931	***
International Education	0.0916		0.0962	
R&D Intensity (% of employees)	1.1532	****	1.1097	****
(R&D Intensity % employees)^2	-1.1596	***	-1.1304	***
Venture Capital Investment at Start-up	0.0276		0.0374	
Business Angel Investment at Start-up	0.0976		0.0765	
New Combinations of Existing Technology	0.1364	**	0.1241	*
Novel Technology Developed Externally	0.1693	**	0.1611	**
Novel Technology Developed Internally	0.0829		0.0661	
Customisation Requirement	-0.0516	***	-0.0531	***
Commercialisation Cost	0.0178		0.0131	
Industry: IT/Com Hardware	0.2265	****	0.2222	****
Industry: Engineering	0.2548	****	0.2536	****
Industry: Life Sciences	0.2036	**	0.2087	***
Industry: Other	0.1863	***	0.1872	***
No. of Observations	354		355	
Log Likelihood	-165.97		-168.41	
Chi-square (df):	109.93 (18)	****	105.82 (18)	****
Pseudo-R^2:	0.2488		0.2391	
Correct classifications (in %):	77.12		76.62	
Maximum Chance Criterion (in %):	67.96		67.96	

Note: The reference category is a software firm selling products that incorporate "tried and tested" technology. The table shows marginal parameter estimates.
**** significant at p<0.001, *** significant at p<0.01, ** significant at p<0.05,
* significant at p<0.10, ± significant at p<0.15 (two-tailed tests)

Table 46: Probit Models to Test the Propensity to Internationalise

Variable	Model II Coefficients		Model IV Coefficients (weighted)	
Firm Size (index of log values at start-up)	0.0980	***	0.1226	***
Age	0.0371	****	0.0431	****
Work Experience in UK for Multinational	0.1424	***	0.1914	***
International Work Experience	0.1035	*	0.1340	**
International Education	0.0916		0.1172	
R&D Intensity (% of turnover)				
(R&D Intensity % turnover)²				
R&D Intensity (% of employees)	1.1532	****	0.6205	**
(R&D Intensity % employees)²	-1.1596	***	-0.4166	
Venture Capital Investment at Start-up	0.0276		0.0462	
Business Angel Investment at Start-up	0.0976		0.0818	
New Combinations of Existing Technology	0.1364	**	0.2492	****
Novel Technology Developed Externally	0.1693	**	0.2589	***
Novel Technology Developed Internally	0.0829		0.2465	***
Customisation Requirement	-0.0516	***	-0.0606	***
Commercialisation Cost	0.0178		0.0523	*
Industry: IT/Com Hardware	0.2265	****	0.2800	****
Industry: Engineering	0.2548	****	0.3091	****
Industry: Life Sciences	0.2036	**	0.2873	***
Industry: Other	0.1863	***	0.2419	***
No. of Observations	354		354	
Log Likelihood	-165.97		-171.48	
Chi-square (df):	109.93 (18)	****	-134.84 (18)	****
Pseudo-R²:	0.2488		0.2822	
Correct classifications (in %):	77.12		75.71	
Maximum Chance Criterion (in %):	67.96		59.30	

Note: The reference category is a software firm selling products that incorporate "tried and tested" technology. The table shows marginal parameter estimates.
**** significant at $p<0.001$, *** significant at $p<0.01$, ** significant at $p<0.05$,
* significant at $p<0.10$, ± significant at $p<0.15$ (two-tailed tests)

Table 47: Probit Models to Test the Propensity to Internationalise

Variable	Model V Coefficients (at least 3 countries)		Model VI Coefficients (at least 10% foreign sales)	
Firm Size (index of log values at start-up)	0.1380	****	0.1256	****
Age	0.0458	****	0.0421	****
Work Experience in UK for Multinational	0.1771	***	0.1872	***
International Work Experience	0.1393	*	0.0994	±
International Education	0.1216		0.1178	
R&D Intensity (% of employees)	1.6076	****	1.5510	****
(R&D Intensity % employees)²	-1.4340	***	-1.3785	***
Venture Capital Investment at Start-up	0.0488		0.0130	
Business Angel Investment at Start-up	0.0847		0.1207	
New Combinations of Existing Technology	0.1399	±	0.1529	*
Novel Technology Developed Externally	0.2054	*	0.2342	**
Novel Technology Developed Internally	0.0916	**	0.0929	
Customisation Requirement	-0.0686	***	-0.0550	***
Commercialisation Cost	0.0211		0.0237	
Industry: IT/Com Hardware	0.3483	****	0.3167	****
Industry: Engineering	0.3670	****	0.3512	****
Industry: Life Sciences	0.2897	***	0.2905	***
Industry: Other	0.2716	***	0.2934	****
No. of Observations	289		300	
Log Likelihood	-129.35		-137.05	
Chi-square (df):	127.19 (18)	****	122.32 (18)	****
Pseudo-R²:	0.3296		0.3086	
Correct classifications (in %):	80.97		80.28	
Maximum Chance Criterion (in %):	61.25		62.67	

Note: The reference category is a software firm selling products that incorporate "tried and tested" technology. The table shows marginal parameter estimates.
**** significant at $p<0.001$, *** significant at $p<0.01$, ** significant at $p<0.05$,
* significant at $p<0.10$, ± significant at $p<0.15$ (two-tailed tests)

6.2.1.2. Results

Based on a comparison of these models, we reach the following conclusions with regard to our hypotheses. H1a could be supported. Our measure of size at start-up is positively related to the observation of international activities. The results of all the models show that, compared to domestic start-ups, the likelihood of international sales increases with larger log values of size measured at start-up. Despite possible problems of endogeneity, we used "size today" in model III to explore the stability of our effects. As is evident from the table, model II and III lead to identical size effects. Furthermore, all other independent variables remained unchanged in terms of direction and statistical significance. Given that we entered the *log values* of firm size into the regression models, the results indicate that the effect of *absolute firm size* decreases, the larger firms are. Overall, it suggests, that a certain size threshold or critical mass in terms of manpower and resources is required in order to internationalise. Once a certain scale of operations has been reached, the marginal effects of absolute values size becomes insignificant. Nonetheless, H1a receives support as we find significant positive effects of the log values of size on the propensity to internationalise. The impact on the different methods to operationalise size will be discussed further in section 6.2.4.

H2a was supported. In all models, both the measures of living experience abroad and work experience in an internationally operating company had a positive, significant impact on the probability to internationalise. It is interesting to note that, in all models, the marginal effects of work experience for an internationally operating company were stronger than the effects of direct work experience in a foreign country. International education also had a positive impact on internationalisation. Its effect, however, is statistically insignificant when the other two measures are entered in the regression as well. Taken individually, the effect of international education is statistically significant. We will discuss the effect of the different measures of international experience in more detail in section 6.2.4.

H3a was not supported. Neither the involvement of venture capitalists nor business angels had a significant impact on the decision to internationalise. H4a hypothesised a curvilinear effect of technological intensity on the probability to internationalise. As already stated above, model I used R&D expenditures as percentage of total sales whereas model II used the percentage of R&D employees. For a curvilinear, inverted U-shaped effect to be present, three conditions must be met. First, the parameter of technology intensity must be positive and significant. Second, the parameter for squared technology intensity must be negative and significant. Third, the turning point of the curve must lie within the observed range of values for technology intensity.[29] In all models

---

[29] We obtain the latter through equalising the first derivative of the R&D intensity function with 0.

except model IV, we can observe a significant positive effect for the variable and a significant negative effect for the squared term, regardless of whether R&D intensity is measured as percentage of turnover or as share of development employees. The turning points are within the range of observed values (82% for R&D intensity as share of turnover, 50% for employees) thus leading us to accept the presence of a curvilinear effect. Only in the weighted model does the squared term lose its significance. This difference can be explained if one recalls the fact that the weights put a greater emphasis on smaller firms and software firms. Among each of the strata, the software firms and the smallest firms have the highest level of employees working on product development.[30] Software firms and firms belonging to the smallest size class report and R&D intensity (employees) of 35% which compares to 21% for the remaining firms. Since the likelihood of international sales is lower for these firms, the correlation of R&D intensity and international sales is less significant. One would therefore expect other factors to account to a greater extent for the variation in the data. Since the squared terms actually measures the decreasing element in the curve - the "penalty" of high R&D levels on the propensity to internationalise - it does not come as a surprise that the weighting increases the standard error of the estimate. For the weighted data, there seems to be a more linear relationship between R&D intensity and international sales. On the unweighted data, however, a curvilinear effect will become apparent. H4a therefore receives partial support.

H5a looked at the innovativeness of the products sold abroad. Compared to the base case of "tried and tested" technology, firms that sell more innovative products have a higher probability to engage in international activities. However, no significant effect was found for the most innovative product category. Nonetheless, hypothesis 5a can be supported. A Wald test was performed in order to test the hypothesis of a joint impact. Compared to the base case of "tried and tested" technology, all three dummy variables that operationalised more innovative product technology were jointly related to international activities ($p<0.01$). The hypothesis of a joint positive impact was supported irrespective of the chosen specification. More innovative technology is thus positively related to internationalisation in our models.

H6a is supported as the degree of customisation is negatively related to internationalisation in all models. H7a looked at the transaction costs associated with commercialising a product. The hypothesis that high transaction costs represented a stronger barrier for non-internationalisers than for internationalisers could not be supported in any of the models. As expected, all models predict that internationalisers are older than domestic start-ups. This is to be expected given an average time lag of two years between firm formation and initial internationalisation reported in the section on descriptive statistics. Compared to the base case of software, firms from all other industries had a higher propensity

---

[30] See also section 5.2.5. on the overcounting of R&D employees among small firms.

to internationalise. While there is a literature on the problems of service firms with regard to internationalisation (see Erramilli and Rao 1993) this finding came as a surprise as more than 90% of service firms were software companies. A priori, they were expected to face relatively few barriers to internationalisation other than, in particular cases, the need to translate their applications. Probably this is explained by the fact that the majority of software firms are small firms involved in contract programming. Rather than venturing abroad, they are more likely to offer and deliver their services locally. On the other hand, since there are software firms that have very high levels of foreign sales, it appears that barriers to internationalisation can be overcome through offering highly standardised packages.

As a next step, we were interested in identifying the effects of the weighting on our regression model. Above all, compared to the maximum chance criterion of 59.3%, the classification ratio of the weighted regression of 75.9% represents a substantial improvement of predictive ability. The results of the weighted model differ in two aspects from the unweighted models. First, the curvilinear effect of research and development intensity becomes insignificant (see also above). Second, the weighted model is the only model where higher costs of commercialisation do actually lead to a higher probability to sell internationally. As the weighting changes the emphasis of the multivariate pattern of small and service firms, we ran a number of regressions on various sub-samples. These regressions (results not shown) clearly identify the overemphasis of software firms as being responsible for the change of the cost of commercialisation coefficient. Software firms experience on average higher costs of commercialisation than firms from the other industry groups. The fact that there are still 56% of software firms with international activities causes this coefficient to become positive in a weighted model. The reduction of the level of significance of technology intensity can be explained by the lower probability of the smallest firms to engage in international sales. Yet, among these firms, one can also observe very high levels of technology intensity as measured by R&D employees. Note also that due to the lower probability of smaller firms and software firms to internationalise, the weighted regression models produce better performance statistics. In order to examine the validity of our explanation, we performed several regressions on the subsample of software firms. The results are displayed in appendix 6. We provide a summary discussion of the effects of the weighting in section 6.2.4. Altogether, the weighting does not fundamentally change the results of our modelling of the probability of international sales.

Models V and VI use more conservative thresholds to operationalise international activities. As stated above, firms are counted as internationalisers if they have entered at least three different foreign markets (model V) or if they generate at least 10% of their total revenues through foreign sales (model VI). Comparing the parameter estimates of these models with the other models, one realises that the effects are stable. Finally, we estimated these models using robust standard errors in order to account for possible effects of heteroscedasticity not accounted for by the log transformations of firm size (results not shown here). None of the robust models changed the sign or level of significance of the coefficients reported here. To summarise, we conclude that, with the exception of the variable commercialisation cost affected by the weighting, the reported effects are stable regardless of the chosen model specification and the chosen threshold for international activities.

6.2.2. The Degree of Internationalisation

6.2.2.1. Methodological Considerations

In this section, we will estimate the degree of internationalisation of the firms in our sample. Our dependent variable, the share of non-domestic revenues, is the most frequently used measure of the degree of internationalisation of a firm. It is closely related to the binary dependent variable estimated in the previous section. In this section, we are actually testing whether the variable vector that accounts for the decision to internationalise can also account for different internationalisation "intensities".

There are a number of approaches that could be used to estimate this variable. One approach, used by numerous studies (see Sullivan 1994, for a review), consists of estimating the chosen indicator of the degree of internationalisation through a standard OLS (ordinary least squares) regression. This approach can be performed on the subsample of internationalisers or on the total sample. If only the international start-ups are retained for this analysis, the results can, of course, only apply to this sub-sample. From a theoretical and managerial point of view, an important issue now arises. Suppose the regression on the sub-population of internationalisers leads to the (rather unexpected) finding that a high degree of international sales is explained by products characterised by high customisation requirements. In the previous section, however, we found that customisation had a significant impact on the decision *not* to compete internationally. What recommendations can be given if the characteristics of those firms with a high degree of internationalisation are relatively similar to those that do not compete internationally at all? Stated in other words, an analytical focus on the subset of internationalisers risks producing findings that may be inconsistent with the determinants of observing international activities in the first place. To avoid the above problem, we can, as an alternative approach, set the value of the dependent value (share of non-domestic revenue) to "0" for the non-internationalisers and perform a standard OLS regression. This approach uses the information on non-internationalisers as well and has been employed, for example, by Reuber and Fischer (1997) and Bloodgood, Almeida and Sapienza (1997).

Yet, at this stage, an additional issue arises. In our case, we have information on the independent variables of both firms with and without international activities. Yet, only for firms with international activities, the dependent variable, the share of non-domestic revenues, is observable. We therefore have what is called a censored sample. Censoring is one instance where the values of variables are limited in their range thus producing biased OLS estimators (Greene 1997). In our case, this is mainly caused by the cross-sectional research design. Given that we sampled firms founded between 1987 and 1997, we ended up with a number of firms whose recorded life span (one or two years) is too short to observe them when they engage in international activities. Setting the value of the non-domestic revenue artificially to "0" will produce biased estimators since the values of this dependent variable for non-internationalisers are – strictly speaking - not observable. In the econometric literature, this problem is known as sample selection. Sample selection occurs when the observation of a dependent variable is not independent from the probability of its occurrence.

A number of different methods have been developed to estimate the determinants of a dependent variable for the entire population of firms based on a censored sample. These models usually estimate a selection equation to determine the probability of observing the dependent variable and a main equation on the dependent variable. Two widely used estimation methods are the Tobit model and the two step Heckman selection model. The Tobit model is actually a special case of sample selection. Here, the selection equation is the same as the main equation being estimated. This would be the appropriate method if internationalisation was a linear phenomenon, i.e. the same factors that discriminate between internationalisers and non-internationalisers are also responsible for a high score of the degree of internationalisation. As we hypothesised that the same variable vector determines the propensity to internationalise and the degree of internationalisation of a firm, the results of the Tobit model should be consistent with the OLS regression.[31] Accordingly, comparing the results of the Tobit and a standard OLS regression could inform our understanding of the validity and stability of the observed effects and state whether sample selection is a problem in the present case.

6.2.2.2. Model Estimation

To shed further light on the determinants of the degree of internationalisation, we will now discuss the results of our estimations in order to identify which factors account for the variation in the share of non-domestic revenue. We will compare

---

[31] Of course, the magnitude of the coefficients will be different. Still, Greene (1980) found that the coefficients of the OLS model, when divided by the degree of censoring, approximate to the coefficients of the Tobit model.

the results and discuss to what extent the differences can be attributed to the different estimation methods.

Table 48 shows the results of the OLS regressions on the sub-sample of firms with international activities (models I to III). In these models, we decided not to use age as a control variable. Instead, we used the number of years a firm has already sold internationally as a predictor. We do so for the following reason: First, this variable can be understood as "age since first international sales" or company experience with international sales. It is highly correlated with firm age ($r=0.64$), but likely to be a better predictor of the degree of internationalisation since it takes into account that firms enter foreign markets at different age levels. Second, from a theoretical point of view, firm experience plays a central role in the process theories of internationalisation reviewed in chapter 2. Accordingly, the extent to which firms engage in international sales is argued to be a function of the past experience with foreign activities. Since we perform these OLS regressions on the sub-sample of internationalisers, we have information on this variable. This is not the case when looking at the entire sample, since the variable can not be established for non-internationalisers. Table 49 shows the results of the OLS regressions performed on the total sample with the share of non-domestic revenue set to "0" for non-internationalisers (models IV to VI). Finally, in table 50 we contrast these OLS regressions with three Tobit models in order to examine the validity of our results and to account for the effects of the censoring (models VII to IX). The models are also estimated using the weights in order to assess the impact of the sampling strategy (models III, VI and IX). In all cases, the models resulted in statistical significant solutions. In the OLS models, the R^2 and adjusted R^2 ranged from 0.19 to 0.30 and 0.13 to 0.26 respectively. The pseudo R^2 in the Tobit models ranged from 0.05 to 0.07.

Table 48: Estimation of the Share of Non-Domestic Revenue
- OLS Regression on International Firms -

Variable	Model I Coefficients		Model II Coefficients		Model III Coefficients weighted	
Firm Size (index of log values at start-up)	0.0274		-0.0067		0.0258	
International Experience of the Firm (in years)	0.2565	****	0.3056	****	0.2391	****
Work Experience in UK for Multinational	0.0646		0.0706		0.0710	
International Work Experience	0.0447		0.0713		0.0487	
International Education	0.0463		0.0071		0.0481	
R&D Intensity (% of turnover)			0.3589	**		
(R&D Intensity % turnover)^2			-0.0573			
R&D Intensity (% of employees)	0.6204	****			0.5681	***
(R&D Intensity % employees)^2	-0.3151	*			-0.3135	±
Venture Capital Investment at Start-up	0.0502		0.0672		0.0481	
Business Angel Investment at Start-up	0.0871		0.0827		0.1003	±
New Combinations of Existing Technology	0.1531	*	0.1756	*	0.1956	**
Novel Technology Developed Externally	0.0957		0.1181		0.1548	
Novel Technology Developed Internally	-0.0149		0.0469		0.0369	
Customisation Requirement	-0.0715		-0.0656		-0.0735	
Commercialisation Cost	0.0781		0.0555		0.0634	
Industry: IT/Com Hardware	0.1430	*	0.0912		0.1111	
Industry: Engineering	0.1892	**	0.1328	±	0.1426	*
Industry: Life Sciences	0.2044	***	0.1501	**	0.1812	**
Industry: Other	0.2458	***	0.1581	*	0.2275	**
No. of Observations	231		231		231	
F-Statistic	3.86	****	3.75	****	2.93	****
df	18; 212		18; 212		18; 212	
R^2	0.2470		0.2416		0.1993	
Adjusted R^2	0.1831		0.1772		0.1313	

Note: The reference category is a software firm selling products that incorporate "tried and tested" technology. The table shows beta coefficients.
**** significant at p<0.001, *** significant at p<0.01, ** significant at p<0.05,
* significant at p<0.10, ± significant at p<0.15 (two-tailed tests)

Table 49: Estimation of the Share of Non-Domestic Revenue
- OLS Regression on all Firms -

Variable	Model IV Coefficients		Model V Coefficients		Model VI Coefficients weighted	
Firm Size (index of log values at start-up)	0.1280	***	0.0975	**	0.1411	***
Age	0.1599	****	0.1694	****	0.1745	****
Work Experience in UK for Multinational	0.1270	**	0.1393	***	0.1537	***
International Work Experience	0.0709		0.0871	*	0.0615	
International Education	0.0646		0.0546		0.0635	
R&D Intensity (% of turnover)			0.3726	****		
(R&D Intensity % turnover)²			-0.1745	*		
R&D Intensity (% of employees)	0.6892	****			0.4593	***
(R&D Intensity % employees)²	-0.4533	****			-0.2534	*
Venture Capital Investment at Start-up	0.0308		0.0291		0.0392	
Business Angel Investment at Start-up	0.0639		0.0612		0.0739	±
New Combinations of Existing Technology	0.1107	*	0.1343	**	0.1280	**
Novel Technology Developed Externally	0.1155	**	0.1255	**	0.1571	***
Novel Technology Developed Internally	-0.0026		0.0377		0.0523	
Customisation Requirement	-0.1123	**	-0.1309	**	-0.1159	**
Commercialisation Cost	0.0436		0.0483		0.0729	
Industry: IT/Com Hardware	0.1870	****	0.1592	****	0.1696	***
Industry: Engineering	0.2388	****	0.2044	****	0.2074	****
Industry: Life Sciences	0.2024	****	0.1735	****	0.2031	****
Industry: Other	0.2140	****	0.1524	**	0.2048	****
No. of Observations	352		352		352	
F-Statistic	7.54	****	6.64	****	7.82	****
df	18; 333		18; 333		18; 333	
R²	0.2871		0.2640		0.2971	
Adjusted R²	0.2485		0.2243		0.2592	

Note: The reference category is a software firm selling products that incorporate "tried and tested" technology. The table shows beta coefficients.
**** significant at $p<0.001$, *** significant at $p<0.01$, ** significant at $p<0.05$,
* significant at $p<0.10$, ± significant at $p<0.15$ (two-tailed tests)

Table 50: Estimation of the Share of Non-Domestic Revenue
- Tobit Regression -

Variable	Model VII Coefficients		Model VIII Coefficients		Model IX Coefficients weighted	
Firm Size (index of log values at start-up)	7.8795	****	6.5952	***	10.0559	****
Age	3.4506	****	3.6712	****	4.2444	****
Work Experience in UK for Multinational	13.5384	****	14.6213	****	17.9507	****
International Work Experience	7.5071	**	9.1635	**	8.2268	*
International Education	9.1450		7.8975		6.7146	
R&D Intensity (% of turnover)			70.2167	***		
(R&D Intensity % turnover)^2			-24.5733	±		
R&D Intensity (% of employees)	136.2137	****			89.1006	***
(R&D Intensity % employees)^2	-111.4290	****			-54.9145	*
Venture Capital Investment at Start-up	4.6199		4.8184		6.7062	
Business Angel Investment at Start-up	12.0750		11.6734	±	14.0679	*
New Combinations of Existing Technology	16.7416	***	19.2948	***	24.6549	***
Novel Technology Developed Externally	21.4477	***	23.9287	***	32.5872	***
Novel Technology Developed Internally	6.6827		10.7940	*	17.4824	**
Customisation Requirement	-3.9317	***	-4.4213	****	-4.3216	***
Commercialisation Cost	1.4131		1.4834		2.9929	
Industry: IT/Com Hardware	24.5434	****	21.9252	****	29.7948	****
Industry: Engineering	33.2199	****	29.7669	****	36.6633	****
Industry: Life Sciences	32.8766	****	29.0679	***	40.9037	****
Industry: Other	27.2351	****	21.1645	****	34.4005	****
No. of Observations	352		352		352	
Log Likelihood	-1231.30		-1236.91		-1078.44	
Chi-square (df):	-144.56 (18)	****	-133.34 (18)	****	164.86 (18)	****
Pseudo R^2	0.0554		0.0511		0.0710	

Note: The reference category is a software firm selling products that incorporate "tried and tested" technology. The table shows coefficient estimates.
**** significant at p<0.001, *** significant at p<0.01, ** significant at p<0.05,
* significant at p<0.10, ± significant at p<0.15 (two-tailed tests)

6.2.2.3. Results

In model I to III which examine the sub-sample of internationalisers, there are few significant factors that impact on the degree of internationalisation. The number of years since their first international sales, or, stated differently, their direct international experience, is strongly related to the degree of internationalisation. The beta coefficients reveal that this is one of the strongest predictors of the degree of internationalisation. This result lends support to process theories which argue that the extent of international activities at a given time is a function of past experience with international activities. When looking at technology intensity, it became apparent that the linear component of the R&D vector is positive and significant in all three models and is the most influential variable according to the beta coefficients. Differences between the models became apparent as the squared component of this vector is significant only when using the share of R&D employees as a measure. However, the turning point of the function is only reached at about 100% R&D intensity by employees, the limit observation of the sample. The hypothesis of a curvilinear effect can therefore not be supported in the sub-sample models.

When looking at the innovativeness of the product, we found that only the products that incorporate "new combinations of existing technology" have a significant positive impact on the share of non-domestic revenue compared to the base case of "tried and tested technology". A Wald test on a joint influence of the technology variables was insignificant. All remaining product related variables turned out to be insignificant as well. Among the industry variables, life sciences firms were the only firms with a consistent positive effect in the models. The dummy variables for engineering and "other firms" were positive in model I, where we operationalised technology intensity as share of R&D employees. Variables that discriminated between internationalisers and non-internationalisers, such as size, international experience and customisation have lost their explanatory effect with regard to the share of non-domestic revenue, with only work experience for an internationally operating firm being marginally significant in model II.

Overall, we conclude that the models on the subsample of internationalisers perform quite poorly as none of the hypothesised relationships could be supported. These results suggests that, when looking just at the subsample of internationalisers, the factors that caused them to venture abroad are of limited value for explaining their degree of internationalisation. It also suggests that, at least as far as the chosen variable vector in our models is concerned, internationalisers are a quite homogeneous type of firm. For example, the Probit regressions in section 6.2.1. showed that the products of international start-ups require less client-specific customisation. Once that these firms sell their products into foreign markets, their marginal customisation requirements lose their power as predictors of subsequent performance. Differences in their strategic orientation and particular events or experiences rather than the more structural characteristics measured here are likely to explain the differences in their degree of internationalisation.[32] This is also evident from the strong effect of experience with cross-border sales on the subsequent degree of internationalisation. The latter lends support to the arguments of internationalisation process models which see organisational outcomes as functions of past experience. We therefore conclude from model I to III that the variable vector that discriminated quite well between internationalisers and non-internationalisers in the previous section loses its power when applied to the question how well the subsample of internationalisers performs in terms of degree of internationalisation. Nonetheless, the findings of the subsample regression are not contradictory to the results on the decision to internationalise, because its significant factors were not *negatively* related to the decision to internationalise in the first place.

As a next step, we looked at the entire sample of firms. A picture consistent with the earlier findings emerges here, since both the OLS regression and the Tobit model produce results which are in direction and significance almost identical to the Probit model on the differences between international start-ups and domestic start-ups. We base our discussion mainly on the results of Tobit model as we believe that its results are more accurate given the degree of censoring in our sample.

In all models that were estimated on the entire sample, firm size was significantly positively related to the share of non-domestic revenue. The same results were obtained when using the summary scale constructed of the log values for size at start-up and at the time of the survey (results of the latter not shown here, but see table 55). H1b can therefore be supported. [33] Since we used the summary scale constructed of the log values for employee and sales, the results suggests that a the

---

[32] Lindqvist (1991) encountered somewhat a similar situation. She came to a similar conclusion after finding out that few variables of her dataset contributed to explaining differences in the share of non-domestic revenue among her sample of firms with international activities.

[33] Since the share of non-domestic revenue is not independent from the level of sales, we then also added the absolute value for "sales today" into the equations. This control variable was not found to be significant in any of the models that were based on size at start-up. However, it was significant and positively related to the degree of internationalisation when entering size at the time of the survey. Since we have already pointed out in section 6.2.1. that the level of total sales at the time of the survey could be at the same time the cause and effect of a high degree of international sales, we cannot make any causal inference here. In any case, the simultaneous use of the summary scale for size and sales today impacted on the level of significance for the firm size index scale. This was to be expected given the high degree of multicollinearity among these variables (correlation $r=0.75$). The remaining variables were not affected in terms of direction and significance. The variable sales today is therefore omitted from the displayed specifications in order to improve the comparability between the models that estimate the different dimensions of internationalisation. A more detailed discussion of the effect of firm size in our models can be found in section 6.2.4.

effect is decreasing with increasing absolute size. Stated differently, firms that generate a high share of non-domestic revenues are found to have minimum size. Work experience for an internationally operating firm was found to have a significant positive impact on the share of non-domestic revenues in all models. The effects for direct international work experience were positive and significant with the exception of model IV and VI. In these specifications, this variable slipped above the chosen significance thresholds. We believe that this is an effect of the censoring that is not accounted for by the OLS regressions and are therefore inclined to accept the positive impact of that variable when looking at the entire sample. International education was not found to be significant in any of the models when entered simultaneously with the other two variables measuring management's international experience. When we omitted the latter two and entered only international education in the regression equations, this variable turned out to be significant. We will discuss this effect in more detail in section 6.2.4. Overall, we find support for H2b.

The presence of venture capital was not significantly related to the degree of internationalisation in any of the models. Marginally significant effects were achieved for business angel investment in the case of the weighted OLS and Tobit models and the unweighted Tobit model that used R&D employees as measure of technology intensity. H3b therefore receives partial support.

In the OLS and Tobit models that used the share of R&D employees as measure of technology intensity (models IV, VI, VII and IX), we found a curvilinear effect of technology intensity on the share of non-domestic revenue. The turning points of the function lay between 61% and 90%. In models V and VIII that used R&D expenditures as a percentage of turnover, we could also identify a curvilinear effect. Yet, only four firms had expenditure levels that were beyond the turning point of this vector. Despite lying within the observed range, the curvilinearity is therefore of limited relevance for practical or predictive purposes. H4b therefore receives only partial support.

Similar effects were observed when looking at the innovativeness of the technology embodied in the products. Compared to the base case of tried and tested technology, more advanced / newer technology was positively related to the degree of internationalisation. While the most advanced technology was not positively related to the base case, the joint impact of the three technology dummies was positive and significant ($p<0.03$). Hypothesis 5b therefore receives support. Like in the Probit models on the differences between internationalisers and domestic firms, the extent of required product customisation was in all models (III to IX) negatively related to a the share of non-domestic revenues. The level of pre- and after sales service requirements, the costs of commercialisation, were not related to the degree of international sales in a significant way. This leads us to accept hypothesis 6b and reject hypothesis 7b.

Finally, the effects of the control variables for age and industry were consistent across the different specifications and corroborated the findings of the Probit model. Accordingly, as expected, older firms are more likely to have higher shares of non-domestic revenues. Furthermore, compared to the base case of software, all remaining firms had higher levels of non-domestic revenues. We then tried to assess the differences between the weighted and unweighted regressions. In all eight models, the weighting produced similar effects and there are hardly any differences in the level of significance of the individual variables. The main difference was found when looking at business angels. This result can be explained because the weighting overemphasises the multivariate pattern of smaller firms that had a much lower likelihood of attracting business angel finance. As the amount of variation explained by that variable increases through the weighting, we identify marginally significant effects in the regressions.

To conclude, the differences between the sub-sample OLS regressions and the models performed on the entire sample were striking. In the latter case, the differences in the degree of internationalisation can, to a large extent, be attributed to the discriminating factors between internationalisers and non-internationalisers. Taking the entire sample as a base for analysis, we could therefore support H8. Yet, we have to be aware that an acceptance or a rejection of this hypothesis is a direct consequence of the method rather than the characteristics of international start-ups. When looking exclusively at the latter as a base for analysis, H8 would clearly have to be rejected. None of the factors that significantly influenced internationalisation had substantial power to explain the subsequent share of non-domestic revenues among the internationalisers.

6.2.3. The Timing of Market Entry

6.2.3.1. Methodological Considerations

In order to test the hypotheses regarding the timing of foreign market entry, we estimated several Cox proportional hazard and Weibull regression models. These models are part of a family of approaches models known as event history analysis (EHA). Event history analysis has two distinct features that recommend its use for the analysis of decision making in a more dynamic context. First, event history analysis allows for a more dynamic consideration of the decision to internationalise as it allows for the incorporation of firm characteristics measured at several time periods preceding foreign market entry. Unfortunately, we do not have such information for the sample firms.

Second, and more important in our case, event history analysis is a superior approach to investigate the probability of an event occurring when the data is censored. In principle, a model specification without data from different time periods is related to a binary choice model, such as a Logit or Probit model. As already mentioned in the previous section, our cross-sectional sample is "cut off" or censored because there are a number of young firms that have currently not internationalised but are likely to do so in the future.[34] Previous research has shown that Logit or Probit models to analyse organisational outcomes can lead to biased estimators when the sample is censored (Hannan and Freeman 1984; Yamaguchi 1991). If, on the other hand, the Cox regression leads to the same results as the Probit model on the decision to internationalise, we can conclude that the results are quite stable and that the censoring is not a problem in the case of our sample.

Event history analysis tries to identify the factors that impact on the occurrence of a particular event ("exits" or "failures" in the terminology of EHA), given different duration times ("times-at-risk" or "spell lengths") between starting time and occurrence. The rate at which an event occurs during the specified period at risk is referred to as hazard rate. The hazard rate usually varies over time and among different groups. Cox proportional hazard models have in the past been applied to modelling foreign market entry decisions of firms (Tan and Vertinsky 1996). It is a non-parametric method estimated using the method of partial likelihood. As opposed to parametric methods such as an exponential regression or a Weibull regression, Cox's method assumes a time dependence of the variates without requiring the researcher to specify its form. Since parametric methods such as the Weibull regression are very sensitive to the specification of time dependence and interaction, Cox's method is, in many cases, more likely to produce robust results (Allison 1984; Yamaguchi 1991). On the other hand, a Weibull regression allows for an interaction with time and the incorporation of an increasing or decreasing hazard rate over time.[35] Graphical inspection of the hazard rate over time usually reveals whether the observed phenomenon is subject to increasing or decreasing hazard over time. For these reasons, we will estimate several Cox and Weibull models. A more formal discussion of the likelihood functions and properties of these models can be found in Yamaguchi (1991) and Greene (1997).

6.2.3.2. Model Estimation

In event history analysis, the factors that impact on the occurrence of an event are estimated. Using the jargon of EHA, a firm is "at risk" of "failing" since inception. In the present context, a failure or exit refers to the first foreign market entry. By the end of the observed time period, a firm will have either failed, that is

---

[34] A further reason for censoring would be the death of an organisation. As these case are not observable at the time of the survey, we have no data on these.

[35] The classical example of the application of the Weibull regression is the question of how quickly a bearing wears out. Given constant use, the risk of failure of a bearing usually increases over time, that is a bearing that has been in use for one year will have a lower risk of failure than a bearing that has been in use for five years. The hazard rate approximating the risk of failure is thus increasing over time instead of being constant.

internationalised, or be treated as censored observation. An important caveat has to be noted. Event history analysis normally requires data that was recorded before observations were at risk or that are not subject to changes over time. While the assumption that categoric variables such as industry and innovativeness of the technology are not subject to changes over time is quite reasonable, a problem appears when looking at technology intensity. On the one hand, one expects high-technology start-ups to devote most of their resources in relative terms on product development when they are young. However, the same argument can be made in the other direction. Early commercial success allows the start-up's management to channel additional resources to research and development activities in order to concentrate on future generation products. Note also that a breakdown of technology intensities in section 5.2.5. revealed that the level of R&D expenditures stayed relatively stable irrespective of the age of the start-up. Thus, if there are changes over time, we do not expect these changes to bias our modelling of the timing of market entry in a consistent way. This property should therefore not impact substantially on the results but could increase the noise in the data. In the worst case, this leads marginal t-statistics to slip outside the accepted significance levels.

Model I and model II (table 51) are identical with one exception. Like in the previous models, we report the results for two different measures of technology intensity. In both models, the starting year for a firm to be "at risk" of international market entry is its year of formation. In model III, we chose a different starting period. Here, a firm starts being at risk after its first sales. We chose this model specification in order to account for those firms that focus exclusively on product development during their first years. By definition, these will enter foreign markets only after product development is finished. In the following table (table 52), we compare model I to a weighted model (model IV) and to a model that uses a different definition of exit (model V). In the latter case, we consider a firm as international when it has entered its first three foreign markets. Finally, in table 53, we report the results of three Weibull regressions in order to identify whether a decreasing or increasing hazard rate invalidates or supports the results of the Cox model.

6.2.3.3. Results

All eight models result in statistically significant solutions. The parameter coefficients should be interpreted as follows: A positive sign indicates that a variable is positively related to early internationalisation. Conversely, a negative coefficient indicates that the variable in question is negatively related to the speed of market entry. When looking at the models, we found that the effects were very consistent irrespective of the model specification. The Weibull and Cox models produce almost identical results.

Table 51: Cox Regression to Estimate the Time to Internationalise

Variable	Model I Coefficients base year: year of formation		Model II Coefficients base year: year of formation		Model III Coefficients base year: first sales	
Firm Size (index of log values at start-up)	0.3288	****	0.2933	****	0.3652	****
Work Experience in UK for Multinational	0.3671	***	0.3904	***	0.4079	****
International Work Experience	0.2144	±	0.2411	±	0.2333	±
International Education	0.1555		0.1465		0.2861	
R&D Intensity (% of turnover)			1.7091	**		
(R&D Intensity % turnover)^2			-1.4387	**		
R&D Intensity (% of employees)	3.0148	****			3.3636	****
(R&D Intensity % employees)^2	-3.0959	***			-3.4630	****
Venture Capital Investment at Start-up	-0.1473		-0.0837		-0.1350	
Business Angel Investment at Start-up	0.2635		0.2619		0.2555	
New Combinations of Existing Technology	0.2362		0.2773		0.2844	
Novel Technology Developed Externally	0.3729	±	0.4950	*	0.4955	*
Novel Technology Developed Internally	0.1314		0.1732		0.1214	
Customisation Requirement	-0.0867	**	-0.1009	**	-0.1149	***
Commercialisation Cost	-0.0113		-0.0174		-0.0254	
Industry: IT/Com Hardware	0.5578	***	0.5552	***	0.7652	****
Industry: Engineering	0.7380	****	0.6883	****	0.7984	****
Industry: Life Sciences	0.6557	***	0.5837	**	0.7271	***
Industry: Other	0.3551	±	0.2705		0.4265	**
No. of Observations	354		354		354	
No. of Failures	242		242		242	
Log Likelihood	-1161.76		-1164.77		-1109.51	
Chi-square (df):	84.53 (17)	****	78.48 (17)	****	106.83 (17)	****
Pseudo R^2	0.0351		0.0326		0.0459	

Note: The reference category is a software firm selling products that incorporate "tried and tested" technology. The table shows parameter estimates instead of hazard ratios.
**** significant at p<0.001, *** significant at p<0.01, ** significant at p<0.05,
* significant at p<0.10, ± significant at p<0.15 (two-tailed tests)

Table 52: Cox Regression to Estimate the Time to Internationalise

Variable	Model I Coefficients base year: year of formation		Model IV Coefficients weighted		Model V Coefficients failure: entry into 3 countries	
Firm Size (index of log values at start-up)	0.3288	****	0.3630	****	0.2801	****
Work Experience in UK for Multinational	0.3671	***	0.4952	***	0.2128	
International Work Experience	0.2144	±	0.2878	±	0.3935	**
International Education	0.1555		0.0959		0.2288	
R&D Intensity (% of employees)	3.0148	****	1.8739	****	3.2360	***
(R&D Intensity % employees)^2	-3.0959	***	-1.4912	****	-3.1441	***
Venture Capital Investment at Start-up	-0.1473		-0.1573		0.0758	
Business Angel Investment at Start-up	0.2635		0.2612		0.3442	
New Combinations of Existing Technology	0.2362		0.5216	**	0.1219	
Novel Technology Developed Externally	0.3729	±	0.6987	***	0.0991	
Novel Technology Developed Internally	0.1314		0.5030	**	-0.0579	
Customisation Requirement	-0.0867	**	-0.0964	***	-0.1073	**
Commercialisation Cost	-0.0113		0.0342		0.0389	
Industry: IT/Com Hardware	0.5578	***	0.5908	****	0.7851	****
Industry: Engineering	0.7380	****	0.8098	****	0.8928	****
Industry: Life Sciences	0.6557	***	0.7626	***	0.6776	**
Industry: Other	0.3551	±	0.4778	*	0.4545	*
No. of Observations	354		354		354	
No. of Failures	242		242		184	
Log Likelihood	-1161.76		-1010.36		-928.35	
Chi-square (df):	84.53 (17)	****	93.89 (17)	****	73.97(17)	****
Pseudo R^2	0.0351		0.0444		0.0383	

Note: The reference category is a software firm selling products that incorporate "tried and tested" technology. The table shows parameter estimates instead of hazard ratios.
**** significant at p<0.001, *** significant at p<0.01, ** significant at p<0.05,
* significant at p<0.10, ± significant at p<0.15 (two-tailed tests)

Table 53: Weibull Regression to Estimate the Time to Internationalise

Variable	Model VI Coefficients Weibull		Model VII Coefficients Weibull		Model VIII Coefficients weighted Weibull	
Firm Size (index of log values at start-up)	0.3153	****	0.2814	****	0.3594	****
Work Experience in UK for Multinational	0.3977	***	0.4195	***	0.5159	***
International Work Experience	0.2412	*	0.2671	*	0.3093	*
International Education	0.1426		0.1366		0.0884	
R&D Intensity (% of turnover)			1.6896	**		
(R&D Intensity % turnover)²			-1.4664	**		
R&D Intensity (% of employees)	3.0813	****			1.9683	**
(R&D Intensity % employees)²	-3.2081	***			-1.6148	*
Venture Capital Investment at Start-up	-0.1425		-0.0767		-0.1416	
Business Angel Investment at Start-up	0.2207		0.2223		0.2247	
New Combinations of Existing Technology	0.1965		0.2488		0.5173	**
Novel Technology Developed Externally	0.3365		0.4728	*	0.6856	***
Novel Technology Developed Internally	0.1062		0.1543		0.5004	**
Customisation Requirement	-0.0943	**	-0.1081	**	-0.1039	**
Commercialisation Cost	-0.0499		-0.0027		0.0477	
Industry: IT/Com Hardware	0.5571	***	0.5533	***	0.5723	***
Industry: Engineering	0.7886	****	0.7304	****	0.8398	****
Industry: Life Sciences	0.7204	***	0.6425	**	0.8144	***
Industry: Other	0.3523	±	0.2636		0.4866	*
No. of Observations	354		354		354	
No. of Failures	242		242		242	
Log Likelihood	125.49		-173.80		-167.26	
Chi-square (df):	-170.45 (17)	****	85.35 (17)	****	100.95 (17)	****
p	1.62		1.58		1.60	

Note: The reference category is a software firm selling products that incorporate "tried and tested" technology. The table shows parameter estimates instead of hazard ratios.
**** significant at p<0.001, *** significant at p<0.01, ** significant at p<0.05,
* significant at p<0.10, ± significant at p<0.15 (two-tailed tests)

Small differences were only found when we changed the model specification and added the weights. In the Weibull regressions, the p-values of around 1.6 indicate an increasing hazard rate over time (bottom table 53). The value of 1.6 should be interpreted as follows: five years after inception, a firm's chances of engaging in international activities are nearly twice as high compared to two years after inception (or, to be precise $(5/2)^{1.6-1} = 1.73$).

In all models, we found that our measure of firm size had a significant positive effect on early foreign market entry. H1c is therefore supported. Like in the previous models on the propensity and degree of internationalisation, we entered the log values of size into the regression equation. The results therefore indicate that the effect of size decreases with increasing absolute values of firm size thus suggesting that a minimum critical mass is required for the initiation of international activities.

International experience was also positively related to early foreign market entry in all models. The results are significant for work experience in an internationally operating firm and work experience abroad. After taking these two factors into account, international education turned out to be insignificant. When we added only the latter in the regression equation, we found positive, significant coefficients in all models for international education (results not shown here). We therefore can support hypothesis 2c.

Hypothesis 3c stated that firms with external sources of equity finance were expected to engage in international sales more rapidly than other firms. None of the models revealed significant positive effects of business angel or venture capitalist investment on the timing of foreign market entry. Note that venture capital was even negatively associated with rapid entry, albeit at an insignificant level. Hypothesis 3c therefore has to be rejected. H4c hypothesised a curvilinear effect of technology intensity on the timing of international sales. This hypothesis can be accepted since we observe a significant curvilinear effect with the turning points of the function well within the observed range of values for this variable. This effect was identified in all models irrespective of the measure and specification.

To our surprise, the innovativeness of a product did have a weaker impact on the timing than on the other dimensions of internationalisation. Compared to the base case, only one category, "product incorporating novel technology developed externally", had was positively related to the timing of market entry. Furthermore, the hypothesis of a joint positive impact of more innovative technology could not be supported ($p<0.48$). We therefore do not find any support for hypothesis 5c in the unweighted models. Note, however, that these variables become significant in the weighted models (models VI and IX).

Like in the models on the probability of engaging in international sales (section 6.2.1.) the extent of required client-specific customisation was negatively related to early foreign market entry. The extent to which a product requires pre- and after-sales services during commercialisation, however, does not impact on the timing of first entry. We therefore accept H6c but have to reject H7c. Among the control variables, there are industry effects consistent with the other models. In essence, compared to the base case of software, firms from all other industries entered foreign markets quicker.

As a next step, we compared these results with the results from two slightly different specifications. In the first case, we chose a different base year as "entry" year for firms becoming at risk of internationalising. Instead of being "at risk" at the time of formation, we chose their first financial year as entry time. This specification is supposed to account for effects from those firms that do not generate any sales during their early years and exclusively focus on product development. In the second case, we chose a more conservative threshold to designate the "exit" of "failure" event. Here, we considered the time span to enter three different foreign markets. Both specifications resulted in almost identical estimators thus supporting the stability of the observed effects.

Finally, we assessed the impact that our sampling strategy had on the results by comparing the weighted and unweighted results. Here, in both the Cox and the Weibull models (model III and model VIII), the weighting had a consistent impact. In essence, the observed difference are the increase of statistical significance for innovativeness and external finance from business angels. The internationalisers among both software and the smallest firms, characterised their products as more innovative than their domestic counterparts, or, stated differently, the differences were more pronounced compared to the remaining firms from other industries and size classes. It does require a reconsideration of our judgement on hypothesis 5c, since the test of the significant positive joint effect of the three "innovativeness" dummy variables could not be supported in the unweighted models. Hypothesis 5c can therefore only be supported in the weighted models.

To conclude, the estimations of the factors influencing the timing of internationalisation produce very similar results to the Probit models on the differences between domestic and international start-ups. The main exception is the innovativeness of the products sold abroad. Since our chosen specifications of the Cox and Weibull regressions are somewhat similar to a binary choice model while having the advantage of accommodating censoring, the results paint a quite clear picture of the factors influencing the different dimensions of internationalisation. The next section will provide a summary discussion of the results of the various models to explain the first three dimensions - probability, degree and timing - of internationalisation.

6.2.4. Discussion: Differences Between International Start-ups and Domestic Start-ups, Degree of Internationalisation and Timing of Foreign Market Entry

Our findings indicate that the key variables that play a role in the internationalisation of start-ups in high-technology industries are international experience of the founders, technology intensity, the extent to which a product requires client-specific customisation and the degree of technological differentiation of the technology incorporated in a product. With the exception of the role of external equity finance and the commercialisation requirements of the exported products, all variables had, by and large, the expected effect on the observed outcomes. The analysis of the first three dimensions of internationalisation revealed a quite clear and consistent picture. This is quite remarkable because we used different econometric approaches to model these dimensions. The only area where the results depended substantially on the chosen method, or to be precise, on the analysis sample, was the estimation of the degree of internationalisation. The analysis revealed that none of the hypotheses could be supported when estimating the regression models on the sub-sample of international firms. Table 54 gives a summary overview of the hypothesised and identified relationships.

Table 54: Summary of Expected and Identified Relationships

Hypothesis	Expected Relation	Propensity to Internationalise	Degree of Internationalisation		Timing of Entry
			International Start-ups only	Total Sample	
Firm Size	+	+	not sig.	+	+
International Exp.	+	+	not sig.	+	+
External Equity	+	not sig.	not sig.	not sig. / +	unweighted: not sig. weighted: +
Technology Intensity	curvilinear	unweighted: curv. weighted: +, lin.	+ linear	curvilinear / linear	curvilinear
Newness of Technology	+	+	not sig.	+	unweighted: not sig. weighted: +
Customisation	-	-	not sig.	-	-
Cost of Commercialisation	-	unweighted: not sig. weighted: +	not sig.	not sig.	not sig.

The fact that we used a stratified random sampling approach rather than a random sampling approach to generate our data did not appear to invalidate our findings. The use of the weights lead to different results in only four instances (see table 54). In the majority of cases, these effects can be attributed to the software firms. Since their characteristics could not be picked up entirely by the industry dummy variables, their over-representation in the weighted models is responsible for the observed differences. In order to check the validity of our reasoning, we therefore performed several regressions on the software firms to model the decision to internationalise, the degree of internationalisation and the timing of internationalisation.[36] The results are displayed in appendix 6. They show that the significant positive effect of the cost of commercialisation on the decision to internationalise can be found among the software firms. Furthermore, the positive effect of the innovativeness of the technology on the timing is also to a large extent a result of the software firms. The remaining difference between weighted and unweighted model (positive effect of business angels on timing) can be attributed to the smaller firms.[37] Nevertheless, we cannot identify major differences between the weighted and unweighted models that would invalidate our conclusions.

Among the industry control variables, we found clear evidence that firms from the manufacturing sector are more likely to internationalise than their software counterparts. A further control variable, age, also had a strong effect on the probability of international sales and the degree of non-domestic revenues. This does actually lend support to the propositions of the internationalisation process

---

[36] An alternative approach would have been to model an interaction term between software and those variables where differences between the weighted and unweighted model appear. As this requires knowledge of the differences, it is – in the absence of well-founded hypotheses - not a suitable approach for hypothesis testing.

[37] Note also that R&D intensity becomes insignificant in each of the subsample regressions in appendix 6. This suggests that R&D intensity does not discriminate between the different dimensions of internationalisation among the software firms. We therefore performed a Probit model on the subsample of all manufacturing firms and compared the test statistics with the Probit model on the total sample. Here, the inclusion of the software actually lead to an *improvement* of the test statistics such as the classification ratio (from 74% to 77% in the case of the decision to internationalise), which is the opposite of what one would expect if the model loses power on the software firms. A more plausible explanation is therefore, that the software firms are a too heterogeneous group. This is caused by the fact the industrial classification systems used by OECD countries do not allow for a more accurate classifications other than "computer-related services". A sizeable, yet unknown proportion of these firms seems to behave more like the relatively homogeneous manufacturing firms. These may well be the firms that sell standardised software packages. The remaining firms, such as contract programmers and software consultants could be responsible for the variation in the model results. Unfortunately, we can only speculate on these groups, as our dataset does not allow us to explore these differences further. Additional research on software firms should therefore develop criteria to divide this heterogeneous group of firms into more homogeneous sub-groups.

theory (Johanson and Vahlne, 1977; 1990) which argues that the degree of internationalisation of a firms is actually increasing over time irrespective of whether strategic decisions in that direction are made.

Table 55: Effect of Different Measures of Firm Size on Dependent Variables

Measurement of Size	Differences between Domestic and International Firms	Degree of Internationalisation (OLS / Tobit, all firms)	Timing of Internationalisation
Start-up			
Employees (absolute)	positive	positive *	positive
Employees (log)	positive	positive	positive
Sales (absolute)	not significant, pos.	not significant, pos.	positive
Sales (log)	positive	positive	positive
Index of abs. values	positive *	positive *	positive
Index of log values	positive	positive	positive
Today			
Employees (absolute)	not significant, pos.	positive *	not significant, pos.
Employees (log)	not significant, pos.	positive *	not significant, pos.
Sales (absolute)	not significant, pos.	positive	positive
Sales (log)	positive	positive	positive
Index of abs. values	positive	positive	positive *
Index of log values	positive	positive	positive

* marginally significant at p<0.15

The impact of several variables on the internationalisation of high-technology start-ups requires further consideration. In order to explore the role of firm size, we ran a series of regressions that used different measures of firm size. Table 55 summarised the role of size in the different models. The table shows that in all regression models, the various measures of firm size had a positive impact on the dependent variables. However, not all measures of size, especially when using absolute values, were related to the various dependent variables at a statistically significant level. Note also that one cannot make inferences about a causal relationship when considering the effect of size measured at the time of the survey. Nonetheless, the results are displayed here because they paint a consistent picture, irrespective of whether start-up size or size today is used. Furthermore, in each of the regression model, the use of different measures for size does not impact on the stability of the effects of the other variables.

As already mentioned, for the models presented in the previous sections, we constructed an index out of the logarithms of employment (in full-time equivalents) and annual sales. We chose to do so because in all regression models using the index constructed out of the log values, we obtain significant results and consistently better test statistics. We therefore concluded that the log transformations resulted in a better fit of our models to the data. [38] The effect of firm size should be interpreted as follows. For the smallest firms, a marginal increase in size leads to significantly higher propensity to engage in international sales, to a higher share of non-domestic revenue and to an earlier entry into foreign markets. However, the positive effect of firm size decreases the larger the firms gets. These results therefore suggest that international activities require a certain minimal scale. Beyond that threshold, additional size differentials do not contribute to explaining the phenomenon of internationalisation. Having said that, plots of the effects of firm size on the three dimensions of internationalisation suggest that this minimal scale is quite low and is actually overcome by the average firm in our sample. For example, based on the log values for size today, the Probit models on the decision to internationalise predict an incremental positive internationalisation probability from 9.4 employees onwards. Note that this value is below the sample median of 12 employees. These findings corroborate the results of Calof (1995) who found that – while being statistically significant – size did not explain a lot of the variation in international activities. While this is not a direct contradiction of internationalisation process theory, it does indicate that scale-related barriers to international sales can be overcome quite easily.

The explanation why small size is not an important barrier to internationalisation for some start-ups could be related to their particular resource endowment. Resource-based approaches argue that organisational outcomes are determined by their resource endowment and accumulated skills. Accordingly, scholars have argued that the international experience of the founders should be given attention when analysing the phenomenon of international entrepreneurship (McDougall, Shane and Oviatt 1994; Oviatt and McDougall 1994). The models presented here confirm the results from studies on international new ventures that identified the international experience of the entrepreneur as key variable (Jolly, Alahuhta and Jeannet1991; McDougall, Shane & Oviatt 1994; Murray 1994; Bloodgood, Almeida and Sapienza 1996; Reuber and Fischer 1997). All three measures of international experience, work experience abroad, work experience in the UK for an internationally operating firm and international education, were positively related to the dimensions of internationalisation at a significant level. [39] Due to the level of collinearity between these variables, their joint inclusion in the models

---

[38] An alternative approach would be to divide the firms up into different size classes and generate dummy variables. When choosing that approach, we produced consistent results.

[39] The exception is the sub-sample OLS model to determine the share of non-domestic revenue.

causes international education to become insignificant in all cases. All variables are significantly correlated between each other at p<0.01. However, they cannot be transformed into a single scale to measure "international experience" as, despite their correlation, they represent quite different aspects of this construct. Accordingly, the alpha score of 0.48 for the hypothetical summary scale is too low to recommend the creation of a single item. Taken individually, though, all three measures are significant. Our results therefore show that international experience does not necessarily have to come from living or working abroad. Work experience in the UK for an internationally operating country turned out to be the strongest predictor among the three operationalisations. The exposure to foreign operations during previous employment is thus likely to lower the psychic barriers to international expansion. Probably, this variable does, in many cases, also comprise the managerial experience of the founder.

An additional variable grounded in resource-based approaches is the degree of technological differentiation of the products. We argued earlier that the degree of differentiation is likely to increase with the newness of the technology incorporated in the products. Our results lend support to the assertion that international new ventures exploit leading edge technology (Jolly, Alahuhta and Jeannet 1991; Boter and Holmquist 1996; Murray 1996). The newness of the technology incorporated in the products turned out to be a significant predictor of international activities. While there is no difference in the timing of market entry, firms whose products incorporate newer technology will have a higher chance of eventually entering foreign markets. Subsequently, they are also likely to achieve higher levels of foreign sales than firms that export products incorporating less advanced technology. An important qualifying remark is warranted here. The analysis of the individual variables revealed that the dummy variable for the most advanced technology category was insignificant in the majority of models. This could indicate a problem related to international technology transfer, such as user acceptance of a new solution. This is a considerable obstacle in domestic transactions (Roberts 1991), but could be amplified in the cross-border setting for two reasons. First, from a buyer's point of view, the firm in question is an unknown start-up without a proven track-record. Second, the manufacturer of the product is a foreign firm, which from a buyer's point of view, raises questions of reliability and product support. The mechanisms of how start-ups overcome these barriers in an international setting should therefore become an area for future research in international entrepreneurship. The analysis of the chosen entry modes in the next section should also shed further light into this apparent dilemma.

Our third proxy variable to operationalise resource-based approaches, the presence of business angel and venture capital finance, did not have a significant effect in most of the models. This result came as a surprise since both variables do not only capture the influx of financial resources but also the value-added through strategic advice and access to complimentary business contacts. There is an obvious a priori explanation for the lack of explanatory power of these variables. Some high-technology start-ups with external equity exclusively focus on product development for a number of years. These firms received external funds to perform resource intensive development activities with uncertain outcomes and do not, in the absence of a commercial product, devote substantial management time and resources to international expansion during their early years. Yet, we expected this effect to be picked up by the curvilinear modelling of technology intensity. To our surprise, this was not the case. Still, while the curvilinear modelling did not impact on the significance level of external equity finance, it has the potential to explain why previous findings on the relationship between technology intensity and international activities have been inconclusive (for example Cooper and Kleinschmidt 1985; Lindqvist 1991; Fujita 1995a). In essence, our results show that up to a certain point, technology intensity is positively related to the three dimensions of internationalisation.[40] However, beyond that level, technology intensity will start to impact negatively on internationalisation as it draws on too many critical resources. This effect is apparent from the majority of models irrespective of the measure. Not surprisingly, however, the curvilinear effect becomes most clear when we chose the share of R&D employees as operationalisation of technology intensity.

The importance of customisation as a barrier to internationalisation echoes findings of studies that examined product characteristics of international start-ups (Murray 1996; Lindell & Karagozoglu 1997; Roberts & Senturia 1997). From a theoretical point of view, the role of customisation is more difficult to untangle. On the one hand, one can argue from a transaction cost point of view and identify high customisation requirements as a condition that gives rise to transaction costs during commercialisation. Conversely, one can adopt a resource-based perspective and argue that the capability to offer standardised products is a precondition for growth and expansion (Roberts 1991). We are inclined to follow Roberts who persuasively argues that substantial R&D investments are required to turn a bespoke concept into "shrink-wrap" standardised products. This reasoning receives some support by looking at the significant, negative correlation between our variables that capture technology intensity and customisation (r=-0.1247 for R&D expenditures, r=-0.1494 for R&D employees; both are significant at p<0.05). Whatever line of argument one adopts, client-specific customisation is clearly negatively related to the probability of engaging in international sales, the degree of non-domestic revenues and the timing of foreign market entry.

Our final set of hypotheses concerned the role of the cost of commercialisation. Here, we could not support the notion that the cost of commercialisation represent important barriers to cross-border relationships. It could be explained if one recalls that the preferred entry mode of the firms in our sample is the use of foreign distributors (42%). This is in contrast with studies which report that the preferred

---

[40] In our models, the observed turning points lie between 50% (probability to internationalise, model I) and 100% (degree of internationalisation, models V and VI).

entry mode of smaller firms is direct exporting (Bamberger and Evers 1994), thus indicating that start-ups in high-tech industry adopt different distribution channels compared to more traditional small firms. Furthermore, these findings do lend support to recent theorising on the use of collaborative market entry modes in knowledge-intensive industries when the motivations of the entrant are influenced by gaining access to complementary capabilities and skills in the target country (Madhok 1997). Given the relative unimportance of size and transaction cost characteristics other than customisation as explanators of international activities, we would argue that even the smallest firm and youngest firms are capable of selling their products abroad if their decision is matched with the appropriate entry mode. Our final area of analysis will therefore examine the determinants of the entry mode choice.

6.3. The Choice of Market Entry Mode

6.3.1. Model Estimation

We will now proceed to analyse the determinants of our fourth dimension of internationalisation, the choice of entry mode. To test our hypotheses, we estimated six Probit models with the entry mode (1=distributor, 0=direct export) as dependent variable. These two entry modes capture 78% of the observed entry modes in our sample (see also section 5.3.3.). We report the marginal parameter coefficients of the models in order to compare the magnitude of the effects of the different variables. We estimated our principal model using firm size at start-up (model I). In model II, we use firm size at the time of the survey as a measure. Model III is identical to model I but is calculated using the weights. In model IV to VI, we explore the stability of our results with different model specifications. Model IV excludes the variable "domestic sales mode" in order to avoid possible endogeneity problems. In model V, only those entry modes enter the analysis that account for at least 10% of total sales of the start-up. Finally, in model VI, we exclude those entry decisions that have been subject to changes over time in order account for the influence of firm-specific learning effects that cannot be captured with available data. Models I to III are displayed in table 56, models IV to VI in table 57.

Table 56: Probit Model of the Entry Mode Decision
- Direct Exporting vs. Distributors –

1=Distributor, 0 = Exporting Variable	Model I Coefficients start-up size		Model II Coefficients size today		Model III Coefficients weighted	
Firm Size (index of log values at start-up)	0.0842	**			0.1146	***
Firm Size (index of log values today)			0.0911	***		
Company Experience with Int. Activities	0.0000		-0.0074		0.0063	
Work Experience in UK for Multinational	-0.0440		-0.0315		-0.0046	
International Work Experience	-0.0669		-0.1018	±	-0.0437	
International Education	0.0146		0.0181		-0.0438	
Domestic Sales Mode: Distributor	0.3844	****	0.3703	****	0.2942	****
R&D Intensity (% of expenditures)	-0.2693	*	-0.2746	*	-0.0646	
New Combinations of Existing Technology	0.1223	±	0.1490	*	0.0865	
Novel Technology Developed Externally	0.3287	***	0.3182	***	0.3547	****
Novel Technology Developed Internally	0.2109	**	0.1997	**	0.2720	***
Customisation Requirement	-0.0600	***	-0.0682	****	-0.0891	****
Commercialisation Cost	-0.0006		-0.0123		-0.0148	
Industry: IT/Com Hardware	0.1504	*	0.1340	±	0.1629	**
Industry: Engineering	0.2069	**	0.1882	*	0.2286	****
Industry: Life Sciences	0.4546	****	0.4554	****	0.5078	****
Industry: Other	0.0647		0.0545		0.1993	**
Country GDP (in absolute terms)	-0.0050	***	-0.0048	***	-0.0053	***
Country Risk	0.0014		0.0013		-0.0002	
No. of Observations	396		398		396	
Log Likelihood	-219.09		-219.28		-216.12	
Chi-square (df):	107.14(18)		109.93 (18)		114.46 (18)	
Pseudo-R²:	0.1965		0.2004		0.2094	
Correct classifications (in %):	73.99		71.36		71.97	
Maximum Chance Criterion (in %):	54.80		54.52		54.80	

Note: The reference category is a software firm selling products that incorporate "tried and tested" technology. The table shows marginal parameter estimates.
**** significant at p<0.001, *** significant at p<0.01, ** significant at p<0.05,
* significant at p<0.10, ± significant at p<0.15 (two-tailed tests)

Table 57: Probit Model of the Entry Mode Decision
- Direct Exporting vs. Distributors -

1=Distributor, 0 = Exporting Variable	Model IV Coefficients without domestic sales mode		Model V Coefficients entries contributing at least 10% of sales		Model VI Coefficients entry modes that have not changed	
Firm Size (index of log values at start-up)	0.0609	*	0.0447		0.1396	****
Company Experience with Int. Activities	0.0003		-0.0215		0.0117	
Work Experience in UK for Multinational	0.0091		-0.1116	±	-0.0521	
International Work Experience	-0.0940	±	-0.0774		-0.0606	
International Education	-0.0047		0.0899		-0.0175	
Domestic Sales Mode: Distributor			0.3573	****	0.4868	****
R&D Intensity (% of expenditures)	-0.2621	*	-0.3110	±	-0.1728	
New Combinations of Existing Technology	0.1438	*	0.0830		0.0695	
Novel Technology Developed Externally	0.2370	**	0.2539	**	0.3745	****
Novel Technology Developed Internally	0.1384	±	0.1812	*	0.1998	**
Customisation Requirement	-0.0832	****	-0.0532	**	-0.0426	*
Commercialisation Cost	0.0374		0.0367		-0.0071	
Industry: IT/Com Hardware	0.1925	**	0.0802		0.1243	
Industry: Engineering	0.1994	**	0.1495		0.2188	**
Industry: Life Sciences	0.4408	****	0.4383	****	0.4770	****
Industry: Other	0.1872	*	-0.0273		0.0283	
Country GDP (in absolute terms)	-0.0042	**	-0.0051	***	-0.0034	*
Country Risk	-0.0005		0.0015		0.0016	
No. of Observations	397		295		337	
Log Likelihood	-237.18		-168.18		-184.29	
Chi-square (df):	72.54	****	72.44 (18)	****	98.57 (18)	
Pseudo-R^2:	0.1326		0.1772		0.2110	
Correct classifications (in %):	69.52		70.71		70.45	
Maximum Chance Criterion (in %):	54.66		50.84		50.45	

Note: The reference category is a software firm selling products that incorporate "tried and tested" technology. The table shows marginal parameter estimates.
**** significant at p<0.001, *** significant at p<0.01, ** significant at p<0.05,
* significant at p<0.10, ± significant at p<0.15 (two-tailed tests)

6.3.2. Results

All model solutions are statistically significant at $p<0.0001$. Among the 396 entry mode choices for which all variables were completed, 217 (55%) firms chose distributors, 179 (45%) firms chose to export directly. The classification ratios suggests that the predictive ability of the estimated models represents a substantial improvement over the maximum chance criterion. The results of the models are very similar. In all models (except model V, see below), the measure of size is positively related to the use of distributors and the effects are highly significant in the statistical sense. This effect was observable irrespective of whether size at start-up or today (model II) was entered in the regression equation. However, when looking at the marginal effects, the real impact of size on the choice of entry mode is quite small. Nonetheless, H9 can be accepted. The direct international experience of the firm at the time of the market entry is not significantly related to the choice of a particular sales mode in any of the models. H10 therefore cannot be accepted. We then looked at the founders' international experience as a surrogate of direct international experience of the firm. As opposed to the hypothesised positive effect, the parameter coefficients turned out to be negative, albeit not always significant. Hypothesis 11 therefore has to be rejected.

Hypothesis 12 was supported. Firms that used distributors domestically also had a higher propensity to use intermediaries for their international sales in all models. A comparison of the marginal effects also shows that this variable had one of the strongest effect among all dummy variables included in the models. H13, following the organisational capability perspective, stated that the products of firms that export directly incorporated newer technologies than those, which entered foreign markets via intermediaries. This hypothesis has to be rejected. Compared to the base case of a product incorporating tried and tested combinations of existing technology, more advanced technology tends to be sold via intermediaries. This effect could be found in all models. H13 therefore has to be rejected.

The models support H14. Products that require extensive customisation are less likely to be sold internationally through intermediaries. H15 cannot be accepted. The measures used to operationalise the costs of commercialisation did not have statistically significant impact on the decision to involve intermediaries in the sales process.

The strength of the industry control variables depended on the model specification. The strongest and most consistent effect was found among the life sciences firms. All other things being equal, life sciences firms rely much more on intermediaries to sell their products abroad when compared to the base case of software. The effects for IT/Com hardware and engineering supported in most models the notion that these firms are more likely to sell via distributors. The entry modes of firms classified as "other" did not differ from software firms in most of the models. Technology intensity was used as a control variable and resulted in a significant negative effect in four of the six models. Accordingly, firms that have higher R&D expenditures have a lower propensity to sell via distributors. However, as the size of the marginal effect in table 56 indicates, firm differences of at least one order of magnitude need to be present in order to have a substantial impact. Finally, among the country variables, only the absolute market size appears to have a significant impact on the entry mode decision. The size of a national market thus seems to be positively related with the propensity to use distributors. The estimates for country risk did not have a statistically significant effect within the model.[41]

In order to examine the validity of our findings, we tested three additional models. A possible danger of the specifications chosen for the models I to III is that they include the domestic sales mode of the start-ups. While we argue that this variable captures at the same time the notions of domestic learning and path dependency advocated by the organisational capability perspective, we accept the criticism that it could be endogenous to the regression model, i.e. it could be determined to a large extent by the other variables in the regression equation. In order to assess the impact of endogeneity on our parameter estimates, we therefore specified a Probit model excluding the domestic sales mode. Model IV reveals that the exclusion of this variable does not invalidate the results of model I. Note, however, that the levels of significance decrease slightly in model IV.

We make a further modification in model V. In this model, we include only those entry modes that represent at least 10% of the total turnover of the firm. Our initial results could be biased due to the inclusion of reactive, unsolicited foreign sales that are not a result of firm-specific factors or managerial action. Choosing a relatively high threshold of 10% should lead to the exclusion of the majority of these cases. Model V produces similar results than the other models, with the exception of the industry dummy variables (except life sciences) and firm size losing their significance. This result indicates that smaller firms are more likely to have unsolicited ad-hoc foreign sales which are carried out mainly through exporting. When these cases are removed from the analysis, firm size ceases to be a predictor for the use of more complex sales arrangements.

A related modification has been made in model VI. Some of the market entries included in models I to V have been subject to changes over time. Accordingly, the current entry mode could be a result of learning effects over time rather than reflecting actual differences in firm or product characteristics. Model VI therefore only includes those entry modes that have not been subject to changes over time. Despite this change, the effects are similar to those reported in model I.

Finally, we estimated a weighted model in order to assess the effect of the sampling strategy. The comparison between model I and III revealed that the main

---

[41] As the two control variables country risk and GPD per capita where highly correlated (r=0.93), we included only country risk in the regression equations.

differences concern the control variables. Industry effects became stronger, thus indicating that software firms had a stronger preference for exporting as foreign sales mode. Furthermore, the R&D intensity control became insignificant. Table 58 gives an overview of the hypothesised and identified relationships.

Table 58: Summary of Hypothesised and Identified Relationships between Independent Variables and the Choice of Foreign Distributors

Hypothesis	Hypothesis	Expected Relation	Entry Mode
Firm Size	H9	+	+
Firm International Experience	H10	+	not significant
Founders' International Experience	H11	+	not significant
Domestic Sales Mode	H12	+	+
Newness of Technology	H13	-	+
Customisation	H14	-	-
Cost of Commercialisation	H15	+	not significant

6.3.3. Discussion

Looking at the sample average, firms did engage in entry modes that were not very resource intensive. But among these low-resource entry modes, the use of intermediaries was more prevalent than direct exporting. Arguably, selling via distributors represents a more complex and advanced managerial arrangement due to the requirement to find, train, incentivise and monitor a third party. We therefore expected, all other things being equal, the use of foreign intermediaries to be more prevalent among more experienced and larger firms. As hypothesised, we found a positive effect of firm size on the propensity to sell via intermediaries. However, an analysis of the marginal effect reveals that - similarly to the statistically significant but weak effect of R&D intensity - the real impact of that variable is quite small. All other things being equal, firm differences of at least one order of magnitude need to be present in order to have a substantial impact on the choice of entry mode. Furthermore, when we chose a more conservative threshold for the inclusion of an entry mode in order to account for unsolicited sales (model V), size ceased to have a explanatory power in the regression model. These results undermine the role of firm size for determining entry mode choices of international start-ups.

The results with regard to experience turned out to be contrary to our hypotheses. Direct firm experience did not have a significant impact on the commitment of the chosen entry mode. As extensive experience with foreign operations cannot automatically be expected among *young* firms initiating their *first* foreign sales, we also tested for international experience, a substitute for direct company experience. This variable did have a significant impact on the choice of entry mode, albeit *not* in the hypothesised direction. This suggests that managers that have lived abroad are actually more likely to sell internationally without the assistance of intermediaries. A possible interpretation of this finding is that internationally experienced managers do not need to rely on the local market knowledge of a distributor in order to commercialise their products abroad. We conclude from these findings that, as far as the high-tech start-ups of our sample are concerned, experiential knowledge, the key variable in the internationalisation process theory (Andersen 1997), is of limited value to explain the entry mode choices of the firms in our sample. This echoes the findings of other researchers (see for example Bell 1995). However, our findings could also provide further evidence for those researchers who claimed that these two different entry modes do not represent distinct levels of commitment determined by past experience but rather result from product- and firm-specific considerations (Andersen 1993; Leonidou and Katsikeas 1996).

In the case of start-ups, the choice of foreign entry modes may therefore represent a compromise between the resources of the start-up and the support requirements of their products and customers. As hypothesised, our results indicate that a high degree of required customisation led to the exclusion of intermediaries during the sales process. Products that require client-specific changes are more likely to be sold directly by the manufacturer. We argue that this is the case because the expertise, skills and tacit knowledge required to adapt a product according to customers' specifications are more likely to reside within the manufacturer and not the intermediary. We further hypothesised that start-ups whose products require extensive pre- and after sales support will be more likely to sell via distributors. However, this hypothesis could not be supported as the level of required support did not affect the choice of entry mode significantly. We would like to offer the following interpretation for this result. The effects of the variables 'customisation' (H14) and 'after-sales support' (H15) are somewhat related which is also manifest in the significant positive correlation between the two. From the distributor's point of view, they both incorporate the notion of having to acquire certain skills in order to guarantee the effective commercialisation of a manufacturer's product. All other things being equal, they should both act as a barrier to the involvement of intermediaries during the sales process. From the point of view of a manufacturer who wants to serve foreign markets, however, the use of a local distributor may be the only practicable way of providing the necessary infrastructure for installation, maintenance, upgrading and/or training of end-users. We tried to decompose this dilemma and argued that highly customised products are more likely to be sold by manufacturers directly because of their familiarity with their core technology. For a distributor, the costs of acquiring those specialised technological skills may be prohibitive and economically irrational. In contrast, the costs of learning how to perform the more standardised tasks of installation, end-user training and maintenance are likely to be much lower because of scale and scope effects, particularly when the distributor has already has a portfolio of related products in place. Therefore, selling a product whose commercialisation requires high levels of support through intermediaries might be less of a barrier. The fact that the two variables have different effects in the regression, though not as clear-cut as expected, on the use of intermediaries (significant negative in the case of customisation vs. insignificant positive for sales support) is therefore an interesting result in itself which goes a certain way to support our reasoning. It suggests that customisation represents a barrier to the involvement of intermediaries whereas the pre- and after sales requirements can be sub-contracted by the start-ups and may even become a source of profit for their distributors.

The newness of the technology incorporated did have a significant impact on the choice of the entry mode, albeit in the opposite direction than we hypothesised. Compared to the base case of mature and tested technologies, transactions involving products that incorporated more innovative technology (and hence a higher degree of tacit knowledge according to the organisational capability theorists) had a higher chance of being dealt with through collaborative arrangements rather than being exported. While this indicates the international market entry forms are actually influenced by product specific factors, the effects derived from our sample of high-tech start-ups directly contradict the theoretical prescriptions and findings on technology transfer modes of larger firms (Davidson and McFetridge 1985). However, they do corroborate the recent findings of Robertson and Gatignon (1998) which report that firms that experienced higher technology uncertainties were more likely to engage in alliances. This result merits further consideration. First, newer technology may not always be more difficult to comprehend, especially if the distributor already has related products in his portfolio. Second, in the absence of resources to build up a wholly owned subsidiary, a distributor may be the only vehicle to a get a product into a local market. Firms may perceive the performance penalty of sharing the margin worth paying if the target market is too distant for the effective provision of back-up services and if there are few growth opportunities in their domestic market. Third, it points out towards a dilemma that especially young firms without an established track record face. The much quoted concept of "liability of newness" posits that young firms face disadvantages as stable relations with clients are not yet established (Stinchcombe 1965; Hannan and Freeman 1984; Brüderl and Schüssler 1990). In cross-border business, relationships this may well result into what we call the "liability of alienness". Buying from an unknown foreign supplier is a risk, especially in such critical areas such as medical technology. Despite the fact that distributors are considered as sub-optimal choices according to the OC and TCE reasoning, it may well be that an established distributor is seen as a mechanism to overcome this liability of alienness and to gain legitimacy in cross-border business relationships.

Our strongest predictor of the respective foreign entry modes was the domestic sales mode. The effect of this variable can be explained in two ways. First, it is a proxy for different strategic and structural influence factors that impact on sales channel choice irrespective of the setting. This variable therefore partly accounts for unobservable effects whose determination was not among the objectives of the study. Second, the explanatory effect of this variable is arguably due to the presence of embedded routines and experiences with the domestic sales mode. This finding does therefore corroborate theoretical propositions that stress the importance of firm-specific routines and the path dependence of organisational outcomes (Madhok 1997). However, further research should use a more refined measure in order to determine to which extent foreign entry decisions are a result of path dependency or company marketing strategy.

7. Conclusions

We started this research by pointing out that there is a dearth of empirical evidence on the extent of international activities among technology-based start-ups. We then reviewed empirical knowledge in the area of international entrepreneurship and examined different theoretical frameworks that could explain the international activities of start-up firms. Unlike other authors (McDougall, Shane and Oviatt 1994; Knight and Cavusgil 1996), we argued that their widespread international operations per se are not inconsistent with the literature of in the field of international business. In the theoretical part of the literature review, we showed that the various aspects of cross-border expansions of entrepreneurial firms can be accommodated quite well within the existing frameworks. We argued further that the question whether existing theories are applicable to the phenomenon could only be answered after a systematic survey of the international activities of start-ups within a clearly defined setting. This allowed us to respond to three major weaknesses in international entrepreneurship research. First, with a few exceptions, the propositions of the exploratory, case-based research have not been subject to empirical testing. Secondly, the quantitative studies paid comparatively little attention to studying the core dimensions of internationalisation, such as degree of internationalisation, timing of market entry and choice of market entry mode. Thirdly, and most importantly, the majority of empirical studies studying the phenomenon did not include a control group of non-internationalisers. This is understandable as most of these studies were exploratory in focus. Yet, for the field of international entrepreneurship to move on, rigorous testing of the claims of previous contributions is required. The present research therefore comes at a timely moment for an empirical test and to suggest avenues for further research. We will now assess our findings and the applicability of different frameworks.

7.1. Implications for the Field of International Entrepreneurship

The project has provided evidence that international activities are much more prevalent among British start-ups than previously thought. Our population estimates suggest that 60% of British high-tech start-ups (67% of the sample) were selling across borders. On average, they entered foreign markets two years after inception. Today they operate in 10 different markets and generate nearly 40% of their revenues from foreign sales. To our knowledge, this is the first study that systematically attempts to assess the prevalence of international activities among high-technology start-ups in a particular country. We believe that our data is quite representative of the British situation since our descriptive results with regard to basic firm characteristics and international activities are similar to the results of a recent exploratory British study that looked at the international activities of high-technology start-ups in the Oxford and Cambridge region (Keeble et al.1998). To our knowledge, this is the most comprehensive survey undertaken so far in the field of international entrepreneurship and the first attempt to systematically establish the prevalence of this phenomenon in a particular country.

When we looked at our data, we could confirm several propositions derived from a review of the empirical, case-based literature in international entrepreneurship and the theoretical literature. Above all, we confirmed that firm size is of limited power to explain the four dimensions of internationalisation (Lindqvist 1991; McDougall, Shane and Oviatt 1994; Calof 1994). While the findings regarding firm size were statistically significant, they indicate that if there are scale-related barriers to internationalisation, they can be overcome quite easily. In fact, the average firm in our sample is well above the required threshold size suggested by our models. One mechanism to overcome scale-related disadvantages could be related to the skills and capabilities of the entrepreneurial team. Here, we found that international experience of the management team of the start-up had a consistent positive impact on the propensity to internationalise, the timing of internationalisation and the share of non-domestic revenues. However, it was not related to the choice of market entry mode. We thus corroborated earlier results (Jolly, Alahuhta and Jeannet 1991; McDougall, Shane and Oviatt 1994; Bloodgood, Almeida and Sapienza 1996; Murray 1996; Reuber and Fischer 1997) but also showed that international experience does not necessarily have to come from direct living, work or education experience. International exposure while working in the UK turned out the best predictor among the different variables measuring international experience. Our results also support the work of researchers who showed that the international start-ups in their sample produced highly innovative products (Jolly, Alahuhta and Jeannet 1991; Boter and Holmquist 1996; Murray 1996). Accordingly, internationalisation is positively affected by the degree of technological differentiation of a product. While this variable did not lead to an earlier market entry, it eventually lead to a higher probability of starting international sales over time. Furthermore, our results support the notion that client-specific customisation affects international activities in a negative way (Jolly, Alahuhta and Jeannet 1991; Murray 1996; Roberts and Senturia 1996). This is to be expected in high-technology industries as customisation frequently requires skills and capabilities close to the technological core of the product (Roberts 1991). These skills are less likely to be resident within the workforce of intermediaries such as distributors. This is not to say that firms that sell highly specialised, customised cannot or should not attempt to internationalise. However, customisation represents a considerable barrier for building up extensive international activities. In summary, firms were more likely to engage in international activities and achieve a higher share of non-domestic revenues if they offer innovative, standardised products.

In addition, we identified strong industry effects which suggest that industry-specific factors such as competition intensity and geographical location of lead markets also play a substantial role in the internationalisation process (Boter and Holmquist 1996; Murray 1996). The life sciences firms in particular scored very high on all dimensions of internationalisation which probably reflects the importance of the US as global lead market in health care. However, a further industry group merits consideration. Our multivariate results reveal that there are quite distinct differences between software firms and the remaining firms. Yet, the extent to which software firms are a homogeneous industry group is questionable, as the firms may range from small contract programmers to larger firms selling standardised packages. The strategy and structure profiles of these firms are probably quite different and it seems obvious that these should result in different internationalisation pattern. Unfortunately, in the absence of a better classification scheme of these firms, we can only speculate about the nature of these differences.

Overall, the research project therefore does lend support to previous empirical work in the field of international entrepreneurship. Furthermore, it improves the validity of previous findings since our results are stable in the presence of a control group of non-internationalisers.

7.2. Theoretical Implications

The question that now arises is how these results can inform internationalisation theory. On an aggregate level, we do find some support for the *internationalisation process* perspective. When considering a regional breakdown, we realised that the majority of start-ups with international activities entered Western European markets first. When looking at individual countries, however, we found that the United States were the most important target market. In any case, the notion that firms have a preference for entering psychologically close countries can therefore be supported. Nonetheless, the importance of the US as target country suggests that market size rather than psychic distance is the key factor determining the geographical pattern of market entries. When looking at structural aspects of market entry, we found that, on average, start-ups engage in low commitment entry modes. Furthermore, changes of entry modes reflect increasing commitment over time instead of decreasing commitment. However, a sizeable proportion of start-ups entered distant foreign markets first or chose resource-intensive entry modes for their initial international expansion. This finding sits uneasily within the expectations of the process model. In addition, we find only partial support for the role of international experience at an organisational level in explaining internationalisation. Organisational experience had a positive impact on explaining the share of non-domestic revenue but did not influence the choice of entry mode. Note, however, that this is not a proper test of process theory since we do not dispose of a longitudinal dataset and the in-depth information on the extent to which decision making in the internationalisation process is influenced by past experience. Still, our results are at odds with the assertion of process models that see experience as key variable. Furthermore, internationalisation process theory claims an accelerated outward expansion process will be observable among larger firms. While we do find evidence for the significant influence of size on the dimensions of internationalisation, the modelling reveals that the actual impact of firm size is quite limited. Scale related barriers, if at all present, appear to be at such a low level that they can easily be overcome, even by a small start-up. our results therefore only partially support the implications of internationalisation process theory.

We come to a similar assessment when looking at *transaction cost* approaches. While they have in the past been applied successfully to the analysis of entry modes of large firms, their implications in the present setting are inconclusive. In our case, the firms that avoid collaborative arrangements - presumably to avoid the associated governance costs – are slightly smaller and sell less innovative, more customised products. It is reasonable to argue that, due to the customisation requirements, these firms face higher governance costs and sales related transaction costs. But should the ability to offer innovative, standardised, off-the-shelf products be seen as a transaction cost minimising device or as an organisational capability to generate rents? Depending on the theoretical stance that one chooses, one can argue both.

In order to avoid these ambiguities, we followed those researchers that recommended the direct measurement of transaction costs (Klein, Frazier and Roth 1990). We decided to ask our respondents to appraise a series of direct measures of transaction costs occurring during the commercialisation process. Here, we found that in none of the models, our measure of costs had a significant impact on any of the dimensions of internationalisation. A possible explanation is that, since they feel they cannot avoid direct transaction costs, some start-ups accept a performance penalty rather than change their action. Yet, a test of this proposition would require data on firm performance which we do not have. The only way to find some support for the TCE logic is to argue that customisation is related to substantially higher transaction costs compared to installation, maintenance and training since it probably requires investment in skills closer to the technological core of the product. Accordingly, customisation turned out to be a substantial barrier to international sales whereas the direct costs of commercialisation didn't. Yet, one doesn't need the theoretical apparatus of transaction costs and its behavioural assumptions to come to that conclusion.

To conclude, we find only limited support for the propositions of transaction cost-based approaches. Firms effectively did not internalise all cross-border transactions of innovative products in spite of the traditional internalisation and transaction cost arguments. Furthermore, a direct operationalisation of transaction costs did not have the expected impact on internationalisation. Finally, the result that standardisation is positively related to internationalisation can be explained through the arguably less restrictive resource- and capability based approaches. This is not to say that firms should act in a way that is inconsistent with TCE. Yet, we would like to echo the opinions of other researchers who argued that there are superior approaches that do not require the analytical framework of TCE and its behavioural assumptions to reach identical conclusions (Goshal and Moran 1996; Madhok 1997).

We found the most consistent effects when we considered the operationalisations of those frameworks that emphasise the role of *firm-specific resources and capabilities* in explaining organisational outcomes. With the exception of external equity, all hypotheses that emphasised the role of imperfectly imitable, firm-specific factors received empirical support. The role of international experience of the founders as a substitute for organisational experience has been confirmed with regard to its positive impact on timing, degree and probability of international sales. We are also inclined to see low client-specific customisation requirements as an ability that facilitates the growth and internationalisation process rather than as a transaction cost minimising device (Roberts 1991).

Our variable that measured the newness of technology requires further discussion. Firms whose products incorporated more advanced technology had a higher chance of engaging in international sales and a higher share of non-domestic revenues in the models that looked at the entire sample. We argued that this was because buyers are more likely to buy from foreign firms when the latter offer innovative technology that indigenous competitors cannot supply. The innovativeness of the technology did, however, not lead to the expected results when looking at the determinants of entry modes. In essence, in accordance with the OC perspective, we argued that the transfer of skills required for the effective cross-border commercialisation is likely to be more difficult when the technology is more innovative. This, in turn, should have a positive impact on the use of direct export as entry mode. To our surprise, we realised that products incorporating more advanced technology were more likely to be sold through local intermediaries. We offered three different interpretations for this result. First, we suggested that the transfer of tacit knowledge during the commercialisation may not be difficult if a specialised distributor has already products that incorporate related technology in his portfolio. Second, distributors may be the only way to provide ongoing support in distant markets. Start-ups may have little choice but to accept lower margins in international sales if the demand in their home market is constrained. Third, distributors may be a mechanism to overcome what we called the "liability of alienness" of a foreign start-up. Since, according to the OC and TCE reasoning, collaborative arrangements are considered as sub-optimal operating modes for the cross-border commercialisation of innovative technology, both theoretical approaches should benefit from modifications in order to apply to the particular situation of new ventures. On second thought, it is therefore not surprising that our hypothesis of the impact of technology on the choice of entry mode could not be supported. Our interpretation is that transaction cost and OC logic do not include organisational legitimacy in their reasoning, which is of particular relevance to start-up companies.

7.3. Areas for Further Research

Our results suggests a number of avenues for further research. First, we pointed out repeatedly that our data does not allow us to examine performance related issues. Longitudinal data is required to analyse how differentials in international activities, such as the choice of entry mode, impact on organisational performance. Furthermore, when looking at the subsample of internationalisers, the variables that discriminate between domestic and international start-ups fail to explain their subsequent degree of internationalisation. Exploratory regressions showed that a proxy variable measuring the proactiveness of the firm had some explanatory power. As this is a very crude variable, future research should investigate more closer the strategy-performance relationship of international new ventures.

Second, further research into collaborative entry modes is warranted. In particular, the mechanisms by which a start-up can incentivise and monitor a foreign partner and collect the vital feedback from end-users merit further consideration. With the exception of the theoretical contribution of Zacharakis (1997), this area is largely unexplored within the context of international entrepreneurship. Further research can build on the extensive work by marketing scholars on the domestic manufacturer – supplier relationship (e.g. Heide and John 1994; Celly and Frazier 1996; Lassard and Kerr 1996). Besides the differences compared to the domestic distributor relationship, the situation faced by small start-ups that venture abroad is quite different compared to larger firm for reasons related to bargaining power (Zacharakis 1997). For growth oriented firms, collaborative relationships may well represent one avenue for successful mid-term expansion until sufficient resources to build up wholly owned facilities are available. In addition, if there is a liability of alienness, foreign partners could be the most effective mechanism to gain legitimacy in cross-border business relationships. To conclude, well functioning relationships with intermediaries could be a weaker form of what Oviatt and McDougall (1994) call innovative, hybrid organisational arrangements which they see as precondition for sustainable international entrepreneurship.

Third, our results suggests that the industry classification of software firms comprises a set of quite heterogeneous firms. Our analysis of the Dun & Bradstreet source data also showed that about 60% of the firms in Butchart industries belong to one the software classification ("computer-related services"). As mentioned in the methodology section, this is partly due to the fact that the standard industrial classification systems used in OECD countries fail to provide a more accurate breakdown of these firms. The multivariate analysis revealed a number of effects, partly uncovered after the weighting, that suggest that software firms, or a subgroup of software firms, behave in a quite distinct way compared to manufacturing firms. In the absence of a more accurate breakdown of these firms, it is difficult to explain the exact nature of these effects. We have the feeling that there are at least two distinct subgroups of software firms. On the one hand, there contract programmers and small developers which largely act as sub-contractors and offer highly bespoke products. On the other, there are those software firms that sell packaged solutions which the customer can individually tailor to his needs. Further research into software firms should shed light on those issues and attempt to develop additional classification criteria that can be easily operationalised in surveys.

7.4. Managerial Implications

Our research has identified a number of practicable implications for the managers of technology-based start-ups. We isolate several findings which we believe professional managers need to understand. First, those firms which sell a highly customised or bespoke product should be prepared to commit appropriate resources to their pre-sales and after-sales service strategy given their greater reliance on direct exports. In giving this advice, we are aware that our research findings show that firms appear to choose a mode of foreign market entry irrespective of the resource implications of the commercialisation process. Similarly, our findings also showed that the size or resource endowment of firms had a very weak, albeit statistically significant, effect on the choice of mode of market entry. In short, it does not appear that resource constraints prevent firms from choosing between the two discussed entry modes. Instead, managers should be aware that the choice is likely to be influenced by the degree of customisation of the product. Firms that seek to derive substantial revenues from international activities should therefore consider whether a high customisation / standardisation ratio impacts on their expansion plans.

Second, it appears that in getting a new, technologically advanced product into the market, start-ups with a necessarily limited record of achievement should collaborate in order to exploit the reputation of an established intermediary. The "liability of alienness" may result in situation where potential customers will not deal with an unknown foreign start-up given the uncertainties of determining the continued product support or even the very existence of the firm. The use of a trusted distributor and its existing sales force may frequently be the only effective way to sell products to professional customers, especially in sensitive areas such as medical technology. Distributors may also be essential for supplying widely dispersed customers in a large market like the USA. However, this issue is wider than just medical technology. It is relevant for all young firms without established track-records that initiate the commercialisation at international level of products or services used in 'mission critical' applications with costly implications for failure or non-performance.

Finally, if international expansion via distributors is perceived as an important strategic goal for the start-up, its managers have to be aware already at the product development stage that successful relationships with intermediaries frequently depend on the ability to transfer the required skills for product support. The potential of the products to generate future revenue streams for the distributor is likely to be a further key issues to consider. Those young firms wishing to use distributors in foreign markets can benefit from using collaborative relationships in their domestic market first. Learning effects in managing relationships with intermediaries may be more easily gained in the domestic market and at less cost. In certain circumstances this learning may also be less risky given, for example, easier communication and/or negligible psychic distance. Even for "born global" firms, market based experimentation in the domestic market may still have these advantages.

We would like to conclude this research project by getting back to the initial question of why Europe has not been able emulate the US success in technology-based entrepreneurship. Besides the familiar arguments that focus on the role of culture, finance and support infrastructures, we suggested an additional avenue of investigation. We argued that, due to the limited potential of their home markets, European high-tech start-ups that have the potential and determination to achieve growth trajectories comparable to their successful US counterparts, have to consider international expansion at inception. We also argued that this project can become the starting point for a longer term research agenda on the performance implications of internationalisation. International expansion, though arguably a more challenging path to growth, can be an opportunity for those firms that understand and are able to manage its resource implications. Our results provide ample support that despite small size and a limited resource-base, the majority of technology-based start-ups manages to *initiate* international sales. The present research lay the foundations for gathering a longitudinal dataset to address performance issues. Thus, we will hopefully be in a position to investigate whether the increased managerial complexity of internationalisation represents a barrier to *long-term* growth of European new, technology-based firms.

Appendix

Appendix 1: The Questionnaire

The Internationalisation of Young, Innovative Firms

A Study by Warwick Business School and the Zentrum für Europäische Wirtschaftsforschung

Company Profile

1. **Please state the year of formation (first legal incorporation) of your company:** 19 ____

    Please note: Third parties will NOT be given access to individual company data. Data will be analysed anonymously and used for research purposes only.

2. **Was your company founded as:**
   - ☐ Independent new firm
   - ☐ Management buy-out
   - ☐ Management buy-in
   - ☐ Subsidiary of another firm
   - ☐ De-merger or spin-out from an existing firm
   - ☐ Other (e.g. merger), please state: _____

    If you have any queries about this survey, please contact Dr Gordon Murray or Oliver Burgel at Warwick Business School:

    Phone: 01203 523914
    Fax: 01203 524628
    E-Mail: gordon.murray@warwick.ac.uk
    o.burgel@warwick.ac.uk
    Project Homepage: http://www.intsme.zew.de

3. **Please indicate the TOTAL turnover of your company:**
   - in the FIRST year your company had sales .... £ _____ Year: 19 ____
   - in your LAST financial year .... £ _____ Year: 19 ____
   - the year end forecast for your CURRENT financial year .... £ _____ Year: 19 ____

4. **Does your company have any international sales?**
   - ☐ Yes Indicate the share of total turnover generated by foreign sales in your LAST financial year: ____ %

     Please indicate the number of foreign countries to which you CURRENTLY sell: _____

     Name the FIRST five countries in which you had international sales and the YEAR of market entry:
     _____
     _____

   - ☐ No Do you consider international sales as a probable option in the foreseeable future? ☐ Yes ☐ No

5. **How many persons were/are employed by your company (including owners)?**
   At the time of start-up: _____   Today: _____ *(please state in full-time equivalents)*

6. **How many employees (including founders) have technical/scientific education at degree level?**
   Today: _____   ☐ None

7. **Does your company carry out research and development activities?**
   ☐ Yes, regularly   ☐ Yes, occasionally   ☐ No

8. **How much did you spend on research and development in your last financial year?** ____ % of total sales

9. **How many employees (including the founders) currently work exclusively or for at least 50% of their time on the development of existing and new products?**

   _____ *(in full-time equivalents)*   ☐ None

Founder(s) Profile

10. **How many persons were founders of the start-up?** _____

    If more than 1, had any of the founders worked together for a period of at least 6 months prior to start-up?

    ☐ Yes   ☐ No

11. **Please indicate whether or not you experienced a shortage of skills at the time of start-up or today:**

	Initially at start-up		Today	
	Not at all ... Strongly		Not at all ... Strongly	
Marketing	☐—☐—☐—☐—☐		☐—☐—☐—☐—☐	
Sales / Distribution	☐—☐—☐—☐—☐		☐—☐—☐—☐—☐	
Financial Management	☐—☐—☐—☐—☐		☐—☐—☐—☐—☐	
General Management / Organisation	☐—☐—☐—☐—☐		☐—☐—☐—☐—☐	
Production, Manufacturing, Logistics	☐—☐—☐—☐—☐		☐—☐—☐—☐—☐	
Research and Development	☐—☐—☐—☐—☐		☐—☐—☐—☐—☐	

12. **Please indicate if any of your founders had international experience of the following kind BEFORE you made your first international sales:**
    - ☐ Work experience abroad
    - ☐ Previous work experience in the UK for an international company
    - ☐ Education abroad

13. **Please indicate whether your company received any of the following forms of external finance in addition to your own funds:**
    (as a % of total EQUITY of the company)

	Initially at start up:	To date:
Venture capital:	☐ yes: _____ %	☐ yes: _____ %
Business angels / informal investors:	☐ yes: _____ %	☐ yes: _____ %
Government / public grants:	☐ yes: _____ %	☐ yes: _____ %

Product Characteristics

Please give the following information about the ***best selling*** product line or product family in your LAST financial year. We define a product line/family as a series of closely related products or services (including various upgrades) whose core elements and technologies are identical. For example, a BMW 7 Series would be a particular product line, a BMW 3 Series would be another one, although there are different models (i.e. BMW 318, BMW 323) within the product line. This product line/family is subsequently referred to in the following part of the questionnaire as *"product or service"*.

14. **Please indicate the share of total turnover of your best selling product in your last financial year and describe the product or service:**

    Share of turnover: _____ % of sales

    Description of product: _____
    _____

15. **Please indicate the year in which this product or service was first sold:** 19 _____

16. **Please indicate whether your product or service is a:**
    - ☐ Capital good or service
    - ☐ Consumer good or service
    - ☐ Component for other products
    - ☐ Product ready to use by end-user *(multiple answers possible)*

17. **How would you best describe the innovativeness of your product or service?**
    - ☐ It incorporates 'tried and tested' combinations of existing technology
    - ☐ It incorporates new combinations of existing technology
    - ☐ It incorporates novel technology that has been developed elsewhere
    - ☐ It incorporates novel technology that had to be developed specifically for this product by your company

18. **Please describe key characteristics of the product / service, particularly the extent to which it requires:**

	low — substantial	does not apply
Technical consultation prior to sales	☐—☐—☐—☐—☐	☐
Individual client customisation	☐—☐—☐—☐—☐	☐
Specific configuration / system requirements	☐—☐—☐—☐—☐	☐
Complex or time-consuming installation	☐—☐—☐—☐—☐	☐
Regular maintenance and/or upgrades	☐—☐—☐—☐—☐	☐
Specialised training required for front-line and sales personnel	☐—☐—☐—☐—☐	☐
Other key characteristics, please specify: _____	☐—☐—☐—☐—☐	☐

19. **Please indicate the estimated time for a competitor to launch a similar product with superior performance or a product with similar performance at a lower price:** _____ months

20. **Please indicate whether your product or service has been:**
    - a) developed primarily for the domestic market ☐ yes ☐ no
    - b) developed with the intention to sell abroad ☐ yes ☐ no *(please answer both questions)*

21. **How is your product or service primarily sold in your home country?**
    ☐ via distributors ☐ direct sales from headquarters ☐ both ☐ other, please specify: _____

22. **Please indicate the intensity of competition that you encounter in the UK market:**

    none — very intense
    Intensity of competition: ☐—☐—☐—☐—☐   Number of direct competitors: _____

200   Appendix

23. Do you produce your product or service in any foreign country?
☐ No, only domestic production   ☐ Yes, only foreign production   ☐ Yes, foreign *and* domestic production

If yes → Indicate the country(ies): _____
        ☐   via a wholly owned production subsidiary
        ☐   via a jointly owned production subsidiary with a local partner
        ☐   via a local subcontractor

24. Have you ever sold this product or service abroad?
☐ Yes
☐ No, but ANOTHER product or service is sold abroad   → go to Question 33
☐ No international activities   → go to Question 35

International Activities / Market Entry

In the following section, we would like to ask you about your THREE MOST IMPORTANT foreign markets for the product or service DESCRIBED ABOVE in your LAST financial year (if you have international sales in only one or two countries, please fill in only for country 1 or country 1 and 2). If you did not generate any international sales with the product described above, please do not fill out this section.

25. In how many foreign countries did you sell this product last year? _____ countries

26. Please indicate how the sales for this product have been distributed during your LAST financial year in your domestic and three most important foreign markets: *(in % of total sales for this product)*

Domestic sales: Foreign country 1:   Foreign country 2:   Foreign country 3:   Rest of the world:
_____ %   _____ %   _____ %   _____ %   _____ %   = *100 %*

27. Please name the country and year of market entry	Foreign Country 1	Foreign Country 2	Foreign Country 3
	19 ____	19 ____	19 ____

28. Please indicate the degree of adaptation necessary to sell this product / service abroad:

	none substantial	low substantial	low substantial
Technical adaptation	☐—☐—☐—☐—☐	☐—☐—☐—☐—☐	☐—☐—☐—☐—☐
Adaptation to regulatory requirements	☐—☐—☐—☐—☐	☐—☐—☐—☐—☐	☐—☐—☐—☐—☐
Packaging and sales documentation	☐—☐—☐—☐—☐	☐—☐—☐—☐—☐	☐—☐—☐—☐—☐
Other important product/service changes required, please specify: _____	☐—☐—☐—☐—☐	☐—☐—☐—☐—☐	☐—☐—☐—☐—☐

29. Please indicate the intensity of competition in the foreign country:

	none very intense	none very intense	none very intense
	☐—☐—☐—☐—☐	☐—☐—☐—☐—☐	☐—☐—☐—☐—☐

Estimate the number of direct competitors   _____   _____   _____

30. Please indicate the sequence of entry / foreign sales modes:

(e.g. A - E, see codes below)

	first entry mode	current sales mode	first entry mode	current sales mode	first entry mode	current sales mode
	_____	_____	_____	_____	_____	_____

Codes for modes of sales:
A   Direct exporting (to end-user)
B   Foreign Agent (sells ad hoc on commission basis)
C   Foreign Distributor (sells on a regular basis)
D   Foreign Sales Subsidiary (joint venture)
E   Foreign Sales Subsidiary (wholly owned)
F   Licensing
G   Other sales mode, please specify: _____

31. Between your CURRENT sales mode and the sales mode used at FIRST market entry, did you use any intermediate stages?

☐ Yes, please specify: _____	☐ Yes, please specify: _____	☐ Yes, please specify: _____
☐ No	☐ No	☐ No

32. Do you expect to use a different sales mode in the foreseeable future? (please use the above codes)

☐ Yes, please specify: _____	☐ Yes, please specify: _____	☐ Yes, please specify: _____
☐ No	☐ No	☐ No

Opportunities and Risks of International Activities

33. Did you receive any form of government assistance provided to assist your efforts to internationalise? (e.g. export grants, use of British Embassy facilities abroad, etc.)
☐ No ☐ yes → please indicate the government scheme or service below:

_____
_____

34. How important were the following motives in influencing your decision to sell abroad?
Please RANK the different items in order of importance (1 = most important benefit, 5 = least important benefit)

_____ Potential of foreign markets to generate long-term company growth
_____ Insufficient sales potential in domestic market
_____ Amortisation of product research and development costs
_____ Learning from internationally leading customers, suppliers or competitors
_____ Reputation benefits of being viewed as an internationally competitive company

35. Please indicate the level of importance of the following COSTS of engaging in international sales that you have identified:

	not present				very significant	does not apply
Costs of accessing information on foreign markets	☐	☐	☐	☐	☐	☐
Costs of identifying and forming commercial relationships	☐	☐	☐	☐	☐	☐
Costs of market-entry and setting up foreign sales channels	☐	☐	☐	☐	☐	☐
Costs of product launch in overseas markets (marketing costs)	☐	☐	☐	☐	☐	☐
Operating costs of the chosen sales mode/channel	☐	☐	☐	☐	☐	☐
Costs of monitoring foreign activities	☐	☐	☐	☐	☐	☐
Other important costs, please specify below	☐	☐	☐	☐	☐	☐

_____

36. What constraints have you experienced during your internationalisation process OR, for firms WITHOUT international sales, which prevent you from going abroad?
Please RANK the different items in order of importance (1= most important constraint, 5= least important constraint)

_____ Scarcity of management time
_____ Limited management experience in international activities
_____ Additional costs of foreign sales caused by country-specific AND NOT customer-specific adaptations
_____ Increased exposure to risk
_____ Others, please specify: _____

37. PRIOR to your FIRST international sales, did you:
☐ have a commitment to international sales in your business plan or forecasts?
☐ undertake country-specific market research?
☐ collaborate on research and development with foreign partners?
☐ already sell to a UK subsidiary of your foreign customers / distributors?

38. What led to your first international sales?
(e.g. an unsolicited order, a contact at a trade fair, any particular event or trigger)

_____
_____

Thank you for your cooperation!

In order to thank responding companies for their assistance with this study, we will be sending out a summary report on the findings of our research. If you would like to receive a copy of the report, please indicate your address:

Name:		
Company Name:		
Address:		
Telephone:	Fax:	E-Mail:

Please put the completed questionnaire in the pre-printed Business Reply envelope and send it to:
Dr Gordon Murray, Marketing and Strategic Management Group, Warwick Business School, Coventry CV4 7AL

Appendix 2: Cover Letter - First Mailing

6th October 1997

Dear Mr X,

We would like to request your collaboration in an important new international research programme from Warwick Business School, in cooperation with the Zentrum für Europäische Wirtschaftsforschung in Mannheim, Germany, on the internationalisation of young innovative firms.

The economic importance of young, high-tech firms in the UK and continental Europe appears eventually to have become widely recognised. Recent reports from the CBI, the Bank of England and the European Commission have each highlighted the important contributions of these firms in the areas of innovation, new employment creation, and export-led international competitiveness. Yet, detailed knowledge of the opportunities and constraints facing these firms as they seek to grow remains wholly inadequate. It is also unclear what role, if any, governments can and should play in fostering the creation, growth and, particularly, the internationalisation of these young innovative firms.

We particularly wish to understand a number of key issues about these firms' internationalisation activities. Why do some firms internationalise, often very rapidly, while other firms with similar resources remain domestic in focus? Is the UK market large enough to sustain long-term growth for these companies? Does a high-technology business need to have an international orientation from start-up? How can these fledgling firms compete alongside established multinationals? What advice and support is available?

These questions are at the heart of our research project, which has attracted widespread support among both policy makers and practitioners. It is our intention to compare the internationalisation experiences of entrepreneurs in two countries with markedly different

continued ...

business attitudes, practices and traditions. Importantly, we wish to feed back the results of our study to both industrial participants and government policy makers. It is our express intention to contribute to the debate on how Europe can best emulate the framework of confidence and support which so characterises new technology start-ups in the USA.

Accordingly, data are needed on both firms which *have and do not have* international activities or foreign sales. We would therefore be most grateful if you, or the appropriate senior manager, would give us 15 minutes to answer the enclosed questionnaire and return it in the prepaid envelope. The deadline date for responses is **Friday 27th October**. If you have any questions or comments on the questionnaire, please feel happy to contact us.

Please note: The data will be aggregated and used anonymously. No third party will be given access to any firm specific information which will remain completely confidential.

We would be delighted to send you a summary of the findings of our research. Also enclosed is a *Hot Topics* paper in order to illustrate one means by which we at Warwick attempt to disseminate the results of our contemporary research studies to a wider audience of practitioners and policy makers. If you are interested, further background information about this study and the participating researchers can be found on our project homepage at http://intsme.zew.de

Yours sincerely,

Dr. Gordon Murray
Strategic Management Group
Warwick Business School

Oliver Burgel
Strategic Management Group
Warwick Business School

encs.

Appendix 3: Cover Letter – First Reminder

4th November 1997

Dear Mr X,

Four weeks ago, we sent you a questionnaire and invited you to participate in an Anglo-German academic research study. The purpose of this study is to investigate why some young and innovative firms rapidly internationalise while other comparable firms remain firmly domestic in their sales focus. We are particularly interested in barriers to internationalisation faced by entrepreneurial young firms.

From our records, we know that you have not returned our questionnaire. Yet, we are particularly interested in firms of the age and business activity of your company. While we fully appreciate the time demands on small and medium sized businesses, we are writing to you again to seek your personal co-operation with this university research project.

All completed and returned questionnaires are highly valuable for our analyses. This applies especially if you have not undertaken international activities and do not intend to do so in the near future. For these firms, completing the survey should only take about 10 minutes.

We are confident that this research will have highly practical outcomes. Our findings, which will be discussed with government departments, will give young firms an opportunity to communicate their experiences to policy makers via both the survey and follow-up case studies. However, we would like to stress that all information will be aggregated and used anonymously to guarantee respondent confidentiality.

We enclose a further questionnaire and a Business Reply envelope. Our deadline for returned forms is Friday, 19th December. We would be happy to respond to any queries or comments about the questionnaire or the wider research programme. If they wish, all research participants will receive a summary of key results on request.

We very much hope that you will support this important work.

Yours sincerely,

Dr. Gordon Murray
Strategic Management Group
Warwick Business School

Oliver Burgel
Strategic Management Group
Warwick Business School

Appendix 4: Cover Letter – Second Reminder

3rd December 1997

Dear Mr X,

A couple of weeks ago, we sent you a questionnaire and a reminder and invited you to participate in an Anglo-German academic research study. From our records, it appears that we have not received your questionnaire.

Please excuse our persistence. To be successful researchers, we have to demonstrate exactly the characteristics of commitment and determination as entrepreneurs. While we fully appreciate the time demands on small and medium sized businesses, we are writing to you again to seek your personal co-operation with this university research project.

The purpose of this study is to investigate why some young and innovative firms rapidly internationalise while other comparable firms remain firmly domestic in their sales focus. We are also investigating the various barriers to internationalisation faced by entrepreneurial young firms.

Therefore, we are particularly interested in firms that have not undertaken international activities and do not intend to do so in the near future. For these firms, completing the survey should take less than 10 minutes.

We are confident that this research will have highly practical outcomes. Our research, which will be discussed with government departments, gives young firms an opportunity to communicate their experiences to policy makers and to voice their concerns. The results of this initiative will therefore lead to a much better appreciation of the challenges that young innovative firms face as they attempt to expand their sales.

We enclose a further questionnaire and a Business Reply envelope. We would be happy to respond to any queries or comments about the questionnaire or the wider research programme. All research participants will receive a summary of key results on request.

We very much hope that you will spare the little time that it takes support this important work.

Yours sincerely,

Dr. Gordon Murray
Strategic Management Group
Warwick Business School

Oliver Burgel
Strategic Management Group
Warwick Business School

Appendix 5: Cover Letter – Third Reminder

Dear Sir or Madam,

In the Autumn of 1997, we wrote to you asking for your assistance in a research programme which we were undertaking. We wished to look at the behaviour of innovative start-ups in the UK and, particularly, whether international expansion represents a viable strategy for these young firms.

Since our original contact, we have received over 400 completed questionnaires. This makes our survey the largest, independent study ever undertaken in Europe which specifically focuses on the commercial circumstances facing high-tech start-ups. **We are enclosing with this letter a brief one page of key research findings to date. In a couple of months, all respondents will receive a detailed copy of our research results and conclusions.**

To ensure the accuracy of our findings, it is imperative that we obtain the highest possible response rate. We would therefore ask you most sincerely if you would fill in and return the enclosed questionnaire.

Question: *Why should you bother to help us?*

Answer: Because it is our intention to ensure that the 'voices' of young high-tech companies are heard clearly in government and other influential circles, including banks and institutional investors. Our research shows that, in several critical ways, young high-tech firms are very different from other types of enterprise. Differences which need to be fully appreciated by policy makers include, for example, the role and importance of exporting; the means of financing start-up and early growth, and the firms' needs for highly skilled and innovative labour. The tax breaks for high-tech start-ups recently proposed by a government working group are just one example of policy initiatives being strongly influenced by academic research. However, without tangible evidence to demonstrate high tech firms' material contribution to the British economy and their legitimate needs as young businesses, their interests are likely to be eclipsed by other more powerful commercial parties.

Many of our respondents have shown considerable dedication and fortitude in order to create and sustain successful businesses in technologies essential for a modern and competitive economy.

Please fill in our questionnaire and help us to tell your story!

Yours sincerely,

Dr. Gordon Murray
Strategic Management Group
Warwick Business School

Oliver Burgel
Strategic Management Group
Warwick Business School

Appendix 6: Regression Table – Software Subsample Regressions

Subsample Regression – Software Firms

Variable	Model I Probit: Decision to Internationalise		Model II Tobit: Degree of Internationalisation		Model III Cox: Timing of Internationalisation	
Firm Size (at Start-up)	0.2548		10.4023	*	0.3816	**
Age	0.1793	***	5.4491	***	0.0990	
Work Experience in UK for Multinational	0.1701		9.9967		0.1051	
International Work Experience	0.4909	±	8.0230		0.4349	
International Education	0.9781	**	32.2426	**	0.7711	*
R&D Intensity % employees	-0.4103		54.0744		-0.558	
(R&D Intensity % employees)²	1.3392		54.0743		1.0431	
Venture Capital Investment at Start-up	0.0291		-6.1104		-0.8053	*
Business Angel Investment at Start-up	0.2687		5.1741		0.3238	
New Combinations of Existing Technology	1.2136	**	49.7564	***	1.3197	**
Novel Technology Developed Externally	1.5802	***	51.3233	***	1.6476	**
Novel Technology Developed Internally	1.4395	***	41.2948	**	1.5799	**
Customisation Requirement	-0.2134	*	-3.3220		-0.1668	±
Commercialisation Cost	0.2690	*	-1.5772		0.1973	
No. of Observations	101		99		101	
Log Likelihood	-47.26		-284.27		-201.13	
Chi-square (df):	43.26 (13)	****	40.79 (13)	****	34.44 (13)	****
Pseudo R²	0.314		0.067		0.079	
% correct classifications	74.26					
maximimum chance criterion	57.43					

Note: The reference category is a software firm with more than 20 employees at start-up. The table shows coefficient estimates.

**** significant at $p<0.001$, *** significant at $p<0.01$, ** significant at $p<0.05$, * significant at $p<0.10$, ± significant at $p<0.15$ (two-tailed tests)

List of Tables

Table 1:	Overview of Case Studies in International Entrepreneurship	19
Table 2:	Overview of Quantitative Studies in International Entrepreneurship	29
Table 3:	Dun & Bradstreet Source Data and Cleaned Primary Database	86
Table 4:	Sample Composition After Stratification	88
Table 5:	Drawing Probability per Strata	89
Table 6:	Response Pattern	92
Table 7:	Comparison of Respondents and Non-Respondents	94
Table 8:	Calculation of Weights per Strata	96
Table 9:	Sample Composition by Industry	98
Table 10:	Firm Characteristics at Start-up	99
Table 11:	Firm Size at the Time of the Survey	101
Table 12:	Firm Size by Industry	101
Table 13:	External Finance	102
Table 14:	Founder Characteristics	104
Table 15:	Shortage of Management Skills	105
Table 16:	R&D Indicators - R&D Intensity	106
Table 17:	R&D Indicators - R&D Employees	107
Table 18:	R&D Indicators - Employees with Technical Education	107
Table 19:	Classification of Best-Selling Product	113
Table 20:	Innovativeness of Technology	113
Table 21:	Average Annual Growth Rates	118
Table 22:	Average Annual Growth Rates by Industry	118
Table 23:	Median Annual Growth Rates	118
Table 24:	International Activities of Sample Firms	122

Table 25:	International Activities of Sample Firms by Industry	123
Table 26:	International Activities of Sample Firms by Size Class	123
Table 27:	Timing and Expected Involvement in International Activities	124
Table 28:	The Degree of Internationalisation – Descriptive Statistics	126
Table 29:	Degree of International Activities by Industry	126
Table 30:	First and Current Entry Modes	129
Table 31:	Evolution of Market Entry Modes	129
Table 32:	Geographical Focus of International Activities (by Target Region)	130
Table 33:	Geographical Focus of International Activities (10 Most Frequently Named Target Countries)	131
Table 34:	Mean Annual Growth Rates of the Sample Firms - Comparison of International Start-ups and Domestic Start-ups	132
Table 35:	Median Annual Growth Rates of the Sample Firms - Comparison of International Start-ups and Domestic Start-ups	132
Table 36:	Motives for Initiating International Sales	135
Table 37:	Preparation and Existing Relationships Prior to the First International Sales	136
Table 38:	Triggers for First International Sales	137
Table 39:	Costs of International Sales	138
Table 40:	Barriers to International Sales	139
Table 41:	Summary of Independent Variables	143
Table 42:	Correlation Matrix of Dependent and Independent Variables	144
Table 43:	Summary of Expected Relationships	145
Table 44:	Probit Models to Test the Propensity to Internationalise	147
Table 45:	Probit Models to Test the Propensity to Internationalise	148
Table 46:	Probit Models to Test the Propensity to Internationalise	149
Table 47:	Probit Models to Test the Propensity to Internationalise	150

Table 48:	Estimation of the Share of Non-Domestic Revenue – OLS Regression on International Firms -	157
Table 49:	Estimation of the Share of Non-Domestic Revenue – OLS Regression on all Firms -	158
Table 50:	Estimation of the Share of Non-Domestic Revenue – Tobit Regression -	159
Table 51:	Cox Regression to Estimate the Time to Internationalise	166
Table 52:	Cox Regression to Estimate the Time to Internationalise	167
Table 53:	Weibull Regression to Estimate the Time to Internationalise	168
Table 54:	Summary of Expected and Identified Relationships	171
Table 55:	Effect of Different Measures of Firm Size on Dependent Variables	173
Table 56:	Probit Model of the Entry Mode Decision – Direct Exporting vs. Distributors -	178
Table 57:	Probit Model of the Entry Mode Decision – Direct Exporting vs. Distributors -	179
Table 58:	Summary of Hypothesised and Identified Relationships between Independent Variables and the Choice of Foreign Distributors	182

List of Figures

Figure 1: Firms by Year of Formation 100

Figure 2: R&D Indicators by Industry 108

Figure 3: R&D Indicators by Firm Age 109

Figure 4: Kernel Density Estimation of R&D Intensity by Industry 110

Figure 5: Kernel Density Estimation of R&D Employees by Industry 111

Figure 6: Degree of Technology Differentiation by Industry 114

Figure 7: Commercialisation Requirements by Industry 115

Figure 8: Average Annual Growth Rates by Firm Age 117

Figure 9: Convergence of Growth Mean and Median by Age Group 119

Figure 10: Kernel Density Estimation of the Share of Non-Domestic Revenue by Industry (Compared to Normal Distribution) 127

Figure 11: Median Employment Growth Rates by Age Groups 134

Bibliography

Aaby, Nils-Erik, and Stanley F. Slater (1989), "Management influence on export performance: A review of the empirical literature," International Marketing Review, 6(4), 7-26.

Acs, Zoltan J., and David B. Audretsch (1991), Innovation and Technological Change: An international comparison. Ann Arbor: University of Michigan Press.

Agarwal, Sanjeev, and Sridhar Ramaswami (1992), "Choice of foreign market entry mode: Impact of ownership, location and internalization factors," Journal of International Business Studies, 23(1), 1-27.

Aharoni, Yair (1966), The Foreign Investment Decision Process. Boston: Harvard University, Division of Research.

Allison, Paul D. (1984), Event History Analysis. Beverly Hills: Sage Publications.

Amemiya, Takeshi (1981), "Qualitative response models: A survey," Journal of Econometric Literature, 19(4), 481-536.

Andersen, Otto (1993), "On the internationalization process of firms: A critical analysis," Journal of International Business Studies, 24(2), 209-231.

---- (1997), "Internationalization and market entry mode: A review of theories and conceptual frameworks," Management International Review, 37(Special Issue 2), 27-42.

Anderson, Erin, and Hubert Gatignon (1986), "Modes of foreign market entry: A transaction cost analysis and propositions," Journal of International Business Studies, 17(3), 1-26.

Anderson, James C., and James A. Narus (1990), "A model of distributor firm and manufacturer firm working partnerships," Journal of Marketing, 54(1), 42-58.

Anglo-German Foundation (1988), New Technology-Based Firms in Britain and Germany. London: Anglo-German Foundation.

Armour, Henry. O., and David J. Teece (1980), "Vertical integration and technological innovation," Review of Economics and Statistics, 60(3), 470-474.

Armstrong, J. S., and Terry S. Overton (1977), "Estimating non-response biase in mail surveys," Journal of Marketing Research, 14, 396-402.

Aulakh, Preet S., and Masaaki Kotabe (1997), "Antecedents and performance implications of channel integration in foreign markets ," Journal of International Business Studies, 27(1), 145-175.

Autio, Erkko (1997), "'Atomistic' and 'systemic' approaches to research on new, technology-based firms: A literature study," Small Business Economics, 9, 195-209.

Autio, E. (1995). Symplectic and Generative Impacts of New, Technology-Based Firms in Innovation Networks: An International Comparative Study. Unpublished doctoral dissertation, University of Technology, Institute of Industrial Management: Helsinki.

Bamberger, Ingolf, and Michael Evers (1994), "Internationalization behaviour of small and medium-sized enterprises - empirical results," in: Product/Market Strategies of Small and Medium-sized Enterprises, Ingolf Bamberger (ed.), Aldershot: Ashgate Publishing.

Barkema, Harry G., and Freek Vermeulen (1998), "International expansion through start-up or acquisition: A learning perspective," Academy of Management Journal, 41(1), 7-26.

Barney, Jay (1991), "Firm resources and sustained competitive advantage," Journal of Management, 17, 99-120.

Barrett, Nigel I., and Ian F. Wilkinson (1985), "Export stimulation: A segmentation study of the exporting problems of Australian manufacturing firms," European Journal of Marketing, 19(2), 53-72.

Beard, Charles, and Chris Easingwood (1996), "New product launch: Marketing action and launch tactics for high technology products," Industrial Marketing Management, 25, 87-103.

Bell, Jim (1995), "The internationalization of small computer software firms - A further challenge to stage theories," European Journal of Marketing, 29(8), 60-75.

Bilkey, W. J. (1978), "An attempted integration of the literature on export behaviour of firms," Journal of International Business Studies, 9, 33-46.

Bilkey, W. J., and G. Tesar (1977), "The export behaviour of small-sized Wisconsin manufacturing firms," Journal of International Business Studies, 8, 93-98.

Blankenburg Holm, Desiree, Kent Eriksson, and Jan Johanson (1996), "Business networks and cooperation in international business relationships," Journal of International Business Studies, 27(Special Issue), 1033-1053.

Bloodgood, James M., Harry J. Sapienza, and James G. Almeida (1996), "The internationalization of new high-potential U.S. ventures antecedents and outcomes," Entrepreneurship Theory & Practice, 20, 61-76.

Bogner, William C., Howard Thomas, and John McGee (1995), "Core competence and competitive advantage: A dynamic theory based model," Working Paper.

Bonaccorsi, Andrea (1992), "On the relationship between firm size and export intensity," Journal of International Business Studies, 23(3), 601-635.

Borch, Odd J., and Michael B. Arthur (1995), "Strategic networks among small firms: implications for strategy research methodology," Journal of Management Studies, 32(4), 419-441.

Boter, Håkan, and Carin Holmquist (1996), "Industry characteristics and internationalization processes in small firms," Journal of Business Venturing, 11, 471-487.

Brüderl, Josef, and Rudolf Schüssler (1990), "Organizational mortality: The liabilities of newness and adolescence," Administrative Science Quarterly, 35, 530-547.

Brush, Candida G., and Pieter A. Vanderwerf (1992), "A comparison of methods and sources for obtaining estimates of new venture performance," Journal of Business Venturing, 7, 157-170.

Buckley, Peter J. (1988), "The limits of explanation: Testing the internalization theory of the multinational enterprise," Journal of International Business Studies, 19(2), 181-193.

---- (1990), "Problems and developments in the core theory of international business," Journal of International Business Studies, 21(2), 181-193.

---- (1993a), "Barriers to internationalization," in: Perspectives on Strategic Change, Luca Zan, Stefano Zambon, and Andrew M. Pettigrew (ed.), Boston: Kluwer Academic Publishers.

---- (1993b), "The role of management in internalisation theory," Management International Review, 33(3), 197-207.

---- (1996), "The role of management in international business theory: A meta-analysis and integration of of the literature on international business and international management," Management International Review, 36(Special Issue 1), 7-54.

Buckley, Peter J., and Mark C. Casson (1976), The Future of the Multinational Enterprise. London: Macmillan Publishers.

---- (1998), "Analyzing foreign market entry strategies: Extending the internalization approach," Journal of International Business Studies, 29(3), 539-562.

Buckley, Peter J., G. D. Newbould, and G. Thurwell (1988), Foreign Direct Investment by Smaller UK Firms. London: Macmillan Publishers.

Burenstam-Linder, Staffan (1961), An Essay on Trade and Transformation. Uppsala: Almqvist and Wiksell.

Butchart R. (1987), "A new UK definition of high-technology industries," Economic Trends, 400, 82-88.

Calof, Jonathan L. (1994), "The relationship between firm size and export behaviour revisited," Journal of International Business Studies, 25(2), 367-387.

Calof, Jonathan L., and Paul W. Beamish (1995), "Adapting to foreign markets: explaining internationalisation," International Business Review, 4(2), 115-131.

Cantwell, John A. (1991), "A survey of theories of international production," in: The Nature of the Transnational Firm, Christos N. Pitelis, and Roger Sugden (ed.), London: Routledge.

Carpano, Claudio, and Chrisman James J. (1995), "Performance implications of international product strategies and the integration of marketing activities," Journal of International Marketing, 3(1), 9-27.

Carpano, Claudio, James J. Chrisman, and Kendall Roth (1994), "International strategy and environment: An assessment of the performance relationship," Journal of International Business Studies, 25(3), 639-656.

Caves, Richard E. (1982), "Multinational Enterprises and Technology Transfer," in: New Theories of the Multinational Enterprise, Alan M. Rugman (ed.), London: Croom Helm.

Cavusgil, S. T. (1980), "On the internationalisation process of the firm," European Research, 8(6), 273-281.

Cavusgil, S. T., and V. H. Kirpalani (1993), "Introducing products into export markets: success factors," Journal of Business Research, 27, 1-15.

Cavusgil, S. T., and Shaoming Zou (1994), "Marketing strategy-performance relationship: An investigation of the empirical links in export markets," Journal of Marketing, 58, 1-21.

Cavusgil, S. T., Shaoming Zou, and G. M. Naidu (1993), "Product and promotion adaptation in export ventures: An empirical investigation," Journal of International Business Studies, 24(3), 479-506.

Chetty, Sylvie K., and R. T. Hamilton (1995), "The process of exporting in owner-controlled firms," International Small Business Journal, 14(2), 12-25.

Collis, David J. (1991), "A resource-based analysis of global competition: The case of the bearings industry," Strategic Management Journal, 12(Summer Special Issue), 49-68.

Conner, Kathleen R. (1991), "A historical comparison of resource-based theory and five schools of thought within industrial organization economics: Do we have a new theory of the firm?," Journal of Management, 17, 121-154.

Conner, Kathleen R., and Prahalad C. K. (1996), "A resource-based theory of the firm: Knowledge versus opportunism," Organization Science, 7(5), 477-501.

Cooper, Robert G., and Elko J. Kleinschmidt (1985), "The impact of export strategy on export sales performance," Journal of International Business Studies, 16(Spring 1985), 37-55.

Coopers & Lybrand, and National Venture Capital Association (1996), Sixth Annual Economic Impact of Venture Capital Study. Boston, MA: Coopers & Lybrand.

Coviello, Nicole E., and Hugh J. Munro (1995), "Growing the entrepreneurial firm: Networking for international market development ," European Journal of Marketing, 29(7), 49-62.

Crick, Dave (1995), "An investigation into the targeting of U.K. export assistance," European Journal of Marketing, 29(8), 76-94.

Cyert, Richard M., and James G. March (1963), A Behavioral Theory of the Firm. Englewood Cliffs: Prentice-Hall.

Czinkota, M. R. (1982), Export Development Strategies: US Promotion Policy. New York: Praeger.

Dalli, Daniele (1994), "The "Exporting" process: The evolution of small and medium sized firms toward internationalization," Advances in International Marketing, 6, 85-110.

Davidson, W. H., and D. G. McFetridge (1985), "Key characteristics in the choice of international technology transfer mode ," Journal of International Business Studies, 16(Summer), 5-21.

Dichtl, Erwin et al. (1984), "The export decision of small and medium-sized firms: A review," Management International Review, 24(2), 49-60.

---- (1990), "International orientation as precondition for export success," Journal of International Business Studies, 21(1), 23-41.

Dierickx, Ingemar, and Karel Cool (1989), "Asset stock accumulation and sustainability of competitive advantage," Management Science, 35, 1504-1511.

Douglas, Susan P., and Samuel P. Craig (1992), "Advances in international marketing," International Journal of Research in Marketing, 9, 291-318.

Douglas, Susan P., and Yoram Wind (1987), "The myth of globalization," Columbia Journal of World Business, (Winter 1987), 19-29.

Dunning, John H. (1980), "Towards an eclectic theory of international production: Some empirical tests," Journal of International Business Studies, 11(1), 9-31.

---- (1993), Multinational Enterprises and the Global Economy. Wokingham: Addison-Wesley.

Eisenhardt, Kathleen M., and Claudia Bird Schoonhoven (1996), "Resource-based view of strategic alliance formation: Strategic and social effects in entrepreneurial firms," Organization Science, 7(4), 136-151.

Eriksson, Kent et al. (1997), "Experiential knowledge and cost in the internationalization process," Journal of International Business Studies, 28(2), 337-360.

Erramilli, M. K., and C. P. Rao (1993), "Service firms' international entry-mode choice: a modified transaction cost analysis approach ," Journal of Marketing, 57(July), 19-38.

Florida, Richard, and Martin Kenny (1988), "Venture capital and high technology entrepreneurship," Journal of Business Venturing, 3(4), 301-319.

Foss, Nicolai J. (1998), "The resource-based perspective: An assessment and diagnosis of problems," Scandinavian Journal of Management, 14(3), 133-149.

Franko, Lawrence G. (1989), "Global corporate competition: Who's winning, who's losing, and the R&D factor as one reason why," Strategic Management Journal, 10(5), 449-474.

Fujita, Masataka (1995a), "Small and medium-sized transnational corporations: salient features," Small Business Economics, 7, 251-271.

---- (1995b), "Small and medium-sized transnational corporations: trends and patterns of foreign direct investment," Small Business Economics, 7, 183-204.

Gatignon, Hubert, and Erin Anderson (1988), "The multinational corporation's degree of control over foreign subsidiaries: An empirical test of a transaction cost explanation," Journal of Law, Economics and Organization, 4(3), 305-336.

Gemünden, Hans G. (1991), "Success factors of export marketing: a meta-analytic critique of the empirical studies," in: New Perspectives on International Marketing, Stanley J. Paliwoda (ed.), London: Routledge.

Goshal, Sumantra, and Peter Moran (1996), "Bad for practice: A critique of the transaction cost theory," Academy of Management Review, 21(1), 13-47.

Granovetter, Mark (1985), "Economic action and social structure: The problem of embeddedness," American Journal of Sociology, 91(3), 481-510.

Grant, Robert M. (1996), "Toward a knowledge-based theory of the firm," Strategic Management Journal, 17(Winter Special Issue), 109-122.

Greene, William H. (1980), "On the asymptotic bias of the ordinary least squares estimator of the Tobit model," Econometrica, 48, 504-514.

---- (1997), Econometric Analysis. New York: Macmillan.

Gulati, Ranjay (1998), "Alliances and networks," Strategic Management Journal, 19(Editor's Choice), 293-317.

Hall, John, and Charles W. Hofer (1993), "Venture capitalists' decision criteria in new venture evaluation," Journal of Business Venturing, 8, 25-42.

Hambrick, Donald C., and Phyllis Mason (1984), "Upper echelons: the organisation as a reflection of its top managers," Academy of Management Review, 9, 193-206.

Hannan, Michael T., and John H. Freeman (1977), "The population ecology or organization," Amercian Journal of Sociology, 82, 929-964.

---- (1984), "Structural inertia and organizational change," American Sociological Review, 49, 149-164.

Heide, Jan B., and George John (1994), "Interorganizational governance in marketing channels," Journal of Marketing, 56(April), 32-44.

Hennart, Jean F. (1989), "Can the 'new forms of investment' substitute for the 'old forms'?," Journal of International Business Studies, 20(2), 211-234.

Hennart, Jean-Francois (1990), "A transaction cost theory of equity joint ventures," Strategic Management Journal, 9(4), 361-374.

Hill, Charles W. L., Peter Hwang, and W. C. Kim (1990), "An eclectic theory of the choice of international entry mode," Strategic Management Journal, 11, 117-128.

Hutt, Michael D., and Thomas W. Speh (1992), Business Marketing Management. Orlando: The Dryden Press.

Hymer, Stephen H. (1976), The International Operations of National Firms: A Study of Foreign Direct Investment. Cambridge, MA: MIT Press.

Itaki, Masahito (1991), "A critical assessment of the eclectic theory of the multinational enterprise," Journal of International Business Studies, 22(3), 445-460.

Johanson, Jan, and Lars-Gunnar Mattson (1993), "Internationalisation in industrial systems - A network approach," in: The Internationalisation of the Firm: A Reader, Peter J. Buckley, and Pervez Ghauri (ed.), London: Academic Press.

Johanson, Jan, and Jan-Erik Vahlne (1977), "The internationalization process of the firm - A model of knowledge development and increasing foreign market commitment," Journal of International Business Studies, 4, 20-29.

---- (1990), "The mechanism of internationalization," International Marketing Review, 7(4), 11-24.

Johanson, Jan, and Finn Wiedersheim-Paul (1975), "The Internationalization of the firm - Four Swedish cases," Journal of Management Studies.

John, George, and Barton A. Weitz (1988), "Forward integration into distribution: An empirical test of transaction cost analysis ," Journal of Law, Economics and Organization, 4(2), 337-355.

Jolly, V. K., Matti Alahuhta, and Jean-Pierre Jeannet (1992), "Challenging the incumbent: how high-technology start-ups compete globally," Journal of Strategic Change, 1, 71-82.

Katz, Jerome, and William B. Gartner (1988), "Properties of emerging organizations," Academy of Management Review, 13(3), 429-441.

Keeble, David et al. (1998), "Internationalisation processes, networking and local embeddedness in technology-intensive small firms," Small Business Economics, 11, 327-342.

Klein, Benjamin, Robert Crawford, and Armen Alchian (1978), "Vertical integration, appropriable rents, and the competitive contracting process," Journal of Law and Economics, 21, 297-326.

Klein, Saul, Gary L. Frazier, and Victor J. Roth (1990), "A transaction cost analysis model of channel integration in international markets," Journal of Marketing Research, 27(May), 196-208.

Knickerbocker, F. T. (1973), Oligopolistic Reaction and the Multinational Enterprise. Cambridge, MA: Harvard University Press.

Knight, Gary A., and S. T. Cavusgil (1996), "The born global firm: A challenge to traditional internationalization theory," Advances in International Marketing, 8(11-26).

Koberg, Sabine S., Rosse Joseph, and Donald Bergh (1994), "Toward a definition and typology of high-technology firms," Advances in Global High-Technology Management, 4(Part A), 3-26.

Kobrin, Stephen J. (1991), "An empirical analysis of the determinants of global integration," Strategic Management Journal, 12(Summer Special Issue), 17-31.

Kogut, Bruce (1988), "Joint ventures: Empirical and theoretical perspectives," Strategic Management Journal, 9(4), 319-332.

---- (1989), "A note on global strategies," Strategic Management Journal, 10, 383-389.

Kogut, Bruce, and Harbir Singh (1988), "The effect of national culture on the choice of entry mode," Journal of International Business Studies, 19(3), 411-432.

Kogut, Bruce, and Udo Zander (1993), "Knowledge of the firm and the evolutionary theory of the multinational corporation," Journal of International Business Studies, 24(4), 625-645.

---- (1996), "What do firms do? Coordination, identity, and learning ," Organization Science, 7(5), 502-523.

Leonidou, Leonidas C., and Constanine S. Katsikeas (1996), "The export development process: An integrative review of empirical models," Journal of International Business Studies, (Third Quarter 1996), 517-551.

Licht, Georg, and Harald Stahl (1995), "Enterprise panels based on credit rating data," in: Techniques and Uses of Enterprise Panels, pp. 163-177 , EUROSTAT: Brussels and Luxembourg.

Lim, Jenn-Su, Thomas W. Sharkey, and Ken I. Kim (1991), "An empirical test of an export adaption model," Management International Review, 31(1), 51-62.

Lindell, Martin, and Necmi Karagozoglu (1997), "Global strategies of US and Scandinavian R&D intensive small- and medium-sized companies," European Management Journal, 15(1), 92-100.

Lindqvist, M. (1991). Infant Multinationals: The Internationalization of Young, Technology-Based Swedish Firms. Unpublished doctoral dissertation, Stockholm: Stockholm School of Economics, Institute of International Business.

Lippman, S. A., and Richard P. Rumelt (1982), "Uncertain imitability: An analysis of interfirm differences in efficiency under competition," Bell Journal of Economics, 13, 418-453.

Little, A. D. (1977), New Technology-Based Firms in the United Kingdom and the Federal Republic of Germany. London, Bonn: Anglo-German Foundation for the Study of Industrial Society.

Madhok, Anoop (1996), "The organization of economic activitiy: Transaction costs, firm capabilities, and the nature of governance," Organization Science, 7(5), 577-590.

---- (1997), "Cost, value and foreign market entry mode: The transaction and the firm," Strategic Management Journal, 18, 39-61.

Mahoney, Joseph T. (1992), "Organizational economics within the conversation of strategic management," Advances in Strategic Management, 8, 103-155.

Mahoney, Joseph T., and J. R. Pandian (1992), "The resource-based view within the conversation of strategic management," Strategic Management Journal, 13(5), 363-380.

Mason, Colin M., and Richard T. Harrison (1995), "Closing the regional equity gap: the role of informal venture capital," Small Business Economics, 7, 153-172.

Mauri, A. J., and M. P. Michaels (1998), "Firm and industry effects within strategic management: An empirical examination," Strategic Management Journal, 19(3), 211-219.

McDougall, Patricia P. (1989), "International versus domestic entrepreneurship: new venture strategic behaviour and industry structure," Journal of Business Venturing, 4, 387-400.

McDougall, Patricia P., and Benjamin M. Oviatt (1996), "New venture internationalization, strategic change and performance: a follow-up study," Journal of Business Venturing, 11, 23-40.

McDougall, Patricia P., Scott Shane, and Benjamin Oviatt (1994), "Explaining the formation of international new ventures: The limits of international business research ," Journal of Business Venturing, 9(Nov. 1994), 469-487.

McKinsey & Company (1993), Emerging Exporters: Australia's High Value-Added Manufacturing Exporters. Melbourne: Australian Manufacturing Council.

Meldrum, M. J. (1995), "Marketing high-tech products: The emerging themes," European Journal of Marketing, 29(10), 45-58.

Melin, Leif (1992), "Internationalization as a strategy process," Strategic Management

Journal, 13, 99-118.

Monteverde, Kirk M., and David J. Teece (1982), "Appropriable rents and quasi-vertical integration," Journal of Law and Economics, 25, 321-328.

Moon, Junyean, and Haksik Lee (1990), "On the internal correlates of export stage development: An empirical investigation in the Korean electronics industry," International Marketing Review, 7(5), 16-26.

Moore, Barry (1994), "Financing constraints on the growth and development of small high-technology firms," in Finance and Small Firms, Alan Hughes, and David J. Storey eds. (pp. 112-144). London: Routledge.

Moran, Peter, and Sumantra Goshal (1996), "Theories of economic organisation: the case for realism and balance," Academy of Management Review, 21(1), 58-72.

Morgan, Robert E., and Constantine S. Katsikeas (1997), "Obstacles to export initiation and expansion," Omega, International Journal of Management Science, 25(6), 677-690.

Moriarty, Rowland T., and Thomas J. Kosnik (1989), "High-tech marketing: concepts, continuity and change," Sloan Management Review, (Summer 1989), 7-17.

Murray, Gordon C. (1995), "Evolution and change: An analysis of the first decade of the UK venture capital industry," Journal of Business Finance and Accounting, 22(8), 1077-1107.

---- (1996), "A synthesis of six exploratory, European case studies of successfully-exited, venture capital financed, new technology-based firms," Entrepreneurship Theory and Practice, 20, 44-60.

Murray, Gordon C., and Jonathan Lott (1995), "Have venture capital firms a bias against investment in high technology companies?," Research Policy, 24, 283-299.

Nicholls, Matt, and Solveig Nyvold (1995), An Empirical Investigation Into the Logic and Means by Which Venture Capital Backed, Emerging Technology Businesses in the UK Internationalise Their Sales Activities. Unpublished MBA dissertation, Warwick Business School.

Nordström, K. A. (1991). The Internationalization Process of the Firm. Unpublished doctoral dissertation, Stockholm: Stockholm School of Economics, Institute of International Business.

North, Douglass C. (1990), Institutions, Institutional Change and Economic Performance. Cambridge: Cambridge University Press.

Nunally, J. C., and I. H. Bernstein (1994), Psychometric Theory. New York: McGraw-Hill.

Oakey, R. (1994). New Technology-based Firms in the 1990s. London: Paul Chapman Publishing.

Oakey, Ray, Roy Rothwell, and Sarah Cooper (1988), The Management of Innovation in High-Technology Small Firms. London: Pinter Publishers.

Ohmae, Kenichi (1990), The Borderless World: Power and Strategy in the Interlinked Economy. New York: Harper.

Organisation for Economic Cooperation and Development (1997), The Oslo Manual - Proposed Guidelines for Collecting and Interpreting Technological Innovation

Data. Paris: OECD.

Oviatt, Benjamin M., and Patricia P. McDougall (1994), "Toward a theory of international new ventures," Journal of International Business Studies, 25(1), 45-64.

---- (1997), "Challenges for internationalization process theory: The case of international new ventures," Management International Review, 37(Special Issue 2), 85-99.

Penrose, Edith T. (1959), The Theory of the Growth of the Firm. New York: John Wiley.

Peteraf, Margaret A. (1993), "The cornerstones of competitive advantage: A resource-based view," Strategic Management Journal, 14, 179-191.

Pitelis, C. N., & Sugden, R. (1991). The Nature of the Transnational Firm. London: Routledge.

Porter, Michael (1980), Competitve Strategy. New York: Free Press.

Porter, Michael E. (1986), Competition in Global Industries . Boston: Harvard Business School Press.

---- (1994), "Toward a dynamic theory of strategy," in: Fundamental Issues in Strategy, Richard P. Rumelt, Dan E. Schendel, and David J. Teece (ed.), Boston: Harvard Business School Press. (pp. 163-177).

Preece, Stephen B., Grant Miles, and Mark C. Baetz (1999), "Explaining the international intensity and global diversity of early-stage technology-based firms," Journal of Business Venturing, 14, 259-281.

Ramaswamy, Kannan, K. Galen Kroeck, and William Renforth (1996), "Measuring the degree of internationalization of a firm: A comment," Journal of International Business Studies, 27(1), 167-177.

Rao, T. R., and G. M. Naidu (1992), "Are the stages of internationalization empirically supportable," Journal of Global Marketing, 6(2), 147-170.

Reid, Stan D. (1981), "The decision-maker and export entry and expansion," Journal of International Business Studies, 12(3), 101-112.

Reuber, A. R., and Eileen Fisher (1997), "The influence of the management team's international experience on the internationalization behaviour of SMEs," Journal of International Business Studies, 28(4), 807-825.

Roberts, Edward B. (1991), Entrepreneurs in High Technology. New York: Oxford University Press.

Roberts, Edward B., and Senturia Todd A. (1996), "Globalizing the emerging high-technology company," Industrial Marketing Management, 25, 491-506.

Robertson, Thomas S., and Hubert Gatignon (1998), "Technology development mode: A transaction cost conceptualization," Strategic Management Journal, 19, 515-531.

Root, Franklin R. (1994), Entry Strategies for International Markets. New York: Lexington Books.

Rosson, Philip J., and Stanley D. Reid (1987), Managing Export Entry and Expansion. New York: Praeger Publishers.

Roth, Kendall (1995), "Managing international interdependence: CEO characteristics in a resource-based framework," Academy of Management Journal, 38(1), 200-231.

Rothwell, Roy, and W. Zegveld (1982), Industrial Innovation and Small and Medium Sized Firms. London: Pinter Publishers.

Sapienza, Harry J. (1992), "When do venture capitalists add value?," Journal of Business Venturing, 7, 9-27.

Saxenian AnnaLee (1991), "The origins and dynamics of production networks in Silicon Valley," Research Policy, 20(5), 423-437.

Shanklin, W. L., and J. K. Ryans (1987), Essentials of Marketing High-Technology. Boston: Lexington Books.

Small Business Research Centre (1992), The State of British Enterprise: Growth, Innovation and Competitive Advantage in Small and Medium Sized-Firms. Cambridge: University of Cambridge.

Stinchcombe, Arthur (1965), "Social structure and organizations," in: Handbook of Organizations, James G. March (ed.), Chicago: Rand McNally.

Storey, David J. (1994), Understanding the Small Business Sector. London: Routledge.

---- (1996), The Ten Percenters - Fast Growing SMEs in Great Britain. London: Deloitte & Touche.

Storey, David J., and Bruce S. Tether (1998), "New technology-based firms in the European Union: An introduction," Research Policy, 29, 933-946.

Sullivan, Daniel (1994), "Measuring the degree of internationalization of a firm," Journal of International Business Studies, 25(2), 325-342.

---- (1996), "Measuring the degree of internationalization of a firm: A reply," Journal of International Business Studies, 27(1), 179-192.

Tallman, Stephen B. (1991), "Strategic management models and resource-based strategies among MNEs in a host market," Strategic Management Journal, 12(Summer Special Issue), 69-82.

Tan, Benjamin, and Ilan Vertinsky (1996), "Foreign direct investment by Japanese electronics firms in the United States and Canada: Modelling the timing of entry," Journal of International Business Studies, 27(4), 655-681.

Tapia, Richard A., and James R. Thompson (1978), Nonparametric Probability Density Estimation. Baltimore: Johns Hopkins University Press.

Teece, David J. (1977), "Technology transfer by multinational firms: the resource costs of transferring technological know-how ," Economic Journal, 87, 242-261.

---- (1981), "The market for know-how and the efficient international transfer of technology ," Annals of the Academy of Political and Social Science, (458), 81-96.

---- (1986), "Profiting from technological innovation: Implications for integration, collaboration, licensing and public policy," Research Policy, 15, 285-305.

---- (1987), The Competitive Challenge: Strategies for Industrial Innovation and Renewal. Cambridge: Ballinger.

Teece, David J., Gary Pisano, and Amy Shuen (1997), "Dynamic capabilities and strategic management," Strategic Management Journal, 18(7), 509-533.

Turnbull, Peter W. (1987), "A challenge to the stages theory of the internationalisation process," in: Managing Export Entry and Expansion, P. J. Rosson, and S. D. Reid (ed.), New York: Praeger.

United Nations Conference on Trade and Development (1993), Small and Medium-sized Transnational Corporations: Role, Impact and Policy Implications. New York: United Nations.

Vernon, Raymond (1966), "International investment and international trade in the product life cycle," Quarterly Journal of Economics, 80, 190-207.

---- (1979), "The product life cycle hypothesis in a new international environment," Oxford Bulletin of Economics and Statistics, 41(4), 255-267.

Wagner, Joachim (1995), "Exports, firm size and firm dynamics," Small Business Economics, 7, 29-39.

Walker, G., and Laura Poppo (1991), "Profit centres, single-source suppliers, and transaction costs," Administrative Science Quarterly, 36(1), 66-97.

Waters, Malcolm (1995), Globalization. London: Routledge.

Welch, Denice E., and Lawrence S. Welch (1996), "The internationalization process and networks: A strategic management perspective," Journal of International Marketing, 4(3), 11-28.

Welch, Lawrence S., and Reijo Luostarinen (1988), "Internationalization: Evolution of a concept," Journal of General Management, 14(2), 34-55.

Wernerfelt, Birger (1984), "A resource-based view of the firm," Strategic Management Journal, 5, 171-180.

Williamson, Oliver E. (1975), Markets and Hierarchies: Analysis and Antritrust Implications. New York: Basic Books.

---- (1981), "The economics of organization: The transaction cost approach," American Journal of Sociology, 87(November), 548-577.

---- (1985), The Economic Institutions of Capitalism. New York: Free Press.

---- (1996), "Economic organisation: the case for candor," Academy of Management Review, 21(1), 48-57.

Wortzel, Laurence H., and Heidi V. Wortzel (1981), "Export marketing strategies for NIC and LDC-based firms," Columbia Journal of World Business, (1), 51-60.

Yamaguchi, Kazuo (1991), Event History Analysis. Newbury Park: Sage Publications.

Yli-Renko, Helena, and Erkko Autio (1998), "The network embeddedness of new, technology-based firms: Developing a systemic evolution model," Small Business Economics, 11, 253-267.

Zacharakis, Andrew L. (1997), "Entrepreneurial entry into foreign markets: A transaction cost perspective," Entrepreneurship Theory & Practice, (Spring), 23-39.